The Trade–Development Nexus in the European Union

This volume offers new perspectives on the evolution of the trade–development nexus in the European Union against dramatic changes in the international context. Without disregarding them, it seeks to go beyond the controversial and extensively researched Economic Partnership Agreements (EPAs). In particular, it focuses on the reform of the Generalised System of Preferences, the negotiation of various Preferential Trade Agreements, the application of trade sanctions, the allegedly ambitious agendas on decent work, Aid for Trade and aid untying, and the implications of the changing balance of power in global economic relations. Taking diverse approaches and, at times, reaching different conclusions, contributors directly or indirectly address one or more of the three general themes of the book: differentiation, coherence and norms.

This book was previously published as a special issue of *Contemporary Politics*.

Maurizio Carbone is Professor of International Relations and Development and Jean Monnet Professor of EU External Policies at the University of Glasgow, UK. He has published on EU external relations, most specifically foreign aid, policy coherence for development, and EU–Africa relations.

Jan Orbie is Professor of EU External Relations in the Department of Political Science and Director of the Centre for EU Studies at Ghent University, Belgium. He has extensively published on the European Union's global role, including the trade–development nexus.

The Trade–Development Nexus in the European Union

Differentiation, Coherence and Norms

Edited by
Maurizio Carbone and Jan Orbie

Routledge
Taylor & Francis Group
LONDON AND NEW YORK

First published 2015 by Routledge

2 Park Square, Milton Park, Abingdon, Oxon, OX14 4RN
605 Third Avenue, New York, NY 10017

Routledge is an imprint of the Taylor & Francis Group, an informa business

First issued in paperback 2020

British Library Cataloguing in Publication Data
A catalogue record for this book is available from the British Library

ISBN 13: 978-1-138-81670-1 (hbk)
ISBN 13: 978-0-367-73914-0 (pbk)

Typeset in Times New Roman
by RefineCatch Limited, Bungay, Suffolk

Publisher's Note
The publisher accepts responsibility for any inconsistencies that may have arisen during the conversion of this book from journal articles to book chapters, namely the possible inclusion of journal terminology.

Contents

Citation Information

The chapters in this book were originally published in *Contemporary Politics*, volume 20, issue 1 (March 2014). When citing this material, please use the original page numbering for each article, as follows:

Chapter 1

Beyond Economic Partnership Agreements: the European Union and the trade–development nexus
Maurizio Carbone and Jan Orbie
Contemporary Politics, volume 20, issue 1 (March 2014) pp. 1–9

Chapter 2

Trading in development: norms and institutions in the making/unmaking of European Union–African, Caribbean and Pacific trade and development cooperation
Tony Heron
Contemporary Politics, volume 20, issue 1 (March 2014) pp. 10–22

Chapter 3

Decent work and indecent trade agendas: the European Union and ACP countries
Mark Langan
Contemporary Politics, volume 20, issue 1 (March 2014) pp. 23–35

Chapter 4

Differentiation within reciprocity: the European Union approach to preferential trade agreements
Stephen Woolcock
Contemporary Politics, volume 20, issue 1 (March 2014) pp. 36–48

Chapter 5

EU trade and development policy beyond the ACP: subordinating developmental to commercial imperatives in the reform of GSP
Gabriel Siles-Brügge
Contemporary Politics, volume 20, issue 1 (March 2014) pp. 49–62

Chapter 6

Sanctions under the EU Generalised System of Preferences and foreign policy: coherence by accident?
Clara Portela and Jan Orbie
Contemporary Politics, volume 20, issue 1 (March 2014) pp. 63–76

Chapter 7
Challenging the European Union: the rising powers and the USA in the Doha Round
Anders Ahnlid and Ole Elgström
Contemporary Politics, volume 20, issue 1 (March 2014) pp. 77–89

Chapter 8
Tensions in the discourse and practice of the European Union's Aid for Trade
Patrick Holden
Contemporary Politics, volume 20, issue 1 (March 2014) pp. 90–102

Chapter 9
Much ado about nothing? The European Union and the global politics of untying aid
Maurizio Carbone
Contemporary Politics, volume 20, issue 1 (March 2014) pp. 103–117

Chapter 10
The value of pointillism*? Integrating trade and development and the European Union as a global actor*
Alasdair R. Young
Contemporary Politics, volume 20, issue 1 (March 2014) pp. 118–126

Please direct any queries you may have about the citations to
clsuk.permissions@cengage.com

Notes on Contributors

Anders Ahnlid is Ambassador and Permanent Representative of Sweden to the European Union in Brussels, Belgium.

Maurizio Carbone is Professor of International Relations and Development and Jean Monnet Professor of EU External Policies at the University of Glasgow, UK.

Ole Elgström is Professor of Politics at the Department of Political Science, Lund University, Lund, Sweden.

Tony Heron is Professor of International Politics at the Department of Politics, University of York, York, UK.

Patrick Holden is Lecturer in International Relations at the School of Government, Plymouth University, UK.

Mark Langan is Senior Lecturer at Politics and Applied Global Ethics (PAGE), Leeds Metropolitan University, Leeds, UK.

Jan Orbie is Professor of EU External Relations at the Department of Political Science, Ghent University, Ghent, Belgium.

Clara Portela is Assistant Professor of Political Science at the Singapore Management University, Singapore.

Gabriel Siles-Brügge is Lecturer in Politics at the University of Manchester, UK.

Stephen Woolcock is Associate Professor at the Department of International Relations, London School of Economics, London, UK.

Alasdair R. Young is Associate Professor at The Sam Nunn School of International Affairs, Georgia Institute of Technology, Atlanta, GA, USA.

Beyond Economic Partnership Agreements: the European Union and the trade–development nexus

Maurizio Carbone[a] and Jan Orbie[b]

[a]*School of Social and Political Sciences, University of Glasgow, Glasgow, UK;* [b]*Centre of EU Studies, Ghent University, Ghent, Belgium*

Without disregarding them, this volume seeks to go beyond the controversial and extensively researched Economic Partnership Agreements to offer new perspectives on the evolution of the trade–development nexus in the European Union against dramatic changes in the international context. In particular, it focuses on the reform of the Generalised System of Preferences, the negotiation of various Preferential Trade Agreements, the application of trade sanctions, the allegedly ambitious agendas on decent work, Aid for Trade and aid untying, and the implications of the changing balance of power in global economic relations. Taking diverse approaches and, at times, reaching different conclusions, contributors directly or indirectly address one or more of the three general themes that are discussed in this introduction: differentiation, coherence, and norms.

Introduction

Seismic shifts have occurred in the international arena in recent years. The financial and economic crisis in Western countries, the rise of emerging powers (most notably China, India, and Brazil), the enhanced agency of developing countries, and the increasing challenges of globalisation have influenced the European Union's (EU) trade and development policies. Moreover, the EU has undertaken a number of institutional reforms, most notably the ratification of the Lisbon Treaty, with the view to acting as a stronger and more coherent actor on the international scene (Niemann and Bretherton 2013, Smith 2013). In the context of these reforms, it has pledged to foster better synergies between its trade and development policies. This attention to the trade–development nexus is not new – linking the two policies has been an important concern since the Treaty of Rome – but what has changed is the way in which this nexus has been interpreted. For instance, when the Lomé Convention was signed in the 1970s, in the context of developing countries' increasing 'commodity power' and pleas for a New International Economic Order, the EU's trade and development arrangement with the African, Caribbean and Pacific (ACP) countries was seen as a model of North–South relations (Arts and Dickson 2004, Orbie 2007). Conversely, the 2000 Cotonou Agreement and its provisions on Economic Partnership Agreements (EPAs) witnessed the change in conventional wisdom on the benefits of trade liberalisation (Elgström 2000). For Young and Peterson (2013), the interaction of the two policies since the beginning of the new century has generated a paradox: on the one hand, a greater emphasis on trade as a tool for development, with particular attention to the concerns of those most in need; and on the other hand, a number of policy initiatives, for instance the conclusion of trade agreements with emerging markets, which have adverse consequences for them.

Against this background, this volume seeks to offer fresh insight on the evolution of the trade–development nexus in the EU. Though we cannot disregard this contentious issue, our intention is to go beyond the EPAs, which has been the almost exclusive focus (cf. Faber and Orbie 2007) of studies that have examined the interaction between the EU's trade and development policies (Storey 2006, Elgström and Pilegaard 2008, Faber and Orbie 2009, Di Caprio and Trommer 2010, Elgström and Frenhoff-Larsen 2010, Ngangjoh-Hodu and Matambalya 2010, Hurt 2012, Langan 2012). The reason is not only that they have already been extensively researched, but also that the EPA agenda, having been outlined at the end of the 1990s, predates the above-mentioned seismic changes. Thus, several other key issues are dealt with in this volume, most notably the reform of the Generalised System of Preferences (GSP), the conclusion of Preferential Trade Agreements (PTAs) with different types of countries and regions, the controversial application of trade sanctions, the allegedly ambitious agendas on decent work, Aid for Trade and aid untying, and the implications of the changing balance of power in global economic relations. Considering the variegated nature of these issues, we decided not to impose an overarching framework on contributors, but to leave them free to choose the theoretical debates with which they wished to engage and to which they wanted to contribute. Taking diverse approaches and, at times, reaching different conclusions, they directly or indirectly address one or more of the three general themes that are discussed in the remainder of this introduction: differentiation, coherence, and norms.

Differentiating against a fast-changing context

The EU has placed differentiation – that is, tailoring trade and development policy to match the level of development and development needs of its partners (Woolcock 2014) – at the centre of its trade–development strategy. In the area of development (assistance), the rise of emerging powers and the changing geography of global poverty (with three quarters of the world's poorest people living in middle-income countries) have stimulated a contentious debate as to the future of development policy and the appropriate policies towards different types of countries (Sumner 2012). Thus, with the 2011 *Agenda for change* (Council of the European Union 2012) the EU has proposed a new focus on 'differentiated development partnerships' and redirecting its aid to poorer countries. In particular, this means that development assistance will have to be phased out in about 20 middle-income countries. This proposal has raised doubts in that differentiation is based on income differences between countries rather than income distribution, and, thus, it fails to take into account inequality (Koch 2013). More generally, the commitments on aid volume and aid effectiveness (Carbone 2013a) have been complemented by a stronger emphasis, although with disappointing results, on 'policy coherence for development' (PCD): a number of non-aid policies are seen as having an equal, if not higher, impact on developing countries (Carbone 2008). At the same time, development policy is becoming more integrated into broader EU external relations (Gänzle *et al.* 2012, Carbone 2013b). This could entail a stronger EU-wide commitment to development, but it could also mean that development considerations will become overshadowed by 'superpower temptations' (Orbie 2012).

In the case of trade policy, the 2012 *Trade, Growth and Development* strategy (European Commission 2012) has stipulated that trade policy should be 'tailored' for 'those countries most in need', with trade preferences seen as a crucial instrument in the fight against poverty. These countries include Least Developed Countries (LDCs) and 'vulnerable economies' (that is, countries lacking product diversification and poorly integrated in the global economy), and those countries covered by the Everything but Arms initiative and various GSP + schemes (e.g. countries that sign up to a series of conventions on core human and labour rights, protecting the environments and other good governance standards). More generally, shifting away from the previous 'harnessing globalisation' discourse (Meunier 2007), the EU has brought economic interests to the core of its external trade agenda (Heron and Siles-Brügge 2012). Thus, faced with the stalled World Trade Organisation (WTO) negotiations and pressures for competitive liberalisation from the USA and Asian countries, it has placed more emphasis on trading with emerging powers rather than developing countries (European Commission 2006). Interestingly, the financial and economic crisis has not halted this tendency, but has instead further reinforced the perceived need to foster free trade (De Ville and Orbie 2014).

In this volume, the issue of differentiation is directly addressed by Woolcock (2014). After systematically assessing the substance of EU trade policy towards a number of partners at different levels of development, he concludes that the EU's PTA policy exhibits differentiation within a general shift towards reciprocity vis-à-vis developing countries and that this needs to be assessed as much at the level of specific policy areas as of partner country. He also argues that commercial competition and sector interests are relatively more important in PTAs with emerging markets and high-income developing countries, whereas norms and institutional factors are relatively more important in shaping those with least-developed or low-income developing countries. Ahnlid and Elgström (2014) show how differentiation has also figured in the EU's discourse in the context of the Doha Development Agenda. In particular, the EU was ready to make concessions to the group of developing countries, but called on emerging powers to shoulder responsibility, liberalise their markets, and contribute to the development objectives of the Doha round (Young 2011).

Differentiation, Siles-Brügge (2014) argues, has also inspired the recent GSP reform, which excludes high- or upper-middle-income countries from being the beneficiaries of EU trade preferential treatment and makes it easier for GSP imports to be graduated. The explanation for the rapid acceptance of this reform rests in the fact that it could appeal to three different groups within the EU that have divergent ideas and interests in relation to the trade–development nexus: protectionists, idealists, and free traders. In the context of the economic crisis, protectionists could be comforted that the new regulation limits imports from major competitors. At the same time, EU discourse emphasises the developmental benefits of the reforms, since trade preferences are henceforth reserved for the poorer countries. In addition, free trade-oriented actors can see merits in the GSP's eligibility restrictions because these provide a strong incentive for third countries to engage in free trade agreements in order to safeguard their access to the European market (see also Bilal *et al.* 2011, Stevens 2012).

Policy coherence and international development

The issue of policy coherence has attracted significant interest in the field of EU studies. When applied to the area of external relations, the central concern seems to be the impact of the EU's action and, closely related to this, how the EU gets to speak with one voice. When applied to the area of international development, the central concern is that the needs and interests of developing countries are taken into account when the EU makes and implements policies. Scholarly attention has concentrated on the former (Gebhard 2011, Portela and Raube 2012, Thomas 2012, Bretherton and Vogler 2013), while the latter has attracted limited interest (Carbone 2009, Gänzle *et al.* 2012). This is a serious oversight, particularly because the two do not necessarily pull in the same direction. In particular, the promotion of PCD has been an explicit commitment for the EU since the Treaty of Maastricht, yet it was only in the mid-2000s that it was placed high on the EU agenda. Achieving PCD is considered a sort of 'mission impossible' (Carbone 2008), because it involves the simultaneous interaction of institutions, ideas, and interests. A classical distinction is between *horizontal* coherence, referring to the synergies (or lack of them) between two (or more) policies, and *vertical* coherence, referring to the (potentially conflicting) interactions between the EU's supranational level and the Member States. Existing literature has paid attention to clashes within the European Commission between Directorate General (DG) Development (renamed DG Devco) and DG Trade (Van den Hoven 2007, Holland and Doidge 2012), and between the European Commission and Member States both in trade (Kerremans 2004, Meunier and Nicolaidis 2006, Elgström and Frenhoff-Larsen 2010, da Conceição-Heldt 2011) and development policies (Carbone 2007, Gänzle *et al.* 2012, Orbie and Lightfoot, forthcoming).

A number of contributions in this volume address the issue of horizontal coherence. With regard to public procurement, Carbone (2014) contrasts DG Development's 'pro-poor' view with DG Trade's focus on export potentials for EU businesses. In the case of the Aid for Trade agenda, Holden (2014) laments the lack of a comprehensive vision of how to link trade and development policies, and highlights the presence of tensions between different discourses within the European Commission, notably regional integration, free market, and pro-poor discourses. In the case of trade sanctions, Portela and Orbie (2014) find a surprising level of coherence between trade, development, and foreign policies, far greater than could be expected. Their findings resonate with arguments made by Heron (2014) , who maintains that the EU's institutional fragmentation may have been overrated. Thus, Siles-Brügge (2014) emphasises the balance of domestic-societal interests, with exporters rather than protectionists being a crucial determinant, in the adoption of the GSP reform. Conversely, the issue of vertical coherence does not figure prominently in this volume, although some contributors make certain relevant observations. For instance, Portela and Orbie (2014) show how different constellations of Member States in the Council managed to block attempts to impose trade sanctions, with the view to protecting their political and commercial interests. Similarly, Carbone (2014) discusses the reluctance of a group of Member States to relinquish sovereignty in the area of aid untying, again with the aim of sheltering domestic firms.

Besides horizontal and vertical coherence, two additional types of coherence are relevant to this volume: *multilateral coherence,* which refers to the EU's interaction with relevant international organisations, and *partner coherence,* which refers to the EU's interaction with developing countries (Carbone 2008). These two forms of coherence have important implications for the nature of the EU as a global actor, as well as for the quality of its partnerships with developing countries. Existing literature on EU external relations has focused on both 'positive synergies' and 'institutional rivalry' with various international organisations (Jørgensen 2009, Jørgensen and Laatikainen 2013), particularly the WTO (Elgström and Pilegaard 2008), the United Nations (Holland 2008), the International Labour Organisation (ILO) (Orbie and Tortell 2009), and the Development Assistance Committee (DAC) (Carbone 2012). Regarding the EU's relations with the developing world, existing literature has emphasised, mostly in relation to the EPA agenda, how the EU's free trade and hard-bargaining approach has constrained the policy space of developing countries and has, in most cases, forced them to surrender policy autonomy (Storey 2006, Di Caprio and Trommer 2010, Hurt 2012).

Several contributors in this volume, directly or indirectly, touch upon multilateral and partner coherence. Portela and Orbie (2014) demonstrate that the EU tends to rely on ILO assessments and that an authoritative condemnation by the ILO facilitates the imposition of trade sanctions by the EU. Langan (2014) argues that by aligning with the policy discourse of the ILO, the European Commission presents its economic agenda as conforming to modern economic thought. Carbone (2014) contrasts the EU's comprehensive approach to aid untying, emphasising the potential positive consequences for firms in developing countries, to that of the DAC, which focuses solely on aid effectiveness. Holden (2014) shows how the EU has adapted the WTO's Aid for Trade agenda to fit with its long-running interest in regional integration.

Heron (2014) explains how the invocation of WTO compliance as an external constraint and driver of reform has ultimately weakened the EU's position vis-à-vis the ACP by limiting its room for manoeuvre in dealing with the scepticism widespread among ACP countries about the prospects of reciprocal free trade. However, Woolcock (2014) notes that, despite their lack of market power and negotiation capacity, the EU has guaranteed more policy space to LDCs than it has for other more developed countries. Conversely, Langan (2014) maintains that the EU's decent work agenda has legitimised its attempt to lock-in ACP countries to its strategic vision and has closed down policy space for more interventionist ACP economic agendas that could align more directly with pro-poor norms.

The EU as a (normative?) actor

The EU has attempted to construct an image of being a 'force for good', promoting a range of different norms in combination with its trade and development policies, including democracy and human rights, regional integration, and social standards (Aggarwal and Fogarty 2004, Scheipers and Sicurelli 2008, Kerremans and Orbie 2009, Manners 2009, Whitman 2011). It has, however, faced numerous challenges – and, unsurprisingly, some view the EU as just another realist power, attempting to guarantee itself access to emerging markets and protecting its market from external competition (Farrell 2005, Storey 2006, Hurt 2012, Langan 2012). Moreover, the increased competition with international actors means that the EU may have given up on its self-proclaimed normative distinctiveness to enter a contemporary version of power politics (Smith 2013). Thus, the EU has concluded trade agreements with a number of strategic partners (for example, China, Russia, Japan, India, and Brazil), which threaten to further erode the value of developing countries' access to the EU market (Young and Peterson 2013).

The dichotomy between norms and interests is one of the central themes of this volume. Although differing in their understanding of what a norm is (as pointed out by Young (2014) in the conclusions to this volume), most authors highlight the lofty objectives in EU discourse: its 'developmental' trade policy (Siles-Brügge 2014); 'pro-poor agenda' in promoting aid untying (Carbone 2014); emphasis on regional integration in aid for trade (Holden 2014); claim to pursue human rights through trade (Portela and Orbie 2014); decent work agenda (Langan 2014); and 'benign partner' role (Ahnlid and Elgström 2014). However, their empirical analyses often qualify the normative dimension by pointing out gaps between discourse and practice. For instance, Ahnlid and Elgström (2014) show that in the negotiation of the Doha Development Round not only has the EU become 'more realistic', but the 'benign partner' role is not always shared by the developing countries it negotiates with. Siles-Brügge (2014) argues that although justified in development terms, the reform of the GSP is driven by commercial interests, with the aim of recapturing lost leverage with emerging economies. Holden (2014) finds no significant evidence that that the EU's Aid for Trade agenda resulted in a decreased focus on the poor, but neither there is evidence of EU discourse on pro-poor AfT being translated into actual achievements. Langan (2014) shows that the EU's discursive commitment to decent work not only fails to translate into the attainment of decent jobs by ACP citizens, but has also had a regressive impact on local economies.

More broadly, there is a need to make a more systematic assessment of the EU's normative power (aspirations) through trade that goes beyond simple 'words versus deeds' contrasts (Whitman 2011, Bailey and Bossuyt 2013). Some attempts are made in this volume. For instance, Siles-Brügge (2014), from a political economy perspective, posits that the EU is primarily driven by 'political economic forces' and that it is mainly concerned with establishing liberal markets in which its firms can successfully compete for business. Langan (2014) uses a 'moral economy perspective' to illustrate the co-optive nature of the EU's engagement with external 'partners' and makes the case for 'alternative development strategies' that give more 'policy space' to developing countries as opposed to trade liberalisation. Ahnlid and Elgström (2014), drawing on role theory, argue that transformed power relations have created a situation characterised by role uncertainty; thus, to the challenge posed to its leadership claims by the rise of powers, the EU has reacted by projecting a more realist approach in international trade negotiations. Heron (2014), by blending economic constructivist and historical approaches, contends that while initially the reform of the EU-ACP trade regime rested on a strong convergence between institutions and ideas, in due course there was significant divergence, with institutional dynamics prevailing over norm-based arguments. Holden (2014), on the basis of critical discourse analysis, documents how the global Aid for Trade agenda has been translated and reconfigured at the EU level.

Another important question within the literature on the EU as a global actor is whether the EU can be seen as a 'norm-maker' or a 'norm-taker' in international politics. Regarding trade and development, many scholars claim that the EU has followed 'neoliberal' development paradigms as developed within international organisations (Arts and Dickson 2004, Farrell 2008, Hurt 2012). However, it has also been argued that the EU has played a major role in forging an international consensus on the aid effectiveness agenda (Carbone 2013a) and the Doha Development Agenda (Van den Hoven 2004, Young 2007, Poletti 2012). Through the EPAs and other bilateral agreements, the EU not only pursues free trade but also regional integration and deep integration involving behind-the-border issues, which arguably reflects a desire to promote the 'European model'.

But when it comes to how to interpret and implement the trade–development nexus more generally, the EU experiences difficulties in formulating a distinctive view. In this sense, the 'EU's enthusiasm for a global conception of trade and development is not strong enough to over-ride its own institutional and geoeconomic dynamics' (Holden 2014). Moreover, as argued by Young (2014) in the conclusion to this volume, the various contributions, directly or indirectly, point to the limits of the EU's effectiveness in a policy domain where its power resources are considerable. Thus, the image that is left hanging is one of considerable uncertainty as to how the EU should deal with the trade–development nexus in the changing global context (see Ahnlid and Elgström 2014). Apart from the general recognition that liberalisation will be beneficial for development, that Aid for Trade is a necessary complement to this, and that a differentiated approach should be pursued, the EU's views on the trade–development nexus are hardly original and still in limbo. Unsurprisingly, the EU's contribution to the post-2015 debate has been rather disappointing: its view on 'a decent life for all' barely mentions trade policy and only in the annex does it become clear that the old recipes that have not worked – that is, trade liberalisation with some exceptions and AfT – are again proposed (European Commission 2013).

Conclusion

The EU is the world's largest trading power and the biggest importer of products from developing countries. Combining the supranational and bilateral policies of its Member States, it is also the largest provider of development assistance. While the EU has promoted close links between its trade and development policies since its inception, its interpretation of the trade–development nexus has significantly evolved. Recent research has mostly focused on how this has played out in the EPAs; hence, this volume adds to the existing literature by shedding light on a number of less researched issues at the intersection of the two policies. What seems to emerge is that, despite the clear recognition that the trade–development nexus should be addressed, the EU does not have a clear or distinctive view on how this should happen. Apart from providing insights into recent changes of the EU's trade–development nexus, this volume makes a contribution to wider debates on the EU as a global actor. Theoretically, the question of 'coherence' directs us towards new-institutionalist explanations, whereas the 'normative power' issue brings our attention to ideas and interests. However, as also suggested in Young's concluding reflections, further research would be needed to provide a more theoretically informed picture of how interests, institutions, and ideas interact in shaping the trade–development nexus within the EU's external relations. While the argument to move beyond institutionalist explanations has been made convincingly by some of the authors in this volume, there is still considerable uncertainty as to the causal mechanisms through which institutions, ideas and interests interact. Empirically, a potential way forward would be to move beyond Brussels-centric analyses and concentrate on the effective impact of the EU's trade–development policies on the ground. This would also require interdisciplinary research involving comparative politics, international relations, and development studies.

Acknowledgements

We want to acknowledge support received from the Glasgow Jean Monnet Chair in EU External Policies, held by Prof. Carbone, and the Centre for EU Studies of the University of Ghent, co-directed by Prof. Orbie, to organise a workshop at the University of Glasgow in March 2013, where most of the contributions to this volume were presented. We also want to thank Niels Keijzer, Svea Koch, Mike Smith, Chris Stephens, and Alasdair Young for sharing ideas and giving helpful comments.

References

Aggarwal, V. and Fogarty, E., 2004. *EU trade strategies: between regionalism and globalism*. Basingstoke: Palgrave Macmillan.

Ahnlid, A. and Elgström, O., 2014. Challenging the European Union: the rising powers and the United States in the Doha Round. *Contemporary Politics*, 20 (1), 77–89.

Arts, K. and Dickson, A.K., 2004. *EU development cooperation: from model to symbol*. Manchester: Manchester University Press.

Bailey, D. and Bossuyt, F., 2013. The European Union as a conveniently-conflicted counter-hegemon through trade. *Journal of Contemporary European Research*, 9 (4), 561–577.

Bilal, S., Ramdoo, I., de Roquefeuil, Q., 2011. *GSP reform: principles, values and coherence*. Maastricht: ECDPM, ECDPM briefing note no.24.

Bretherton, C. and Vogler, J., 2013. A global actor past its peak? *International Relations*, 27 (3), 375–390.

Carbone, M., 2007. *The European Union and international development: the politics of foreign aid*. London: Routledge.

Carbone, M., 2008. Mission impossible: the European Union and policy coherence for development. *Journal of European Integration*, 30 (3), 323–342.

Carbone, M., ed., 2009. *Policy coherence and EU development policy*. London: Routledge.

Carbone, M., 2012. Au-delà de l'aide: la cohérence des politiques de développement de l'Europe. *Revue Internationale de Politique de Développement*, 3, 197–212.

Carbone, M., 2013a. Between EU actorness and aid effectiveness: the logics of EU aid to sub-Saharan Africa. *International Relations*, 27 (3), 341–355.

Carbone, M., 2013b. International development and the European Union's external policies: changing contexts, problematic nexuses, contested partnerships. *Cambridge Review of International Affairs*, 26 (3), 483–496.

Carbone, M., 2014. Much ado about nothing? The European Union and the global politics of untying aid. *Contemporary Politics*, 20 (1), 103–117.

da Conceição-Heldt, E., 2011. Variation in EU member states' preferences and the commission's discretion in the doha round. *Journal of European Public Policy*, 18 (3), 403–419.

Council of the European Union, 2012. Council conclusions 'Increasing the impact of EU development policy: an agenda for change'. *3166th Foreign Affairs Council Meeting*, Brussels, 14 May.

De Ville, F. and Orbie, J., 2014. The European commission's neoliberal trade discourse since the crisis: legitimizing continuity through subtle discursive change. *British Journal of Politics and International Relations*, 16 (1), 149–167.

Di Caprio, A. and Trommer, S., 2010. Bilateral graduation: the impact of EPAs on LDC trade space. *Journal of Development Studies*, 46 (9), 1607–1627.

Elgström, O., 2000. Lomé and post-lomé: asymmetric negotiations and the impact of norms. *European Foreign Affairs Review*, 5 (2), 175–195.

Elgström, O. and Pilegaard, J., 2008. Imposed coherence: negotiating economic partnership. *Journal of European Integration*, 30 (3), 363–380.

Elgström, O. and Frenhoff-Larsen, M., 2010. Free to trade? Commission autonomy in the EPA negotiations. *Journal of European Public Policy*, 17 (2), 205–223.

European Commission, 2006. *Global Europe: competing in the world.* COM 567, 4 October.

European Commission, 2012. *Trade, growth and development: tailoring trade and investment policy for those countries most in need.* SEC 87, 27 January.

European Commission, 2013. *A decent life for all.* COM 92, 27 February.

Faber, G. and Orbie, J., eds., 2007. *European Union trade politics and development: 'Everything but Arms' unravelled.* London: Routledge.

Faber, G. and Orbie, J., eds., 2009. *Beyond market access for economic development: EU–Africa relations in transition.* London: Routledge.

Farrell, M., 2005. A triumph of realism over idealism? Cooperation between the European Union and Africa. *Journal of European Integration*, 27 (3), 263–283.

Farrell, M., 2008. Internationalising EU development policy. *Perspectives on European Politics and Society*, 9 (2), 225–240.

Gänzle, S., Grimm, S. and Makhan, D., eds., 2012. *The European Union and global development: an 'enlightened superpower' in the making?* Basingstoke: Palgrave.

Gebhard, C., 2011. Coherence. *In*: C.J. Hill and M. Smith, eds. *International relations and the European Union.* 2nd ed. Oxford: Oxford University Press, 101–127.

Heron, T., 2014. Trading in development: norms and institutions in the making/unmaking of EU-ACP trade and development cooperation. *Contemporary Politics*, 20 (1), 10–22.

Heron, T. and Siles-Brügge, G., 2012. Competitive liberalisation and the 'global Europe' services and investment agenda. *Journal of Common Market Studies*, 50 (2), 250–266.

Holden, P., 2014. Tensions in the discourse and practice of the European Union's Aid for Trade. *Contemporary Politics*, 20 (1), 90–102.

Holland, M., 2008. The EU and the global development agenda. *Journal of European Integration*, 30 (3), 343–362.

Holland, M. and Doidge, M., 2012. *Development policy of the EU.* London: Palgrave.

Hurt, S.R., 2012. The EU-SADC economic partnership agreement negotiations. *Third World Quarterly*, 33 (3), 495–510.

Jørgensen, K.E., ed. 2009. *The European Union and international organizations.* New York: Routledge.

Jørgensen, K.E. and Laatikainen, K.V., eds., 2013. *Routledge handbook on the European Union and international institutions. performance, policy, power.* Abingdon: Routledge.

Kerremans, B., 2004. What Went Wrong in Cancun? A principal-agent view on the EU's rationale towards the Doha Development Round. *European Foreign Affairs Review*, 9 (3), 363–393.

Kerremans, B. and Orbie, J., 2009. The social dimension of European Union trade policies. *European Foreign Affairs Review*, 14 (5), 629–641.

Koch, S., 2013. *From poverty reduction to mutual interests? The debate on differentiation in EU development policy.* Discussion Paper. Berlin: Deutsches Institut für Entwicklungspolitik.

Langan, M., 2012. Normative power Europe and the moral economy of Africa–EU ties. *New Political Economy*, 17 (3), 243–270.

Langan, M., 2014. Decent work and indecent trade agendas: the European Union and ACP countries. *Contemporary Politics*, 20 (1), 23–35.

Manners, I., 2009. The social dimension of EU trade policies: reflections from a normative power perspective. *European Foreign Affairs Review*, 24 (5), 785–803.

Meunier, S., 2007. Managing globalization? the EU in international trade negotiations. *Journal of Common Market Studies*, 45 (4), 906–925.

Meunier, S. and Nicolaïdis, K., 2006. The European Union as a conflicted trade power. *Journal of European Public Policy*, 13 (6), 906–925.

Niemann, A. and Bretherton, C., 2013. EU external policy at the crossroads: the challenge of actorness and effectiveness. *International Relations*, 27 (3), 261–275.

Ngangjoh-Hodu, Y. and Matambalya, F., 2010. *Trade relations between the EU and Africa*. London: Routledge.

Orbie, J., 2007. The European Union and the commodity debate: from trade to aid. *Review of African Political Economy*, 34 (112), 297–311.

Orbie, J., 2012. The EU's role in development: a full-fledged development actor or eclipsed by superpower temptations? *In*: S. Gänzle, S. Grimm and D. Makhan, eds. *The European Union and global development: an 'enlightened superpower' in the making?* London: Palgrave, 17–36.

Orbie, J. and Tortell, L., 2009. The new GSP + beneficiaries: ticking the box or truly consistent with ILO findings? *European Foreign Affairs Review*, 14 (5), 663–681.

Orbie, J. and Lightfoot, S., forthcoming. The Europeanization of development policy. *In*: A. Hadfield, I. Manners, and R.W. Whitman, eds. *The foreign policies of the EU member states*. Abingdon: Routledge.

Poletti, A., 2012. *The European Union and multilateral trade governance: the politics of the doha round*. London: Routledge.

Portela, C. and Raube, K., 2012. The EU polity and foreign policy coherence. *Journal of Contemporary European Research*, 8 (1), 3–20.

Portela, C. and Orbie, J., 2014. Sanctions under the EU Generalised System of Preferences and foreign policy: coherence by accident? *Contemporary Politics*, 20 (1), 63–76.

Scheipers, S. and Sicurelli, D., 2008. Empowering Africa: normative power in EU–Africa relations. *Journal of European Public Policy*, 15 (4), 607–623.

Siles-Brügge, G., 2014. EU trade and development policy beyond the ACP: subordinating developmental to commercial imperatives in the reform of GSP. *Contemporary Politics*, 20 (1), 49–62.

Smith, M., 2013. Foreign policy and development in the post-Lisbon European Union. *Cambridge Review of International Affairs*, 26 (3), 519–535.

Stevens, C., 2012. The proposed new GSP. *In*: ODI, *The next decade of EU trade policy: confronting global challenges*. London: Overseas Development Institute, 22–23.

Storey, A., 2006. Normative power Europe? economic partnership agreements and Africa. *Journal of Contemporary African Studies*, 24 (3), 331–346.

Sumner, A., 2012. Where do the poor live? *World Development*, 40 (5), 865–877.

Thomas, D.C., 2012. Still punching below its weight? coherence and effectiveness in European Union foreign policy. *Journal of Common Market Studies*, 50 (3), 457–474.

Van den Hoven, A., 2004. Assuming leadership in multilateral economic institutions: The EU's 'Development Round' discourse and strategy. *West European Politics*, 27 (2), 256–283.

Van den Hoven, A., 2007. Bureaucratic competition in EU trade policy. *In*: G. Faber and J. Orbie, eds. *European Union trade politics and development: 'Everything but Arms' unravelled*. London: Routledge, 60–73.

Whitman, R.W., ed., 2011. *Normative power Europe: empirical and theoretical perspectives*. Basingstoke: Palgrave.

Woolcock, S., 2014. Differentiation within reciprocity: the EU approach to preferential trade agreements. *Contemporary Politics*, 20 (1), 36–48.

Young, A.R., 2014. The value of pointillism? Integrating trade and development and the EU as a global actor. *Contemporary Politics*, 20 (1), 118–126.

Young, A.R., 2007. Trade politics ain't what it used to be: the European Union in the doha round. *Journal of Common Market Studies*, 45 (4), 789–811.

Young, A.R., 2011. The rise (and fall?) of the EU's performance in the multilateral trading system. *Journal of European Integration*, 33 (6), 715–729.

Young, A.R. and Peterson, J., 2013. 'We care about you, but . . . ': the politics of EU trade policy and development. *Cambridge Review of International Affairs*, 26 (3), 497–518.

Trading in development: norms and institutions in the making/unmaking of European Union–African, Caribbean and Pacific trade and development cooperation

Tony Heron

Department of Politics, University of York, York, UK

This paper offers a contribution to recent debates on European Union (EU) external trade and development policy, with a specific focus on the African, Caribbean and Pacific (ACP) group of countries. The question asked is why the EU encountered such difficulties in the attempt to translate its normative preferences for freer trade and closer economic integration into a series of binding agreements? Drawing on both economic constructivist and historical institutionalist insights, it is argued that the case for reform initially rested on a strong convergence between institutions and ideas, enabling the EU to discursively present desired policy reforms as necessary to satisfy World Trade Organisation trade rules. However, in due course, the institutional dynamics behind the latter began to diverge from the EU's policy preferences and blunt its norm-based argument – thus creating the space for transnational coalitions to, first, question and, ultimately, undermine aspects the EU's trade and development prospectus for the ACP.

Introduction

This volume comes in the wake of unwelcomed anniversaries for both the World Trade Organisation (WTO) Doha Development Agenda (DDA) of 2001 and the European Union–African, Caribbean and Pacific (EU–ACP) Cotonou Agreement of 2000. In both cases, the new millennium saw the launching of a bold prospectus for redefining trade and development cooperation between rich and poor countries that has since founded. Although the two are defined by different institutional trajectories, negotiation objectives and political dynamics, what they share is that, in the end, each failed to come up with a package of measures capable of simultaneously satisfying the desire to promote and extend the liberalisation of trade with that of clarifying and strengthening rules on 'special and differential' treatment (SDT) for developing countries. In the case of the DDA, even though the latest WTO Ministerial Conference, held in the Indonesian island of Bali between 5 and 7 December 2013, did reach agreement on a limited range of issues from the original Doha package (trade facilitation, agriculture and cotton, plus one or two development measures), this represented a weak and partial imitation of what was pledged back in 2001. In the case of the Cotonou Agreement – the main empirical focus of this paper – the EU-CARIFORUM Economic Partnership Agreement (EPA) concluded in October 2008 remains the only agreement of its kind. Whatever the final outcome of the negotiations, it is fair to say that the trade component of the Cotonou Agreement looks increasingly likely to fall short of the ambitious plans laid out in 2000.

How, then, do we account for these suboptimal outcomes? How far do the DDA and Cotonou share intrinsic features, which explain the difficulty each has had in translating trade and development principles into substantive agreements? At least insofar as the former is concerned, the ongoing problems in the EPA negotiations have prompted scholars to focus on the political dimension (Del Felice 2012, Hurt *et al.* 2013, Trommer 2013, Siles-Brügge 2014). A common theme in this recent literature has been highlighting the active role of the ACP, in alliance with transnational advocacy coalitions, in rebutting the EU's depiction of the EPAs as 'non-coercive' and 'development-friendly' and to, instead, portray them as coercive, driven by self-interest and potentially deeply damaging to the ACP. In other words, the failure of the EU's trade and development prospectus for the ACP has not occurred by chance.

This insight undoubtedly provides a welcome corrective to the early literature, which (either explicitly or implicitly) presupposed that the EU's market and financial power would be sufficient to bring the EPAs into being. However, it arguably does not go far enough in uncovering why the EU's prospectus has proven to be so vulnerable to rebuttal. Put another way, how is it that in spite of the obvious power asymmetries involved and the ostensible commitment of the ACP to closer economic integration the EU has encountered such difficulties translating its free trade preferences into concrete agreements? In addressing this puzzle, the main contribution of this paper is to reconsider something that in the past was assumed to be integral to the reform process: namely the need to conform to the WTO's multilateral trade norms and legal disciplines. Although the extant literature has been sceptical about the importance of this – that is, when weighed against the independent, political and commercial interests of the EU – few scholars have sought to understand WTO compatibility itself as anything other than a strategic asset in the EU's attempts to persuade sceptical ACP states of the merits of reciprocal free trade.

In this paper, we turn this conventional orthodoxy on its head by looking more carefully at the political implications of WTO compliance for the full realisation of the EU's post-Lomé vision – especially in the light of the parallel difficulties that the WTO itself has encountered in delivering a package of trade and development measures capable of satisfying the institution's disparate membership. Theoretically speaking, the paper blends insights from both economic constructivist and historical institutionalist approaches to demonstrate how the invocation of WTO compliance as an external constraint and driver of reform actually served to weaken the EU's position by exposing the limited and uneven nature of its policy leverage over the ACP, alongside the difficulties of crafting trade and development cooperation agreements in accordance with WTO trade norms (Heron and Murray-Evans 2013). On the one hand, the paper takes seriously the independent causal role of ideas in determining political outcomes, particularly in moments of economic crisis and institutional uncertainty (Blyth 2002). On the other hand, it also recognises the constraining effects of policy institutionalisation and path dependency in delimiting the space and opportunity available to agents employing ideas- or norm-based arguments to justify radical policy change. Following Parsons (2007), ideas and institutions are thus conceived as operating according to separate but connected logics, where neither is entirely independent from nor reducible to the other.

Put in more straightforward language, the paper argues that the promotion by EU policy actors of trade reciprocity via the Cotonou Agreement and the EPAs rested on a strong convergence between institutionalised (legal) norms and the EU's separate norm-based (policy) preferences – the first referring to the legal imperatives created by WTO rules and the second the EU's desire to recast its relationship with the ACP in line with neoliberal conceptions of development – which was initially present but soon began to dissipate. Although the presumed necessity of WTO compliance initially enabled EU actors to conflate the desirability of the EPAs with the requirements of WTO trade law, in due course path-dependent institutional practices associated with the former served to blunt the effectiveness of this discursive strategy. Once the institutional landscape and the EU's discursive strategy were revealed to be at odds with one another, the EU's norm-based advocacy of the EPAs had limited reach – thus creating the discursive space for transnational activists to, first, question and, ultimately, undermine important aspects of the EU's development prospectus for the ACP.

To explain and substantiate this interpretation, the rest of the paper proceeds in three stages. First, the next section (re-) examines the relationship between the exigencies of WTO compatibility and the shift towards reciprocity in EU–ACP trade relations. Here, the key point is to show that the creation of the WTO not only highlighted the incompatibly between discriminatory trade preferences and the most-favoured nation (MFN) principle, but also an unresolved tension between this and the organisation's nominal commitment to SDT for the developing countries. In other words, while the WTO's enhanced legal disciplines drew a line under General Agreement on Tariffs and Trade (GATT)-inconsistent trade preferences typified by Lomé, these disciplines provided few clues as to how the latter could be rendered WTO compatible in a manner consistent with SDT principles, which was the ostensible objective of the Cotonou Agreement. In the second section of the paper, we apply this insight to three features of the EPAs – the legal ambiguity concerning eligibility for preferential treatment, the limited and uneven nature of the EU's policy leverage and the blurring of the boundaries between the EU's developmental and commercial priorities – with the aim of showing why the EU's trade and development prospectus for the ACP has been less successful than expected. A brief concluding section assesses the wider implications of the approach taken for understanding the likely future shape and direction of the EU's external trade and development agenda.

The rise and fall of Lomé

First, then, what was the significance of the creation of the WTO for the demise of Lomé and the difficulties that its successor – the Cotonou Agreement and the EPAs – eventually ran into? The prevalent interpretation found in the extant literature has been to dismiss the importance of WTO compatibility, or at least to demonstrate that EU policy-makers possessed a much greater range of policy options for dealing with the strengthening of multilateral trade rules than they were willing to acknowledge (Stevens 2008). This much is not in doubt. But what remains underexplored in these accounts in the extent to which appeals to WTO compliance as an external driver of trade reform ultimately proved to be self-defeating, by limiting the EU's room for manoeuvre in dealing with the scepticism widespread among the ACP about the prospect of reciprocal free trade (McQueen 1998). In order to understand why this was the case, we need to consider the peculiar way in which SDT was accommodated within the GATT – and therefore the WTO – and how this ultimately served to limit the scope for crafting trade and development cooperation agreements that at the same time conformed to other WTO rules.

Although SDT is indelibly associated with the GATT, the concept was not actually enshrined in the organisation's legal texts until 1979 (Heron 2013). By this point, the principles underpinning it had already been operationalised de facto in the form of two sets of institutional practices that came to define the relationship between rich and poor countries under the GATT: namely asymmetrical reciprocity and unilateral trade preferences. Asymmetrical reciprocity, on the one hand, referred to the institutional practice whereby the developed countries waived developed countries of their obligations under Article I to offer reciprocal market access. This institutional practice did not, it is important to note, amount to a legally definable obligation; rather, it was part of a highly informal process by which the enforcement of GATT disciplines was over time applied to the developing countries with less and less consistency (Hudec 1987).

Unilateral trade preferences, on the other hand, referred to the institutional practice by which the developed countries granted one-way market access to the developed countries, above and beyond that offered on a MFN basis to all GATT members. Although such preferences were omitted from the GATT at the time of its creation, calls for their inclusion became progressively louder as the numerical balance of the organisation's membership began to shift in favour of the developing countries in the late 1950s and 1960s. This culminated in the creation of the generalised system of preferences (GSP) in 1968, made permanent by 1979 Enabling Clause. Yet, as in the case of asymmetrical reciprocity, GATT disciplines governing unilateral preferences were never placed on an entirely secure legal footing. For one, although the Enabling Clause legally empowered the contracting parties to grant non-reciprocal trade preferences (provided that they were offered to all developing countries and did not discriminate between them) there was nothing requiring them to do so. In fact, all decisions regarding the duration of preferences, graduation, product coverage and preference margins were left entirely to the discretion of the preference-granting country (Hoekman and Özden 2005). The most significant anomaly with the GSP was the legal ambiguity surrounding eligibility for preferences. While providing the legal grounds for preferential treatment in favour of developing countries, the logically prior task of defining a 'developing' country was never satisfactorily resolved. Although the narrower concept of 'least developed' was codified under the Enabling Clause (referring to those countries formally classified as such by the United Nations), developing country status under the GATT became a matter of self-declaration – a practice that continues to this day under the WTO. In other words, aside from the least developed countries (LDCs), the concept of a 'developing' county in relation to preferential trade came to have close to no legal standing in the multilateral trading system.

Ultimately, these informal institutional practices and ad hoc decision-making procedures would leave a lasting legacy on Europe's trade and development relations with its former colonies – not only during the Lomé period but also after the creation of the WTO and the introduction of the enhanced dispute settlement understanding (DSU), shortly after which EU policy-makers sought to redefine relations with the ACP on the basis of reciprocal free trade. Although the European Economic Community (EEC) itself constituted a legally permitted form of trade discrimination under Article XXIV, its formation also brought the former African colonies of France and Belgium into the GATT fold. The reason this was significant is that, prior to the Treaty of Rome, these colonies benefited from trade preferences covered by a derogation enshrined in Article I of the GATT. The formation of the Customs Union meant that all members would now in effect grant these preferences, even though only France and Belgium were legally entitled to offer them. At the time, the EEC justified this anomaly by arguing that each arrangement constituted a separate 'free trade area' and was thus authorised under Article XXIV. This was a dubious defence, not least since even though these arrangements were nominally reciprocal they did not come close to satisfying GATT legal requirements for the prompt and complete liberalisation of 'substantially all trade' (Hudec 1987, p. 49).

The UK's accession to the Common Market in 1975 necessitated extending the geographical focus of existing preferences to ACP, although not as it turned out South Asian, Commonwealth states. But rather than simply do this or take the opportunity to bring existing preferences into line with the GATT, policy-makers decided upon a much more ambitious global regime even more odds with the MFN principle. The Lomé Convention – the first protocol (1975–1979) in particularly – now stands in retrospect as something of a highpoint in the attempt to recast North–South relations in the light of the demand for a new international economic order (NIEO) (Brown 2000). Unlike the GSP, preferences granted under Lomé were legally contractual and therefore could not be altered or withdrawn unilaterally. The Lomé regime also reflected some of the other demands emanating from the NIEO, including a substantial aid delivery mechanism in the form of the European Development Fund (EDF), plus compensatory mechanisms to assist countries suffering price fluctuations for primary commodities (STABEX) and to guarantee the production of certain minerals (SYSMIN). Finally, Lomé was governed by an elaborate set of joint EEC-ACP institutions, including a Council of Ministers, Committee of Ambassadors and Joint Parliamentary Assembly.

In sum, Lomé constituted something of a paradox in the postwar trade architecture. Although its existence was difficult to square with multilateral legal disciplines it appeared to rest on precisely what the GSP lacked: a set of specified legal obligations according to which preferences and other forms of SDT could operate. Yet, Lomé was also a product of its time in that its very existence rested on the unique institutional environment of the GATT, wherein the dominant mode of trade diplomacy often rested on a tenuous link to the legal norms and procedures on which it was supposedly based. In this respect, Lomé shared something in common with the GSP in that neither scheme was been built on secure legal foundations. The accommodation of the special and differential needs of the developing countries was achieved on the basis of a series of informal concessions that stopped short of actual policy changes altering the legal obligations of the developed countries towards the developing countries. Although Part IV of the GATT and even more so the 1979 Enabling Clause were designed to correct this anomaly, the centrepiece of these reforms – the GSP – was arguably beset by as many legal ambiguities as schemes like Lomé that functioned more or less outside of the GATT.

The significance of these anomalies only became fully apparent following the creation of the WTO in 1995. In other words, with the installation of a more legally robust dispute settlement system such trade preferences were more likely to be – and indeed in Lomé's case *were* – deemed in violation of the MFN principle. Although much was made subsequently about the role of the DSU in precipitating the demise of Lomé – not least by the EU itself – the original dispute was provoked, not principally by the legality or otherwise of the regime itself, but by the creation of the single banana market in 1992 as part of the implementation of the Single European Act (Ravenhill 2004, Alter and Meunier 2006). Nevertheless, the upshot was that the banana regime was found by three separate panels – 1993, 1994 and 1997 – to contravene various aspects of GATT trade law, including Article I (non-discrimination), Article III.4 (national treatment), Article XIII (non-discrimination in the application of quantitative restrictions), Article XXIV (free trade areas) as well as Article V of the General Agreement on Services and aspects of EU competition law. Most significantly, by ruling the banana protocol in contravention of Article I, the GATT, in effect, signalled that the entire Lomé regime was open to legal challenge – a challenge, moreover, made far more likely to succeed in the light of the impending introduction of the DSU. The 1994 panel not only found that the protocol contravened the MFN principle, it was also unconvinced by the EU's defence that Lomé fell under the rubric of Article XXIV. The reason for this was that the absence of reciprocity meant that these trade arrangements could not possibly satisfy the GATT legal requirements for the prompt and complete liberalisation of 'substantially all trade'. Crucially, the panel also concluded that since neither Part IV nor the Enabling Clause mention Article XXIV, no recourse could be made to SDT as the basis for exemption from the MFN requirement. Finally, because SDT under the GATT and WTO operated on the idiosyncratic principle of 'self-declaration' the only other basis on which to offer non-reciprocal preferences – that is, short of a legal waiver – was to extend these to all developing countries or limit them to those classified by the UN as LDCs.

The EU's immediate response to all of this was to seek and subsequently obtain a five-year waiver for Lomé in what was one of the very last acts of the Uruguay Round. At this point, the EU possessed the option to seek a further waiver – for which numerous precedents under both the GATT and WTO existed – but soon intimated that its intention would be to recast the entire Lomé system in a way which would render it compatible with Article XXIV. After considering a number of alternative ways of achieving this objective (including the standard application of GSP, a single agreement based on the principle of uniform reciprocity as well as a series of 'differentiated' FTAs involving individual regions and countries), the Cotonou Agreement ultimately settled on the formulae of replacing Lomé with separate EPAs based on six ACP 'regions' identified later by the European Commission. In order to make this possible, the EU sought an extension to the WTO waiver (subsequently granted during the 2001 Doha ministerial in Qatar) in order to allow the ACP sufficient breathing space to prepare for the EPA negotiations, to begin in September 2002 and end no later than 31 December 2007. The Cotonou Agreement, however, made special provisions for LDCs, which would be granted Lomé-equivalent duty – and quota-free (DFQF) preferences under what became the 'Everything but Arms' (EBA) agreement of 2001. By replacing Lomé with reciprocal EPAs for non-LDCs while offering unilateral DFQF treatment to eligible LDCs, the EU appeared to resolve the problem of WTO incompatibility since the regime would now be legally consistent with both the Enabling Clause and – via Article XXIV – the MFN principle. In short, the Cotonou Agreement appeared to offer a prospectus for how SDT might be operationalised under the new global trade architecture, heralded by the arrival of the WTO.

From Lomé to Cotonou to the EPAs

As it turned out, the expiry of the WTO waiver on 31 December 2007 came and went without a single reciprocal agreement having been signed. In 2011, the European Commission reported that only 36 out of 79 ACP states had even signed an 'interim' EPA, with only 18 (4 outside of the Caribbean) deemed to have taken sufficient steps to ratify and implement these agreements (Bilal and Ramdoo 2011). The one exception to this pattern was CARIFORUM. In this case, local trade officials were evidently persuaded that, in the absence of the legal protection afforded by the waiver, the conclusion of a reciprocal agreement was essential to safeguarding remaining preferences from further WTO litigation (CRNM 2008). In addition, regional elites broadly shared the view of EU officials that a comprehensive agreement, while not strictly necessary for satisfying multilateral trade rules, would improve access to the EU market for non-traditional Caribbean exports, thus fostering economic diversification and lessening the region's long-standing dependence on agricultural commodities blighted by preference erosion and declining terms of trade. Finally, the relatively advanced stage of regional integration in the Caribbean, coupled with relative homogeneity in terms of the sensitivity of individual member states to the effects of preference erosion, meant that the insistence on a region-based agreement caused few problems for CARIFORUM, at least compared with the situation elsewhere. In sum, the CARIFORUM agreement was a product of a relatively strong convergence between legal and institutional norms as enshrined in the WTO and the neoliberal policy preferences of EU policy-makers and their CARIFORUM counterparts (Heron 2011).

While it is certainly true that the relatively advanced nature of regional integration in the CARIFORUM region, combined with relative homogeneity in terms of sensitivity to the effects of preference erosion, provides part of the answer to why the region was willing to sign a comprehensive EPA when the rest of the ACP was not, endogenous factors alone cannot explain this variation. Rather, it is the case that, over time, the EU's strategic appeals to WTO compliance as an external driver of the reforms had the unintended effect of complicating what was already a complicated process. Despite the fact that critics were quick to recognise the fact that Article XXIV was a good deal more ambiguous and hence flexible than EU policy-makers were willing to acknowledge – especially in relation to what was precisely meant by 'substantially all trade' (South Centre 2008, Trommer 2013) – few considered the full implications of this. This related not just to the ability of EU policy-makers to plausibly invocate WTO compliance as an external constraint, but also to its appropriateness as a legal mechanism for crafting free trade agreements consistent with principles of SDT, which was claimed to be at the heart of the EPAs. In the next section, we apply this insight to three anomalous features of the EPAs – the legal ambiguity concerning eligibility for preferential treatment, the limited and uneven nature of the EU's policy leverage, and the blurred boundary between the EU's developmental and commercial priorities – which, when combined, hold the key to understanding why the EU's trade and development prospectus for the ACP has met with less success than might have otherwise been expected.

The legal ambiguity concerning eligibility for preferential treatment

In recent years, it has become something of a truism to attribute the general failure of the EU's post-Lomé trade and development agenda for the ACP to Trade Commissioner Pascal Lamy's fateful decision in 2001 to grant DFQF treatment to the LDCs unilaterally under the EBA (see, among others, Ravenhill 2004, Stevens 2008). To do so, however, begs an obvious question: in designing a successor to Lomé, why did the EU seek to differentiate between LDCs and non-LDCs with respect to eligibility for preferential treatment in the first place and how is it that it has been unable to reconcile this objective with the promotion regionally based agreements? A common answer to these questions centres on the issue of policy incoherence brought about by the competing bureaucratic interests and overlapping competences of DG Trade, on the one hand, and DG Development, on the other (Carbone 2007, van den Hoven 2007). While this interpretation in not entirely wide of the mark, it does rather neglect the fact that the 1996 *Green Paper on Relations between the EU and the ACP Countries* – which established the principle of differentiation – was authored entirely by officials in DG Development and before DG Trade had responsibility for the ACP (Siles-Brügge 2014).

Other explanations, instead, focus on the sheer diversity and complexity of the ACP as a source of the difficulties. Ravenhill (2004, p. 135), in this vein, refers to the general absence in the ACP of 'a coincidence between geography and level of development', meaning that the two categories of countries – LDCs and non-LDCs – are scattered across each region (the Caribbean being the only partial exception to this rule), which in turn made it almost impossible to construct a regional order that at the same time corresponded with the legal requirements of multilateral trade rules. This characterisation is almost certainly true. If pushed too far, however, it serves to reify the distinction between these categories and thus confirm the Commission's version of events, regarding the necessity of WTO compliance and appropriateness of Article XXIV as the means to achieve this. Although the demise of Lomé was prompted by the GATT rulings against it, the normative thrust behind the mooted reforms was the belief that Lomé failed to achieve basic development objectives because the lack of reciprocity served to inhibit the types of policy reform that were by this point deemed essential for economic development. The corollary to this logic was that the introduction of reciprocity would not only produce a more legally robust trade regime but – and this is the crucial point – would expose the economies of the ACP to the exigencies of the global trade system, thus creating an environment conducive to market-oriented policy reform.

In order to achieve this, EU policy-makers discursively presented WTO compliance as an immovable and external constraint, setting the policy parameters inside of which post-Lomé trade arrangements would, by necessity, have to be conceived. The problem with this is that it oversold the robustness of GATT norms and rendered them unproblematic in a way that reduced the EU's room for manoeuvre, arguably making the goal of reciprocal free trade harder rather than easier to achieve. To put the point another way, the difficulties that the EU encountered in prosecuting its post-Lomé trade vision do not stem, at least not primarily, from the diversity and complexity of the ACP but from the fact that eligibility for trade preferences in accordance multilateral trade disciplines is something that was never adequately addressed, either under the GATT or WTO. Although Article XXIV seemed to offer a neat solution to the GATT inconsistency of Lomé it makes no mention of SDT and hence provided no guidance as to how 'development-friendly' free trade agreements might be rendered WTO compatible beyond the simple matter of reciprocity. Further, because Article XXIV was nested in the wider system of multilateral trade regulation in which SDT relied for most part on voluntary concessions (from the developed countries) and self-declaration (from the developing countries), the only basis on which development provisions could be enshrined in the EPAs was if they applied solely to LDCs. But since the EU chose to interpret Article XXIV as requiring region-based agreements, achieving this was all but impossible (again, outside of the Caribbean) given the heterogeneous nature of the ACP.

The limited and uneven nature of the EU's policy leverage

Although the European Commission's 1996 *Green Paper* – which anticipated Cotonou and hence the EPAs – set out a number of alternative options, the trade component of the Cotonou Agreement adopted the formulae of replacing Lomé with separate EPAs based on six regional configurations. The EU's decision to opt for this region-based solution to the problem of WTO compliance appeared justified on legal, normative and practical grounds. That is to say, once EU policy-makers dismissed out of hand the prospect of seeking a further WTO waiver, Article XXIV was deemed to be the only possible means of satisfying multilateral trade rules. While, in theory, this did not require a region-based solution – agreements based on uniform or differentiated reciprocity had just as much chance of satisfying this requirement – this was apparently ruled out on the grounds of practicality, given the heterogeneity and complexity of the ACP group that, by this point, numbered more than 70 countries. However, it is difficult to ignore the fact that this blueprint coincided with a growing enthusiasm among EU policy-makers for the external promotion of neoliberal development norms, especially regional integration (Heron and Murray-Evans 2013). Elements of neoliberal policy conditionality had begun creeping into EU–ACP development cooperation from the mid-1980s (Brown 2000); however, this was mainly in relation to EDF resources while the centrepiece of Lomé – non-reciprocal market access – was to all intents and purposes immune from these initial reform pressures. Indeed, it was precisely for this reason that EU policy-makers sought to introduce reciprocity in the belief that greater exposure to global market pressures would help to promote the types of policy reform that, it was believed, would spur economic growth and diversification. Hence, the Cotonou Agreement and, even more so, the EPAs rested on the ability of the EU to exercise the policy leverage afforded by the ACP's dependence on preferences to impose domestic and regional reforms. By invoking WTO compliance as an external constraint the beneficiaries of Lomé would be left with little alternative but sign reciprocal EPAs or else incur the loss of preferential access to a primary export market.

The flaw in this strategy, which became apparent more or less as soon as the EPA negotiations began in earnest in 2002, was twofold. On the one hand, the policy leverage afforded by the ACP's dependence on preferences only extended as far as each beneficiary was equally dependent on preferences and hence similarly exposed by liberalisation. On the other hand, even if this were the case – which it was not – there would still be incongruence between the desire to secure reciprocity at a regional level and the fact that the policy levers used to achieve this could only be deployed at a national level. This incongruence, furthermore, was accentuated by the principle of 'differentiation' enshrined in the Cotonou Agreement and later implemented through EBA, which ensured that there would be zero costs for LDCs because preferential access was guaranteed whether they signed an EPA or not. The limited and uneven nature of the EU's policy leverage helps to explain why, in public at least, the

European Commission was keen to downplay any coercive element to the agreements and to, instead, emphasise the desirability of the EPAs based on their 'comprehensive' nature above and beyond ensuring continuity of preferential market access. Yet, this discursive tactic ran into two immediate problems. The first was that, as EU policy-makers were all too aware, although the ACP as a whole viewed pro-market economic reforms as necessary for development (with greater or lesser degrees of enthusiasm) the group had been sceptical from the outset about the prospect of reciprocal free trade with the EU (McQueen 1998). In the absence of coercion, it therefore seemed unlikely that many would be persuaded by the case for enshrining these commitments in a new contractual arrangement with the EU – a case, moreover, not helped by the latter's insistence on the inclusion of a raft of WTO-plus provisions that served to confirm the suspicion among many that the desired reforms were ultimately driven by commercial self-interest (Murray-Evans 2013). The second, closely related point is that by emphasising the 'non-coercive' and 'development-friendly' nature of the EPAs, the EU's norm-based argument was open to contestation by critics of the negotiations, which portrayed the agreements in a far more negative light. This is an issue we shall return to shortly, after first considering the consequences of the entanglement of the EU's development and commercial trade objectives.

The blurring of the boundaries between the EU's 'development' and 'commercial' priorities

We now turn to what has been one of the most contentious and politically divisive aspects of the entire EPA process – the inclusion of the so-called Singapore issues. These issues did not become central to the negotiations until the mid-2000s, following the collapse of the WTO Cancún ministerial in September 2003 and in the context of the growing entwinement of the EU's commercial and development agendas associated with the advancement of the Lisbon Agenda. It was at this point that the role of the WTO as an external driver of the reforms diverged most starkly from the EU trade and development prospectus for the ACP. This, in turn, provided the discursive space for transnational advocacy coalitions to counter the EU's case for the necessity and desirability of the EPAs. We can recall from our earlier discussion that, although the abandonment of Lomé hinged on the necessity of WTO compliance, the decision was informed by a more or less independent set of normative convictions, concerning the desirability of reciprocity and market-oriented policy reform. Although conformity with Article XXIV required reciprocal liberalisation for trade in *goods*, this did not extend to the Singapore issues since these issue areas were still to be agreed upon at the multilateral level. The Cotonou Agreement nonetheless made reference to these issues, albeit vaguely, as potential areas of negotiation, reflecting the EU's desire to use the EPAs to promote a wider set of economic reforms. Furthermore, while unrelated to Article XXIV, the inclusion of the Singapore issues was, at least at this stage, premised on the belief that it was very much in keeping with the general negotiating direction in which the WTO appeared to be heading. Indeed, the publication of the aforementioned *Green Paper* coincided with the launching of a separate strategy paper (European Commission 1996, Faber and Orbie 2009, Heron and Siles-Brügge 2012), which formed the basis for the EU's Millennium – and later Doha – Trade Round objectives first enunciated at the Singapore ministerial in 1996.

Following the debacle at Cancún in 2003, however, the three most controversial Singapore issues (competition policy, transparency in government procurement and investment) were dropped from the Doha agenda, thus signalling a clear divergence between the EU's EPA agenda and the underlying legal and institutional parameters on which the agreements were supposedly based. But this divergence was not simply a matter of chance. Rather, the collapse of the

Cancún reflected the path-dependent institutional dynamics of the entire WTO negotiating process, regarding the content and indeed the overall desirability of a further round of multilateral liberalisation (Narlikar and Wilkinson 2004). The key summative point is that the majority of developing county delegations approached Cancún – and the Seattle ministerial before it – believing that their developed country counterparts had failed to deliver promises made during the previous Uruguay Round – what had become known as the 'implementation issues' – but were now seeking to open up negotiations in the 'Singapore issues' without first addressing these grievances.

The EU's eventual response to Cancún was informed by an ongoing internalisation and strategic deployment of a discourse of 'global competitiveness' as a pretext for neoliberal policy reform (Tsoukalis 1997, Rosamond 2002). In 2006, the EU launched its *Global Europe* trade strategy, the essential thrust of which was that the internal dimension of the Lisbon Agenda needed to run in tandem with a more offensive external trade strategy, where the Singapore issues would be a priority (Hay 2007). *Global Europe* suggested that the ACP countries were peripheral to Europe's main commercial interests in Asia and Latin America. Specifically, the European Commission (2006, pp. 10–11) made a clear distinction between its 'main trade interests' and trade agreements with peripheral countries, wherein the primary motive would be promoting sustainable development through the gradual regional and global integrations of these countries into the world economy, in a manner consistent with WTO rules. However, it is striking that the arrival of Peter Mandelson at DG Trade in the aftermath of the Cancun ministerial coincided with the increased prominence of the Singapore issues in the EPA negotiations (Heron and Siles-Brügge 2012).

Measured against the continuation and extension of its EPA strategy based on comprehensive national and regional trade policy reforms, the collapse of Cancun represented the most striking divergence between the EU's legal case for the abandonment of Lomé and its normative preferences for a successor regime based on reciprocity and free trade. This had the effect of blunting the EU's strategic appeals to WTO rules as an external constraint that rendered the EPAs necessary as well as desirable. In other words, the more the EU emphasised the Singapore issues, the less traction was to be gained from continuing to invoke the necessity of WTO compliance, since this obviously went beyond what was strictly required to satisfy multilateral trade rules, particularly once these issues had been dropped from the WTO agenda altogether. On top of this, the entwinement of the EU's 'commercial' and 'development' agendas raised the costs of signing up to an EPA for ACP countries. These costs came not only in the form of reciprocity and compliance with the EU's insistence on reforms associated with the Singapore issues, but also a raft of other requirements, including an 'MFN clause' and a ban on export taxes (Heron and Murray-Evans 2013). The EU's justification for the inclusion of these measures in the negotiations – namely that it did not want to be put at a competitive disadvantage as a result of having signed the EPAs – was difficult to square with the oft-cited claim by its officials that there were no 'offensive interests' at stake in the negotiations. The MFN clause in particular caused consternation for those ACP countries and regions for which the EU was not the dominant trade partner or which hoped to form future trade partnerships with emerging powers. Overall, the increasing prominence of the Singapore issues in the negotiations after Cancun meant that Commission officials now had to rely more and more on moral suasion to convince the ACP of the merits of 'comprehensive' EPAs, particularly in the case of LDCs and non-preference-dependent countries.

All told, the effect of the divergence between EU preferences and the trajectory of developments in the WTO was to expose the former to a rhetorical onslaught from the critics of the EPAs – ACP governments, sceptical EU member states, nongovernmental organisations and activists – which mobilised to effectively rebut the European Commission's depiction of the

EPAs as 'non-coercive' and 'development-friendly' and to, instead, portray them as coercive, driven by self-interest and potentially deeply damaging to the ACP. Although opposition to the EPAs from elements of global civil society began almost as soon as the talks got under way in September 2002 (Traidcraft 2003, ActionAid 2004), there is no doubt that the increasing prominence of the Singapore issues in the negotiations after Cancún meant that the Commission could no longer hide behind the pretext of WTO compatibility and was forced to make the case for the desirability of the EPAs even in the absence of their necessity (Heron and Murray-Evans 2013). In this context, opposition groups were able draw on what Schimmelfennig (2001) calls 'rhetorical action' – the strategic use of norm-based arguments – to, first, question and, ultimately, undermine important aspects of the EU's case. In promoting the complementarily of 'development' and 'competitiveness' discourses in order to downplay the coercive element and emphasise the positive-sum nature of the EPAs, EU policy-makers were, in short, hoisted by their own petard.

Conclusion

As an example of North–South trade diplomacy, the failure of the EPAs to make much headway in recent years presents students of International and European Political Economy with a striking analytical puzzle: that is, in spite of the obvious power asymmetries involved, alongside the policy leverage afforded by its market and financial power, the EU has largely failed to translate its free trade preferences into a series of comprehensive trade and development cooperation agreements with the ACP. In this paper, we have addressed this puzzle through reference to the institutional legacies and path dependencies generated by the GATT and the WTO – and to show how these have, to put it mildly, complicated the attempts by EPA advocates to invoke multilateral trade rules as a constraint on and driver of the reform process. At the end of December 2013, the final outcome of the EPA negotiations is still to be fully determined. We nevertheless know enough at this stage to relate the findings presented here to the wider pattern – and hence likely future shape and direction – of the EU's external trade and development agenda. The European Commission has now earmarked the deadline 1 January 2014 (since extended by the European Parliament to 1 October 2014) for ending the EPA negotiations altogether, by which point, it is hoped, the former will have 'succeeded' in the primary objective of rendering its trade and development co-operation arrangements with the ACP compatible with WTO rules. But, as we have made clear, this objective was the bare minimum of what the EPAs set out to achieve, in respect of the liberalisation of trade, regulatory harmonisation and other policy reforms associated with neoliberal conceptions of development. In this sense, the shortcomings of the EPAs reflect the wider difficulties that all WTO members have encountered agreeing to specific policy measures simultaneously capable of accommodating 'trade' and 'development' objectives within the institution's rules based system. This suggests that EU policy-makers will need to rethink external trade and development priorities – against the backdrop of a noticeable shift in global trade dynamics away from multilateralism towards more fragmented patterns of diplomacy, which are only likely to further entrench the arbitrary and ad hoc nature of trade-related development assistance for countries both inside and outside the ACP.

References

ActionAid, 2004. *Trade traps: why EU-ACP Economic Partnership Agreements pose a threat to Africa's development*. Johannesburg: ActionAid International. Available from: www.actionaid.org.uk/doc_lib/trade_traps.pdf [accessed 25 February 2013].

Alter, K.J. and Meunier, S., 2006. Nested and overlapping regimes in the transatlantic banana trade dispute. *Journal of European Public Policy*, 13 (3), 362–382.

Bilal, S. and Ramdoo, I., 2011. The honeymoon is over. *Trade Negotiations Insights*, 10 (7), 1.

Blyth, M., 2002. *Great transformations: economic ideas and political change in the twentieth century*. Cambridge: Cambridge University Press.

Brown, W., 2000. Restructuring north-south relations: ACP-EU development cooperation in a liberal international order. *Review of African Political Economy*, 85, 376–383.

Carbone, M., 2007. EBA, EU trade policy and the ACP: A tale of two north-south divides. *In*: G. Faber and J. Orbie, eds. *European Union trade politics and development: 'Everything but Arms' unravelled*. London: Routledge, 43–59.

Caribbean Regional Negotiation Machinery (CRNM), 2008. *CRNM note on CARIFORUM Economic Partnership Agreement: what Europe is offering Africa*. Barbados: CRNM. Available from: www.thecommonwealth.org/files/177256/FileName/RNM%20COMSEC%200408.pdf [accessed 5 June 2009].

Del Felice, C., 2012. Power in discursive practices: the case of the STOP EPAs campaign. *European Journal of International Relations*, OnlineFirst June 14, 1–23. doi:10.1177/1354066112437769

European Commission, 1996. The global challenge of international trade: a market access strategy for the European Union, COM (96) 53 final.

European Commission, 2006. Global Europe: competing in the world, COM (2006) 567 final.

Faber, G. and Orbie, J., 2009. The EU's insistence on reciprocal trade with the ACP Group: economic interests in the driving seat? *In*: G. Faber and J. Orbie, eds. *Beyond market access for development: EU-Africa relations in transition*. London: Routledge, 38–64.

Hay, C., 2007. What doesn't kill you can only make you stronger: the Doha development round, the services directive and the EU's conception of competitiveness. *Journal of Common Market Studies*, 45 (1), 25–43.

Heron, T., 2011. Asymmetric bargaining and development trade-offs in the CARIFORUM-European Union Economic Partnership Agreement. *Review of International Political Economy*, 18 (3), 328–357.

Heron, T., 2013. *Pathways from preferential trade: the politics of trade adjustment in Africa, Caribbean and pacific*. London: Palgrave.

Heron, T. and Siles-Brügge, G., 2012. Competitive liberalisation and the 'global Europe' services and investment agenda: locating the commercial drivers of the EU-ACP Economic Partnership Agreements. *Journal of Common Market Studies*, 50 (2), 250–266.

Heron, T. and Murray-Evans, P., 2013. European policy diffusion and the global south: a constructivist institutionalist analysis of the EU-ACP Economic Partnership Agreements. Paper prepared for *Sheffield Political Economy Research Institute Annual Conference*, Sheffield, UK, 1–3 July.

Hoekman, B. and Özden, C., 2005. Trade preferences and differential treatment of developing countries: a selective survey. *World Bank Policy Research Paper No. 3566*.

van den Hoven, A., 2007. Bureaucratic competition in EU trade policy: EBA as a case of competing two-level games? *In*: G. Faber and J. Orbie, eds. *European Union trade politics and development: 'Everything but Arms' unravelled*. Abingdon: Routledge, 60–73.

Hudec, R., 1987. *The developing countries in the GATT legal system*. London: Trade Policy Research Centre.

Hurt, S.R., Lee, D. and Lorenz-Carl, U., 2013. The argumentative dimension to the EU-Africa EPAs. *International Negotiation*, 18 (1), 67–87.

McQueen, M., 1998. Lomé versus free trade agreements: the dilemma facing the ACP Countries. *The World Economy*, 21 (4), 421–443.

Murray-Evans, P., 2013. Agency in the tightest of corners: Southern African responses to the Economic Partnership Agreements. Unpublished manuscript, University of York.

Narlikar, A. and Wilkinson, R., 2004. Collapse at the WTO: a Cancun post-mortem. *Third World Quarterly*, 25 (3), 447–460.

Parsons, C., 2007. *How to map arguments in political science*. Oxford: Oxford University Press.

Ravenhill, J., 2004. Back to the nest? Europe's relations with the African, Caribbean and Pacific group of countries. *In*: V.K. Aggarwal and E.A. Fogarty, eds. *EU trade strategies: between regionalism and globalism*. London: Palgrave Macmillan, 118–147.

Rosamond, B., 2002. Imagining the European economy: 'competitiveness' and the social construction of 'Europe' as an economic space. *New Political Economy*, 7 (2), 157–177.

Schimmelfennig, F., 2001. The community trap: liberal norms, rhetorical action, and the eastern enlargement of the European Union. *International Organization*, 55 (1), 47–80.

Siles-Brügge, G., 2014. *Constructing European Union trade policy: a global idea of Europe*. London: Palgrave Macmillan.

South Centre, 2008. *Market access for trade in goods in the Economic Partnership Agreements (EPAs). Fact sheet 17*. Geneva: South Centre.

Stevens, C., 2008. Economic Partnership Agreements: what can we learn? *New Political Economy*, 13 (2), 211–223.

Traidcraft, 2003. *Economic Partnership Agreements: The EU's new trade battleground.* London: Traidcraft Exchange. Available from: www.traidcraft.co.uk/Resources/Traidcraft/Documents/PDF/tx/campaigns_epas_eu_trade_battleground.pdf [accessed 25 February 2013].

Trommer, S., 2013. Legal opportunity in trade negotiations: international law, opportunity structures and the political economy of trade agreements. *New Political Economy*, 19 (1), 1–21.

Tsoukalis, L., 1997. *The New European economy revisited.* Oxford: Oxford University Press.

Decent work and indecent trade agendas: the European Union and ACP countries

Mark Langan

Politics and Applied Global Ethics (PAGE), Leeds Metropolitan University, Leeds, UK

The European Commission has promised to promote decent work in the African, Caribbean, and Pacific (ACP) countries through pro-poor direct investment and livelihood-creating trade deals. Aligning with the discourse of the International Labour Organisation, the European Commission seeks to achieve 'fair globalisation' in which economic growth is translated into decent jobs. Applying a moral economy perspective, however, the article argues that there is a disjuncture between the norms espoused under the Decent Work Agenda and the tangible implications of European interventions in ACP economies. Specifically, Economic Partnership Agreements will have deleterious consequences for the lives of many poorer producers and workers in ACP countries. The provision of Aid for Trade for decent work, moreover, may not deliver meaningful decent work opportunities in ACP countries. In this analysis, the article explores the emergent normativity-outcomes gap in this sphere of European Union external relations.

Introduction

The European Union (EU) has long portrayed itself as a benevolent development actor in its trade relationship with the African, Caribbean, and Pacific (ACP) countries. From colonial Association to the Cotonou Agreement (2000–2020), economic ties between the 'partners' have been moralised in relation to development norms. Whether couched in terms of EurAfrican integration under the Yaoundé Accords (1963–1975), interdependence under the Lomé Conventions (1975–2000), or smooth integration into global markets under Cotonou, ACP–EU trade has been envisioned as a basis for poverty elimination for vulnerable peoples (cf. Gruhn 1993, Kawasaki 2000, Brown 2002). Historically, European policy-makers have taken great care to update these moral development underpinnings. Memorably, trade between the EU and the ACP countries became infused with the developmental discourse of the New International Economic Order in the 1970s (Gruhn 1976, pp. 241–244). This discursive shift was materially cemented by newly established instruments such as the System for the Stabilisation of Export Earnings (STABEX) which provided a concession through which policy-makers could embed, and diffuse, legitimating norms (cf. Mailafia 1997). ACP–EU trade relations were thus represented as responsive to the demands of the Third World.

This article examines the EU's current pledges to the International Labour Organisation's (ILO) Decent Work Agenda as a means of aligning ACP–EU ties to legitimating development norms. Specifically, it considers how the *moral economy* of ACP–EU ties has been (re)constructed in the Post Washington Consensus (PWC) through recourse to decent work discourse. As Sayer (2007, p. 262) explains, '"moral economy" studies the moral norms and sentiments that structure and influence economic practices ... the term "moral economy" can also refer to the object of this kind of inquiry ... [this approach pays] close attention to how economic arrangements affect well-being'. Given the European Commission's attempts to implement far-reaching Economic Partnership Agreements (EPAs) involving deep liberalisation in ACP economies, decent work discourse can be seen as a strategic means of downplaying concerns surrounding premature market-opening, while reaffirming Europe's progressive intent to assist 'the poor'. By aligning with the policy discourse of the ILO, moreover, the European Commission can represent its economic agenda as conforming to modern development thought (cf. Fine 2001, Stiglitz 2004, Ngwonya and Richardson 2012).

Importantly, this moral economy critique examines whether the EU's discursive commitment to decent work materially translates into the attainment of decent jobs on the part of ACP citizens. In so doing, it addresses wider debates in European studies concerning emergent 'normativity-outcomes gaps' in EU external relations. This moral economy approach sits in critical juxtaposition to liberal institutionalist accounts of Europe's *benevolent* 'normative power' that often exhibit a *prima facie* acceptance of European norms (Langan 2012).[1] Specifically, the article considers the impact of EPAs for decent work prerogatives in two case study sectors – poultry and cut-flower production. Focus on poultry enables analysis in a strategic *import-competing* sector which is vital for food security, as well as for backward linkages between local agriculture and processing facilities. Meanwhile, the focus on cut-flowers highlights not only the 'locking-in' of ACP states' dependence on developmentally dubious export sectors, but also provides insight into a sector often held by European policy-makers as a 'success story' of ACP states' *progressive* integration into global markets (Langan 2011). Together, the case studies provide an illustrative snapshot of the disjuncture between norms and tangible outcomes in the moral economy of ACP–EU ties in relation to 'decent work'. Importantly, however, the article also examines Europe's attempts to utilise Aid for Trade to support decent work – since the linking of these two policy agendas is central to the construction of the moral economy of contemporary ACP–EU ties. Aid for Trade for decent work is seen as particularly problematic in terms of finances and non-disbursement. Therefore, while the EU's decent work discourse is seen as a strategically sound attempt to reconstruct the moral economy of ACP–EU ties in the PWC, outcomes for 'the poor' appear to conflict with ostensible norms. An emergent normativity-outcomes gap is considered in this sphere of EU external actorness, with resonance for critical studies in other areas of EU external relations.

The article is structured as follows. It first examines the moralised Decent Work Agenda amidst the ILO's attempts to more fully integrate core labour standards within the PWC. The article then examines the role of decent work discourse in the (re)construction of the moral economy of ACP–EU co-operation. Thereafter, the article provides critical assessment of the tangible implications of the functioning 'moral economy' in terms of the case study sectors – poultry and cut-flowers – as well as Aid for Trade for decent work.

Decent work, the ILO and the PWC

All economic systems are founded upon ostensible norms governing what is deemed morally acceptable in terms of fair relations between agents; what is deemed as an appropriate distribution of economic output; as well as questions concerning the relationship of economic activities to broader societal welfare (Keat 1993, Bernstein 2007, Sayer 2007). The study of 'moral economy', in this context, seeks to identify such norms (whether explicitly or implicitly held), and to then examine potential disjuncture between founding norms and tangible outcomes. A moral economy perspective, with this critical focus, is relevant whether in the study of the 'moral economy' of the domestic household; the 'moral economy' of national austerity; or in terms of the 'moral economies' of North-South trade. It seeks to explore issues surrounding justice, (in)equality, as well as validations of economic systems that often bear scant relation to founding norms (Sayer 2004).[2] Moreover, it deals with matters of *discourse*, in terms of the discursive embedding of norms within economic systems (Langan 2012).

In the context of North–South trade, therefore, it is revealing to apply a moral economy critique to the study of 'decent work' prerogatives that have recently been popularised within the donor community, notably among European elites. The ILO has played the leading role as 'norm entrepreneur' here and has had success in raising donor awareness of core labour standards as part of a broader PWC. Given concerns surrounding the social consequences of structural adjustment programmes (SAPs) in the Washington Consensus, the ILO repackaged its labour rights agenda for fuller integration within donor policies. Initially invoked within an internal strategy document, 'decent work' soon gained discursive traction as a multi-faceted policy approach. The formal Decent Work Agenda, launched by ILO Director-General Somavia in 1999, encompassed four policy pillars: (i) increase employment in productive sectors; (ii) promote respect of core labour standards; (iii) inclusion of social dialogue; (iv) provision of social protection (ILO 2006, pp. 1–4).

This four-pronged 'decent work' approach became the focal point of the ILO's engagement with the donor community. Importantly, it fitted neatly with broader PWC thought – understood as the intent to justify continued free market policies in the Global South on the basis of greater concern for socially equitable growth (Őnis and F Şenses 2005, p. 277). For instance, the donor community from the mid-1990s onwards promised greater assistance to private sector development in developing countries – as part of what later became known as Aid for Trade (Page 2006, Sunassee Lam 2008). The ILO Decent Work Agenda cemented this emergent 'pro-poor' free market discourse. Not only would competitiveness in the global South be addressed, but, moreover, the jobs created through economic growth would now more directly improve the lives of 'the poor'. Aid for Trade and the Decent Work Agenda would emerge as central pillars of what might accurately be deemed the moral economy of the PWC.

This PWC discourse has been firmly espoused by the ILO in its communications on decent work. The ILO (2006, pp. 3–5) explains that there is 'growing acceptance of the idea that employment and labour market issues are a decisive, but neglected, link between economic growth and poverty reduction'. It also explains that respect for decent work can promote 'industrial peace and improved productivity' (ILO 2007, p. 27). In so doing, it makes clear that there is an explicit business case for decent work. Indeed, the ILO (2009, p. 2) further states that 'sound labour legislation, social dialogue bodies and collective bargaining, equality commissions, dispute resolution mechanism, labour inspectorates, and an informed and effective judiciary ... create an enabling environment for macroeconomic stability, productivity and competitiveness'. The Decent Work Agenda will thereby ensure pro-poor *and* competitive business growth in free markets in alignment with the rationales of the PWC. Second-generation liberalisation measures aimed at completing free market structures are therefore presented as morally legitimate, in the sense of aligning with 'pro-poor' norms.

Given its strategically timely focus, the Decent Work Agenda has gained traction among the wider donor community. Perhaps the ILO's most evident achievement here has been the (belated) inclusion of decent work within the UN Millennium Development Goals. The World Bank, meanwhile, has itself integrated decent work criteria into its *Doing Business* rankings. Haworth and Hughes (2009, p. 1) argue that this 'marks a sea-change in their assessment ... and is another marked shift from the premises underpinning the ailing Washington Consensus'. The IMF (2010), moreover, emphasises decent work as a sound strategy for ensuring a sustainable recovery in the wake of global financial crisis. Reflecting this apparent consensus, civil society institutions such as the International Trade Union Confederation (ITUC 2006) have also welcomed decent work objectives. A 'common sense' acceptance of decent work objectives is thereby apparent in the legitimisation of free market structures.

Interestingly, however, there is pressure from Northern trade unions that the current generation of North–South free trade agreements (FTAs) should include binding 'social clauses' which would allow signatories to be suspended from a trade agreement if core labour standards are violated (Bhagwati 2007). This has found a degree of sympathy within the donor community, particularly in the context of WTO negotiations where Northern states sought to incorporate a social clause in the mid-1990s. This was fiercely resisted, however, by developing countries who suspected that social clauses would be abused for protectionist purposes (Raju 2008). Accordingly, the Decent Work Agenda is currently silent on any form of sanction-invoking social clause.

The decent work agenda and ACP–EU ties

Within the donor community, the EU institutions have been particularly effusive as to the need to integrate the Decent Work Agenda into existing trade and development activities. Specifically, decent work initiatives have played a crucial role in re-upholstering the moral economy of ACP–EU relations in an era of *reciprocal* free trade. This reflects the Cotonou Agreement's championing of EPA free trade agendas which, if fully implemented, would enact far-reaching liberalisation across ACP economies. Notably, this marks a significant departure from the *non-reciprocal* terms of the earlier Lomé Conventions. The decent work agenda therefore plays a key role in downplaying concerns as to the impact of liberalisation and its meaning for ACP workers. In so doing, it realigns the ACP–EU partnership to long-standing norms concerning poverty reduction and a fair post-colonial relationship. The significance of decent work discourse in the reconstruction of the moral economy of ACP–EU ties in a PWC setting becomes clear from analysis of key strategic documents. The *Africa–EU strategic partnership* (AU–EU 2007, p. 13), for instance, firmly states that 'the promotion of decent work in Africa' will be 'jointly addressed' with a view to improving 'living and working conditions'. The *EU-Caribbean partnership for growth, stability and development*, meanwhile, sets out commitments to 'social cohesion and decent work opportunities' (European Commission 2006a). In broader policy terms, the European Commission's (2006b) *Promoting decent work for all*, commits Europe to the promotion of pro-poor employment in open markets. Such documents confirm Europe's discursive commitment to decent work in order to realise the social dimension of a fair globalisation.

Crucially, the Decent Work Agenda has been fully integrated into EU communications on EPA implementation. The European Commission (2010, p. 8) makes clear that EPAs will positively *improve* conditions for decent work. It insists that 'trade liberalisation should help to achieve goals such as high growth, full employment, poverty reduction, and the promotion of decent work' (2006b, pp. 7–8). It further states that it 'will put more of its commercial weight behind efforts to promote social standards and decent work in bilateral and multilateral trade negotiations' (2006b). The European Commission's *Report on the EU contribution to the promotion of decent work in the world,* meanwhile, celebrates that 'in the context of EPAs, the EU-Cariforum Economic Partnership Agreement of December 2007, includes a substantive chapter on trade and sustainable development' (European Commission 2008, p. 27). This pro-poor emphasis is reaffirmed by Karel de Gucht, the current Commissioner for Trade, who insists that 'free trade agreements can open new avenues to secure improvements in the protection of human rights, including labour rights. Trade policy can help, not hinder, legitimate social concerns' (European Commission 2010). Furthermore, the conclusion of EPAs will apparently result in a greater number of decent jobs throughout former colonies (European Commission

2013b). While certain sectors may find themselves uncompetitive in open markets, nevertheless, comparative advantages will ensure that, on the whole, ACP economies will thrive in post-EPA contexts. Job creation within export-orientated sectors such as horticulture, for instance, are regularly cited as examples of how the private sector can deliver decent work opportunities in free trade structures (Ulmer 2004, European Commission 2011, p. 6). As such, these strategic EU communications present free market policies (the EPAs) as being morally legitimate in relation to both internal and external (civil society/ACP) audiences (Langan 2012, p. 243). That is, the moral economy of ACP–EU ties is constructed in such a manner as to cement EU policy-makers' commitment to the on-going roll out of free market reform as part of an ethical drive towards poverty reduction. Meanwhile, the 'common sense' of pro-poor free trade (as projected within decent work discourse) seeks to ameliorate external actors who might contest liberalisation agendas. This constitutes a significant co-optive, ideational power element in the EU's pursuit of trade deals, as well as a vital element in explaining path dependency in terms of EU negotiators' commitment to free market principles.

It is also important to recognise, however, the strategic role played by the co-joining of decent work discourse with narratives of Aid for Trade in the moral economy of ACP–EU relations. This reflects the significance of both thematic discourse(s) in the broader PWC itself (Langan and Scott forthcoming). Aid for Trade will (ostensibly) support businesses to become more competitive and (hence) more capable of employing large numbers of poorer people in life-affirming work. Aid for Trade will also support the creation of enabling infrastructure – such as roads and electricity pylons. This will apparently create decent jobs in ACP firms that benefit from improved infrastructural assets. It will also create direct employment through infrastructural projects. The European Commission (2007, p. 19), for example, cites its support to road construction in Africa as a key source of livelihood creation. In a similar vein, Aid for Trade for capacity-building within ACP trade ministries, labour inspectorates, and trade unions, will promote the governance context in which decent work can be upheld. This Aid for Trade agenda – when combined to decent work objectives – plays a significant role in the (re)construction of the moral economy of ACP–EU co-operation in an era of *reciprocal* trade.

With parallels to earlier phases of ACP–EU relations, meanwhile, norms are diffused and embedded through material aid-giving – symbolising the EU's intent to realise fairer relations. For example, the European Commission has granted €14.75 million towards TACKLE, a joint project with the ILO providing child workers with access to educational opportunities that facilitate their exit from the labour market (EuropeAid 2008, pp. 1–2, ILO 2012, p. 27). In terms of the delivery of Aid for Trade, meanwhile, the European Commission makes clear that it will offer additional resources for EPA implementation. In addition to all-ACP Aid for Trade instruments such as the Centre for the Development of Enterprise, the European Commission promises that Regional Indicative Programmes (RIPs) and National Indicative Programmes (NIPs) will include greater resources for ACP states' transition to free markets upon conclusion of EPAs. Indeed, the Cariforum countries, as the only sub-region to have yet signed a full EPA, were promised substantial RIP and NIP resources for trade capacity-building and promotion of decent work (Mission of Jamaica to the EU 2010). EPAs are thereby (again) presented in the 'moral economy' as an opportunity for pro-poor development.

Europe's pursuit of EPAs has, however, often met with uncertainty on the part of ACP governments, European civil society, and academics. ACP representatives notably expressed grave reservations in October 2006 about the impact of EPAs upon livelihoods (see South Centre 2006, pp. ix-8). The Nigerian Minister of Commerce, Aliyu Modibo Umar, claimed that tariff liberalisation will 'probably destroy the little development that some ACP countries have managed to achieve over the past years' through deindustrialisation (South Centre 2006, 5) The collapse of import-competing textiles production in sub-Saharan Africa amidst the importation of cheap second-hand clothing from the EU is often cited here as an historical example of how tariff liberalisation might undermine decent work (EcoNews Africa and Traidcraft 2005, p. 11). This leads to broader concerns surrounding collapsing ACP *policy space* to protect infant industries from competition. The British TUC (2012, p. 2), for instance, emphasises that 'developing countries need the policy space, fiscal resources and technical assistance to drive economic diversification into key value-adding parts of global supply chains that can provide green and decent jobs for all'. Moreover, there are concerns that Aid for Trade is financially anaemic and, in certain cases, promotes business activities that undermine decent work objectives.

EPAs: creating decent jobs in ACP countries?

In order to critically examine the moral economy of ACP–EU ties in relation to decent work objectives, it is necessary to examine the empirical realities of EU trade policies with regard to their impact on poorer workers. As stated, concerns surrounding EPAs can usefully be considered in case studies of poultry production (an import-competing sector) and the cut-flower industry (an export-orientated sector). Both sectors provide illustrative snapshots of ACP–EU trade networks and draw attention to an emergent normativity-outcomes gap in this area of EU external relations. ACP poultry production is particularly useful to consider in terms of decent work goals since it is a labour-intensive industry that is vital for domestic food security. It also bridges agricultural production with processing facilities, thereby creating opportunities for establishment of backward linkages between urban centres and rural hinterlands. There is particular concern in such strategic import-competing sectors that ACP states should retain the right to place high tariffs upon products emanating from the EU (Langan 2009). Historical evidence demonstrates that during nascent economic development that there is a need to protect domestic producers from cheap foreign imports (Ellington 2004). Prominent economists such as Chang (2003) argue, in this context, that the imposition of premature trade liberalisation will in fact 'kick away the ladder of development'. Namely, high-value sectors (such as poultry processing facilities) will fail upon trade liberalisation as foreign import surges force local producers out of the market. Such events are seen to have deleterious consequences for decent work – causing unemployment in relatively high-skilled, well remunerated sectors such as poultry – and forcing developing countries to instead rely on the attraction of foreign investment in 'predatory' export industries dependent on low-paid labour (such as cut-flower production).

There is considerable evidence that these fears will be borne out upon EPA implementation. In broad macro-economic terms, Milner *et al.* (2009, pp. 8–9) explain that 'increased imports from the EU will tend to induce falls in production and employment in domestic import-competing sectors'. In the case of Mauritius, for example, they predict that full EPA implementation will result in job losses of up to 6.5% of the existing agricultural workforce as subsidised agricultural produce from the EU enters the market, undercutting local smallholders. This would be exacerbated with job losses of up to 15.5% in manufacturing, as cheap imports enter the domestic market. They estimate that this would result in around 6500 direct redundancies, not including job losses among the indirectly employed, for instance, transportation workers (Milner *et al.* 2009, p. 10). In the specific case of poultry production, meanwhile, it is claimed in the Ghanaian context alone that 200,000 jobs are currently exported on an annual basis 'through importation of chicken'. Trade unions here cite tariff reductions brought about in 2003 as the main source of industry woes (Bagooro 2011, pp. 9–13). Accordingly, they claim that 'the unemployment situation in the country will worsen if Ghana signs the EPAs'. This reflects their concerns that the current 20% tariff levied upon EU finished products will be reduced to 0% within 25 years upon the implementation of EPAs (Bagooro 2011).

In the Senegalese poultry sector, meanwhile, there are similar concerns. Up to 10,000 jobs were directly created in Senegalese poultry production from the late 1990s to mid-2000s while tariffs upon foreign imports remained high. This also led to the creation of indirect employment, for instance, in slaughterhouses (Dorémus *et al.* 2004, pp. 5–9). Since the onset of tariff reductions in the mid-2000s, however, 'producer organisations estimate that about 70% of commercial farms have disappeared, and with them, 1500 to 2000 jobs'. The locking-in of further tariff reductions under EPAs is thus seen as a threat to the continuation of production (Nunn and Price 2004). This situation is repeated in the Ivory Coast where poultry imports surged from 2152 tons in 2001 to 15,400 tons in 2003 upon tariff reductions, 'destroying more than 15,000 jobs in the local poultry sector' (Dorémus *et al.* 2004, pp. 6–9). Moreover, there is evidence that the signing, or initialling, of interim EPAs from late 2007 onwards has encouraged higher imports of EU poultry. The European Commission confirmed to the European Parliament (2012) that 'over the last decade, EU poultry exports to sub-Saharan Africa were relatively stable between 200,000 and 300,000 but increased to about 440,000 tonnes in 2011'.

Perhaps most notably, the European Commission's own Sustainability Impact Assessment (SIA) on West African agro-industry finds significant evidence of likely job losses and social hardships faced by producers upon EPA implementation. The SIA explained that between 60% and 70% of West African employment is within the agricultural sector and warned that:

> competition from EU imports can depress local markets for some agricultural products such as onions, potatoes, poultry and cereals. Sustained high levels of imports, or import surges can flood local markets and threaten growth levels of local production or discourage the development of a local processing industry. (Pricewaterhouse Coopers 2006, p. 30)

The SIA also explained that this retrenchment would likely have 'spin-off effects' in terms of job losses in related sectors. For example, it explained that a decline in poultry production would lead to the decline of the feed sector. Importantly, the SIA also predicted that imports of poultry would increase by up to 150% upon the full implementation of an EU EPA with West African countries. With clear implications for decent work objectives, the report also explained that family owned, small-scale farms in the region would likely cut back upon social provisions such as medical expenditure, spending on clothing and food, and education expenses, in order to make efficiencies savings in the wake of reduced incomes (Pricewaterhouse Coopers 2006, p. 30; p. 48). The *moral economy* of ACP–EU ties is thus seen to fall tangibly short of ostensible norms concerning the well-being of poultry workers (and other import-competing sectors) within liberalised trade structures.

In addition to loss of decent jobs in import-competing industries, meanwhile, there are also grounds for scepticism surrounding EPAs' ability to deliver decent work in the separate context of export-orientated sectors. Whereas the European Commission firmly states that ACP exports in sectors such as horticulture and EPZ-manufacturing will thrive within open markets (and secured for the long-term under EPAs), nevertheless, there is concern as to whether such industries do in fact contribute positively to decent work commitments. As stated earlier, it is illustrative to consider the case of cut-flower production given that it is often held up as a 'success story' within liberalised ACP–EU trade networks (European Commission 2011, p. 6; Ulmer 2004). Indeed, free trade arrangements such as EPAs act to 'lock in' developing countries into reliance on such export-orientated sectors where they (apparently) hold comparative advantages. The cut-flower sector in Kenya, for example, established itself as a significant non-traditional export industry in the aftermath of SAP implementation in the 1990s. While higher value import-competing manufacturing sectors declined upon tariff liberalisation, the cut-flower sector took advantage of relatively low tariff access to European markets to supply supermarket retailers with commodities such as roses and chrysanthemums, as well as to create jobs for local citizens (mostly women) (Embassy of the Republic of Kenya in Japan 2013).

The competitiveness of this export-oriented sector, however, depends upon the continued availability of low cost labour and preferential tariff access to Europe. This means that there are concerns about: (i) the quality of jobs on offer, and (ii) whether the industry has long-term viability.[3] On the first question of the quality of jobs, it is worth noting the Kenyan Women Workers' Association who highlight alleged misuse of pesticides, as well as continuing low rates of pay (cited in War on Want 2009). Despite efforts by the Kenyan Floriculture Council, wages remain low. As of 2012, monthly salaries remained around US$43 – little over $1 a day for women labourers engaged in intensive work (often) within oppressive greenhouse conditions (Wafula 2012). Moreover, the Kenyan Human Rights Commission raises questions surrounding lack of sick pay and maternity leave, as well as allegations of sexual harassment on the farms (cited in Karongo 2012). These concerns are mirrored in neighbouring Uganda where one trade unionist recounted the story of one woman worker: 'One lady ... she lost one of her eyes. She was taken to one of the hospitals in Kampala and they say it is the effects of the chemicals ... she has not yet been compensated' (cited in Langan 2011, p. 1227). Such accounts are corroborated by a report for the Ugandan Workers' Education Association:

> Workers have been exposed to many health hazards. They include among others chemical exposure. Several workers both male and female have been exposed to chemicals at their places of work. Skin, throat and respiratory health complications are some of the problems that have been reported in some of the workers. (cited in Langan 2011, p. 1227)

The second concern – regarding industry precariousness in relation to tariff levels – also raises issues relating to the difficulties of promoting decent work within liberalised trade networks. Kenya currently stands at a crossroads in terms of whether it will agree to ratify, and implement, a full EPA. The European Commission recently insisted that countries, like Kenya, that had merely initialled an EPA would have to ratify full adoption and implementation by 1 January 2014. Otherwise such ACP states would default to the Generalised System of Preferences (GSP), which would have devastating consequences for Kenyan exports in sectors such as cut-flowers. Kenya's flower exporters would face an EU tariff of 9% under the GSP, compared to the 0% rate currently enjoyed. Given existing structural deficiencies this would leave Kenyan producers in an uncompetitive position, with clear implications for jobs. Importantly, these concerns surrounding the precariousness of export industries within free markets are relevant across a number of other ACP sectors, such as garment production. Moreover, not only are tariff levels a constant worry, but investors may also choose to relocate production if trade unions or government policies threaten to raise labour costs. The threat of investor flight within export-oriented sectors works to suppress the realisation of 'decent work' within the moral economy of ACP–EU relations. Agreements such as the EPAs 'lock-in' ACP states to these free market structures where attempts to improve workers' plight is met with swift discipline in the form of investor flight. ACP countries must continue to 'race-to-the-bottom' or else lose many (exploitative) jobs that they currently possess (Nunn and Price 2004).

Finally, it is important to examine Aid for Trade for decent work in the moral economy of ACP–EU ties. Again, Aid for Trade – when co-joined with the Decent Work Agenda – provides a strategic discursive platform for (re)aligning ACP–EU relations to long standing norms concerning poverty reduction. Interestingly the ILO (2012, p. 13) praises the role of EU funded all-ACP aid instruments in supporting Aid for Trade for decent work. Notably, the ILO highlights the joint ILO–EU Pro€invest programme and its efforts to 'improve advocacy skills, services delivery and network building' for employers' organisations. It also highlights the aforementioned TARGET programme (ILO 2012). It would be misguided, however, to consider Aid for Trade in isolation from the revenue losses incurred upon EPA implementation. Aid for Trade monies are promoted on the basis that they provide revenue conducive to stimulating business activities capable of fulfilling decent work criteria. Such monies may act only to stabilise ACP economies, however, in the context of declining government revenues (and policy space) to independently support their own domestic producers (Langan and Scott forthcoming).

Considering the EU's lauded Pro€invest initiative for ACP businesses, for example, it is notable that its overall finances came to only €110 million under the 9th European Development Fund (EDF). This represents the equivalent of merely €278,000 per ACP state per annum. Meanwhile, the financial resources of combined all-ACP Aid for Trade instruments under the 9th EDF amounted to less than €1 million per ACP per annum. This is in the context of EPA adjustment costs amounting to €9.2 billion (Milner cited in Langan 2009, pp. 422–425). Again, the European Commission's SIA provides more detail, estimating that removal of tariffs on top 50 affected products will lead to losses of up to US$27.3 million in Ghana, $11.5 million in Benin, and $7.5 million in Senegal. These figures respectively represent 5.44%, 15.23%, and 4.64% of government revenues derived from import tariffs (Pricewaterhouse Coopers 2006, pp. 49–51).

Concerns surrounding Aid for Trade are particularly resonant in the context of the Cariforum countries. As mentioned, Cariforum states were promised significant additional aid monies as part of EPA implementation efforts. Girvin (2012, p. 759) argues that Aid for Trade acted as vital leverage to persuade Cariforum states to agree to the EPA. In this context, the European Commission (2012, p. 96) points to the fact that €194 million was committed to the region in 2011, much of which was directed to Aid for Trade. In addition, the European Commission indicates that €56 million was given as part of Sugar Accompanying Measures to Guyana, Jamaica, and Trinidad and Tobago in 2011 (European Commission 2012b). A high degree of dissatisfaction has, however, been expressed among Caribbean officials. The Ambassador and Head of Mission of Jamaica in the EU (2010, p. 6) expressed her concerns surrounding lack of aid disbursement. In the case of the Sugar Accompanying Measures, moreover, there is concern that these have failed to support those most affected by job losses amidst liberalisation of the Sugar Protocol. Instead, they are utilised to improve the competitiveness of existing sugar production, rather than to assist smallholders who have faced redundancies (Ngwonya and Richardson 2012, pp. 2–3).

There is also regional concern that the European Commission has exacerbated Cariforum countries' position in global markets by not only insisting upon EPA liberalisation (with an incumbent threat to import-competing industries such as cement) but by also endangering successful export sectors such as rum and sugar. For example, the Caribbean rum trade is fearful of EU FTAs with Latin America. A recent report by the Commonwealth Secretariat (2012, p. viii) explains that if the EU maximises free trade deals with Central America, Peru, Columbia, and Mercosur, that Caribbean rum exports will fall by 5.5%, 'corresponding to €1.3 million per year'. This is concerning for decent work objectives, given that the rum industry directly employs over 10,000 workers. The sector is particularly significant for individual Caribbean states such as Barbados where rum represent 13.3% of total exports (Commonwealth Secretariat 2012, p. 2).

In this context, Aid for Trade appears to be granted on shifting sands upon which certain Caribbean industries are sinking, either due to import-competition under EPAs, or else due to preference erosion. It is also necessary to note here fears within the Caribbean (in particular) that the EU's recently espoused principle of differentiation in its future approach to the EDF will mean fewer ongoing resources for Aid for Trade. This will likely occur even where an

EPA has been signed (ECDPM 2012, pp. iv-11). Indeed, many Caribbean states qualify as middle-income developing countries and may lose out as the European Commission acts to 'graduate' certain countries from EDF allocations, or at least to focus spending more squarely upon LDCs. Given that the Cariforum states signed the EPA on the understanding of ongoing support for adjustment, the movement to differentiation appears to breach an implicit understanding of the developmental nature of the EPAs. Again, the moral economy of ACP–EU relations seems to bear scant relation to nominal 'decent work' prerogatives in the PWC.

A clear normativity-outcomes gap is, therefore, apparent in this important sphere of EU external relations. Europe's utilisation of decent work discourse seeks to reassure both internal and external audiences as to the appropriateness of reciprocal trade for 'the poor'. Despite donors' common sense commitment to decent work objectives in the PWC, however, the case of ACP–EU relations demonstrates that such policy agendas may in fact do more to justify inequitable trade arrangements, than to meaningfully reform free markets to better meet the needs of vulnerable peoples. In fact, by providing a moralised framework for the roll-out of second-generation liberalisation, EU decent work agendas may close down policy space for more interventionist ACP economic agendas that would more closely align with pro-poor norms. As such, there is a need for critical accounts of Europe's norm-laden engagement with vulnerable 'partners' in similar fields of EU external relations. Such studies would be facilitated by a moral economy perspective that moves beyond liberal institutionalism's prima facie evaluations of EU norms. A moral economy perspective can examine the co-optive ideational power of EU engagement with external partners, consider issues of path dependency on the part of European elites, as well as highlight normativity-outcomes gaps in terms of regressive impacts on the 'poor'

Conclusion

The article has examined the moral economy of ACP–EU ties in relation to decent work and ACP states' movement to full market liberalisation under EPAs. It has considered the emergence of the ILO Decent Work Agenda as a moral bulwark of the PWC as donors seek to represent ongoing free market reforms in developing countries as contributing to human development. A discursive focus on decent work, combined to Aid for Trade, is understood to cement PWC visions of poverty reduction taking place within liberalised North-South trade regimes. Specifically, EU commitments to decent work are seen to (re)construct the moral economy of ACP–EU ties via strategic visions of ACP states achieving 'smooth and gradual integration' into globalised markets. They are also understood to align EU development policies more closely to the overarching PWC, and to legitimise attempts to lock-in ACP countries to liberalised forms of ACP–EU trade (via EPAs) in relation to both internal and external audiences.

Despite the discursive significance of EU commitments to decent work, however, the article's moral economy critique has raised questions concerning the disjuncture between norms and outcomes within the 'moral economy' of ACP–EU co-operation. It has highlighted the regressive impact of EPAs in two case study sectors (poultry and cut-flower production) as well as the anaemia of Aid for Trade in relation to decent work objectives. Tariff liberalisation under EPAs is particularly seen to threaten import-competing sectors such as poultry production, with a severe loss of livelihoods. Export-orientated sectors such as cut-flower production, meanwhile, are seen to offer insecure, low-paid jobs quite removed from the 'decent work' envisioned in ILO and EU policy communications. A gaping normativity-outcomes gap becomes apparent as the regressive realities of free market systems substantially depart from ostensible pro-poor norms

In terms of Aid for Trade, meanwhile, the article has questioned whether this form of aid meaningfully supports opportunities for decent work. There are concerns that Aid for Trade merely stabilises ACP economies in the context of reduced tariff revenues faced upon EPA implementation. Aid for Trade monies are not therefore 'new' – nor are they secure given the European Commission's recent articulation of its intended principle of differentiation in relation to EDF resources. Aid for Trade instruments, in this context, are seen to do more to embed legitimising norms within the moral economy of ACP–EU relations than to tangibly promote decent work opportunities in ACP countries. Aid for Trade – co-joined with decent work discourse – acts to reconstruct the moral economy of ACP–EU ties, despite the fact that this 'moral economy' operates in a fashion which materially transgresses ostensible norms.

The EU's ability to achieve decent work objectives in the moral economy of ACP–EU ties is therefore brought into question. The implementation of EPAs is seen to 'kick-away-the-ladder' of development in terms of retraction in key import-competing sectors. Job creation in low-value and low-pay export industries such as cut-flower production are, meanwhile, understood to pose a serious challenge to core labour standards given these sectors' emphasis on exploiting vulnerable (women) workers. Furthermore, Aid for Trade is seen as a means of leverage for the conclusion of regressive EPAs. These aid resources are not understood to offer substantial avenues for the widespread realisation of decent work in ACP countries. Instead they are seen to do more to reconstruct legitimations for regressive free market structures. ACP governments, in this context, would do well to reconsider current movements towards the implementation of full EPAs. More viable strategies for creating decent jobs may be found in alternative development strategies in which ACP states exercised the policy space to protect an emergent domestic industrial and agricultural base, and to reject premature liberalisation. In terms of broader European studies, moreover, the application of moral economy critiques would do well to move beyond liberal institutionalist accounts to instead illustrate the co-optive power realities of EU engagement with external 'partners', as well as to highlight emergent normativity-outcomes gaps.

Acknowledgements

Many thanks to Elizabeth McCaig and Vijay Simha Pandrapragada. Thank you also to the reviewers for their suggestions.

Notes

1. For an in-depth critique of liberal institutionalism, with particular emphasis on Ian Manners' account of 'normative power', see Langan (2012).
2. This parallels debates surrounding the conflict of norms and interests in EU studies. As Storey states, however, it is important to avoid a binary reductionism in terms of a 'norms *versus* interests' debate (cited in Langan 2012, p. 263).
3. Uganda would likely retain its 0% tariff access for cut-flowers to European markets for the short to medium term since it is a Least Developed Country (LDC) and would therefore qualify for the Everything But Arms trade arrangement even if it failed to ratify a full EPA.

References

AU–EU, 2007. The Africa-EU strategic partnership: a joint Africa-EU strategy. Available from: www.africa-eu-partnership.org/sites/default/files/eas2007_joint_strategy_en.pdf [accessed 1 March 2013].

Bagooro, S., 2011. *Report of the national civil society forum on the EPA*, Accra, 25 August, Accra: Third World Network-Africa.

Bernstein, H., 2007. Capitalism and moral economy: land questions in sub-Saharan Africa. Paper for Conference on 'Poverty and Capital', Global Poverty Research Group and Brooks World Poverty

Institute, University of Manchester, 2–4 July 2007. Available from: www.sed.manchester.ac.uk/research/events/conferences/povertyandcapital/bernstein.pdf [accessed 8 October 2009].

Bhagwati, J., 2007. Trade liberalisation and 'fair trade' demands: addressing the environmental and labour standards issues. *The World Economy*, 18 (6), 745–759.

Brown, W., 2002. *The European Union and Africa: the restructuring of North–South relations*. London: I.B. Tauris.

Chang, H.J., 2003. *Kicking away the ladder*. London: Anthem Press.

Commonwealth Secretariat, 2012. *The impact of EU bilateral trade agreements with third countries on the Caribbean rum sector*. London: Commonwealth Secretariat.

Dorémus, C., Gaudard, C., Horman, D., Hermelin, B., and Grodent, J., 2004. *Chicken exports: Europe plucks Africa! a campaign for the right to protect agricultural markets*. Brussels: SOS Faim.

ECDPM, 2012. Differentiation in ACP-EU cooperation: implications of the EU's Agenda for Change for the 11th EDF and beyond. ECDPM Discussion Paper No. 134. Maastricht: ECDPM.

EcoNews Africa and Traidcraft, 2005. *EPAs through the lens of Kenya*. London: Traidcraft.

Ellington, L., 2004. *Learning from the Japanese economy*. Stanford: Stanford University. Available from: http://spice.stanford.edu/docs/122 [accessed 1 March 2013].

Embassy of the Republic of Kenya in Japan, 2013. *Kenya cut flowers industry – background*. Toyko: Embassy of the Republic of Kenya in Japan. Available from: http://www.kenyarep-jp.com/business/industry/f_index_e.html [accessed 1 March 2013].

EuropeAid, 2008. *EC and ILO launch project to tackle child labour in African, Caribbean, and Pacific countries*. Brussels: EuropeAid.

European Commission, 2006a. *An EU-Caribbean strategic partnership for growth, stability and development*. Brussels: European Commission.

European Commission, 2006b. *Promoting decent work for all: the EU contribution to the implementation of the decent work agenda in the world*. Brussels: European Commission.

European Commission, 2007. *Promoting employment through EU development cooperation: commission staff working document*. Brussels: European Commission.

European Commission, 2008. *Report on the EU contribution to the promotion of decent work in the world*. Brussels: European Commission.

European Commission, 2010. *EU trade commissioner and ETUC general secretary discuss labour standards and trade policy*. Brussels: European Commission.

European Commission, 2011. *Economic Partnership Agreements (EPAs): African, Caribbean, and Pacific voices speak up for trade and development*. Brussels: European Commission.

European Commission, 2012. *Annual report on the EU's development and external assistance policies and their implementation in 2011*. Brussels: European Commission.

European Council, 2006. *Council conclusions on decent work for all – council meeting, Brussels, 30 November and 1 December 2006*. Brussels: European Council.

European Parliament, 2012. *European parliament – parliamentary questions on 31st May 2012: answer given by Mr Ciolos on behalf of the commission*. Brussels: European Parliament.

Fine, B., 2001. Neither the Washington nor the post-Washington consensus. *In*: B. Fine *et al.*, eds. *Development policy in the 21st century: beyond the post-Washington consensus*. London: Routledge, 1–27.

Girvin, N., 2012. Social movements confront neoliberalism: reflecting on a Caribbean experience. *Globalizations*, 9 (6), 753–766.

Gruhn, I., 1976. The Lomé convention: inching towards interdependence. *International Organization*, 30 (2), 241–262.

Gruhn, I., 1993. *The evolution of African–European relations*. Washington: European Community Studies Association.

Haworth, N. and Hughes, S., 2009. Decent work and the ILO: extending the agenda. Paper for the ILERA 15th World Congress. Available from: www.google.co.uk/search?q=ilera&ie=utf8&oe=utf8&aq=t&rls=org.mozilla:en-GB:official&client=firefox-a [accessed 1 March 2013].

ILO, 2006. *Implementing the global employment agenda: employment strategies in support of decent work: vision document*. Geneva: ILO.

ILO, 2007. *Decent work agenda in Africa 2007–2015 – eleventh African regional meeting, Addis Ababa, April 2007, report of the Director General*. Geneva: ILO.

ILO, 2009. *Develop a global partnership for development*. Geneva: ILO.

ILO, 2012. *The ILO and the EU, partners for decent work and social justice: impact of ten years of cooperation*. Geneva: ILO.

IMF, 2010. *The challenges of growth, employment, and social cohesion*. Washington: IMF.
ITUC, 2006. *Call to action for decent work, decent life*. Brussels: ITUC.
Karongo, C., 2012. Women violated in Kenyan flower sector – KHRC, 15 February 2012. Available from: www.capitalfm.co.ke/news/2012/02/women-violated-in-kenyan-flower-sector-khrc/ [accessed 1 March 2013].
Kawasaki, S., 2000. *Origins of the concept of the 'Eurafrican community'*. Tokyo: Tokyo Kasei University. Available from: www.kasei.ac.jp/library/kiyou/2000/2.KAWASAKI.pdf [accessed 8 October 2009].
Keat, R., 1993. *Every economy is a moral economy*. Edinburgh: University of Edinburgh. Available from: http://www.russellkeat.net/research/ethicsmarkets/keat_everyeconomymoraleconomy.pdf [accessed 8 October 2009].
Langan, M., 2009. ACP-EU normative concessions from Stabex to private sector development. *Perspectives on European Politics and Society*, 10 (3), 416–444.
Langan, M., 2011. Uganda's flower farms and private sector development. *Development and Change*, 42 (5), 1207–1239.
Langan, M., 2012. Normative power Europe and the moral economy of Africa-EU ties: a conceptual reorientation of 'normative power'. *New Political Economy*, 17 (3), 243–270.
Langan, M. and Scott, J., forthcoming. The aid for trade charade. *Cooperation and Conflict*.
Mailafia, O., 1997. *Europe and economic reform in Africa: structural adjustment and economic diplomacy*. London: Routledge.
Milner, C., Morrissey, O., and Zgova, E., 2009. EU-ACP Economic Partnership Agreements and ACP integration. Credit Research Paper, No. 05/09. Nottingham: University of Nottingham.
Mission of Jamaica to the EU, 2010. Cariforum's experience with the EPA, M.G. Roberts Ambassador/Head of Mission of Jamaica to the EU at ESA-EU Information Seminar on EPAs, Malawi, 26–27 July.
Ngwonya, P. and Richardson, B., 2012. Aid for trade and African agriculture: the Bittersweet taste of Swazi sugar. Available from: http://ccs.ukzn.ac.za/files/Aid%20for%20Trade%20and%20African%20agriculture.pdf [accessed 1 March 2013].
Nunn, S. and Price, A., 2004. Managing development: EU and African relations through the evolution of the Lomé and Cotonou agreements. *Historical Materialism*, 12 (4), 203–230.
Őnis, Z. and Şenses, F., 2005. Rethinking the emerging post-Washington consensus. *Development and Change*, 36 (2), 263–290.
Page, S., 2006. Bringing aid and trade together. *In*: S. Page, ed. *Trade and aid: partners or rivals in development policy?* London: Cameron May, 11–34.
Pricewaterhouse Coopers, 2006. *Sustainability impact assessment of the EU-ACP Economic Partnership Agreement – West Africa: agro-industry*. London: Pricewaterhouse Coopers.
Raju, K., 2008. Social clause in WTO and ILO core labour standards: concerns of both India and other developing countries. Social Science Research Network. Available from: http://papers.ssrn.com/sol3/papers.cfm?abstract_id=1195305 [accessed 1 March 2013].
Sayer, A., 2004. Moral economy. Department of Sociology, Lancaster University. Available from: www.comp.lancs.ac.uk/sociology/papers/sayermoral-economy.pdf [accessed 8 October 2009].
Sayer, A., 2007. Moral economy as critique. *New Political Economy*, 12 (2), 261–270.
South Centre, 2006. *High level conference on EU-ACP trade relations: the development challenges of economic partnership agreements*. Brussels: South Centre.
Stiglitz, J., 2004. *The post Washington consensus*. Columbia: Institute for Public Policy Dialogue.
Sunassee Lam, A., 2008. Aid for trade and the European development fund. *In*: D. Njinkeu and H. Cameron, eds. *Aid for trade and development*. Cambridge: Cambridge University Press, 273–292.
TUC, 2012. *A decent job? Assessing DFID's contribution to achieving decent work*. London: TUC.
Ulmer, K., 2004. Are trade agreements with the EU beneficial to women in Africa, the Caribbean, and the pacific? *Gender and Development*, 12 (2), 53–57.
Wafula, C., 2012. MPs to discuss wage rise for flower farm workers. *The Daily Nation*, 26 December.
War on Want, 2009. *Defending the rights of flower workers in Kenya*, 13 February. London: War on Want.

Differentiation within reciprocity: the European Union approach to preferential trade agreements

Stephen Woolcock

Department of International Relations, London School of Economics, London, UK

Recent statements on European Union (EU) trade policy towards developing countries (DCs) have stressed the need for differentiation between trading partners depending on their level of development. But what does this mean in practice? This article assesses the substance of EU trade policy towards a number of partners at different levels of development on the basis of the texts of recent preferential trade agreements (PTAs). It argues that EU PTA policy exhibits differentiation within a general shift towards reciprocity vis-à-vis DCs and that this needs to be assessed at the level of specific policy areas as much as partner country. It also suggests that the factors shaping EU policy vary from case to case with commercial competition and sector interests relatively more important in PTAs with emerging markets and high-income DCs and norms and institutional factors relatively more important in shaping those with least developed or low-income DCs.

Introduction

A central theme to the 2012 Communication on trade and development proposed by the Directorate General for Trade of the European Commission and endorsed by the Council was one of differentiation (European Commission 2012a). Differentiation in this context means tailoring European Union (EU) trade policy to match the level of development and development needs of the EU's trading partners. How this concept is defined – and perhaps more importantly implemented in practice – will determine the balance between reciprocity and development objectives in EU trade policy. But it is also important in shaping a key element of the EU's trade policy per se and – in so far as the EU is a key player – the nature of the international trading system in general.

From the mid-1990s the EU has sought to shape the international trading system. But the leadership aspirations of the EU within the World Trade Organisation (WTO) have been frustrated by the lack of progress in the Doha Development Agenda (DDA). There are a number of causes for this impasse in the DDA, including the shift in the balance of current – and especially the potential for – economic growth and therefore market power towards the emerging markets, the use of the Single Undertaking in negotiations, the burgeoning of preferential trade agreements (PTAs) and governments too ready to take the safe political option of responding to domestic interests rather than seek joint gains in negotiations. Underlying many of these causes, however, has been the problem of how to differentiate between countries in terms of their commitments (to liberalisation) and binding rules according to their level of development or role in international trade and investment.

There is no expectation that the least developed countries (LDCs) should accept commitments on a par with established developed economies. The challenge is 'differentiation' between established developed economies, emerging markets and higher income or large developing economies that have prospects for growth (WTO 2013). In its autonomous trade policy, the EU has offered duty-free-quota-free (DFQF) access to LDCs under its Everything But Arms (EBA) policy. Much of the writing on EU trade policy in the context of development has therefore concentrated on this end of the spectrum and stressed the shift towards more reciprocity in the Economic Partnership Agreements (EPAs). But what does EU policy of differentiation look like across the whole spectrum from LDCs through to the more developed emerging markets? This article addresses this question by looking at the detail of a range recent EU PTAs. It does so because current policy is, for better or worse, being shaped by PTAs.[1] The focus on PTAs also provides an opportunity to assess EU policy across all trade and investment topics, including in particular the 'WTO-plus' or trade rules topics that do not feature in current WTO negotiations or in many autonomous measures such as EBA. It also looks at what differentiation is retained in PTAs, where one would expect the greater use of asymmetric market power favouring the EU to lead to more reciprocity.

The article starts by offering a framework for assessing the factors shaping EU trade and investment policy and PTAs in particular. This is followed by a discussion of the concrete provisions in EU PTAs and what these tell us about differentiation. There is then a discussion of some refined hypotheses concerning the relative importance of factors shaping EU policy.

What factors shape the EU PTA policy?

A full understanding of EU trade policy requires some assessment of the factors shaping EU policy towards trade and PTAs. The prevailing *norms* in trade and development will feed into EU policy. In the recent past, EU policy has been shaped by conflicting views on the benefits of trade for development between those arguing for a continued pursuit of neo-liberal policies (De Ville and Orbie 2014) or that preferences have not contributed significantly to the trade performance of developing economies such as the African Caribbean and Pacific (ACP) states and those who continue to favour 'policy space' for development (Di Caprio and Trommer 2010). The promotion of regionalism as a means of development through region-to-region agreements is another example of normative views shaping the EU trade objectives (Agawal and Fogarty 2004). EU trade has also been shaped by its internal policies that go to make up the *acquis communautaire*. These led to a consensus among the Member States on an approach that placed liberalisation within a framework of rules governing trade and ensure competition. In terms of development, clear predictable rules have been seen as crucial to attracting investment and thus sustainable development. Sustainable development has also been defined to include both the promotion of core International Labour Organisation (ILO) standards and compliance with multilateral environmental agreements.

Other domestic factors influencing EU policy-making take the form of interests and institutions. The balance between offensive and defensive sector interests is the starting point for any analysis of trade policy and it has been argued that these interests also shape EU policy vis-à-vis developing countries (DCs) (Heron and Siles-Brügge 2012). Structural shifts in the balance of growth and trade in the world economy have also influenced EU PTA policy. This takes the form of a broad EU public policy *interest*, as defined in recent EU policy statements such as 'Global Europe' in 2006 (European Commission 2006) and reaffirmed in 'Trade and Growth in World Affairs' in 2010 (European Commission 2010), in maintaining the EU position in the global economy by means of ensuring access to world markets, in particular those emerging or DC markets that have growth potential. LDCs only account for a fraction of DC trade (less than Euro 100bn exports of a total of Euro 4500bn in 2010). The G-20 group of emerging and DCs accounted for more than half of all developing world exports (Euro 2750bn in 2010). Countervailing interests are also at work in the EU in the shape of non-governmental organisations arguing for development over commercial interests.

Decision-making in EU trade and development policy is determined by the *institutional framework* within which it is made (Meunier and Nicolaidis 2006). Responsibility for EU trade with the ACP states was shifted from Directorate General (DG) Development to DG Trade in the European Commission, a move that has been seen as a source of a shift to trade and away from development (Gavas and Maxwell 2009). More recently the implementation of the Lisbon Treaty (Treaty of the Functioning of the European Union (TFEU)) has brought further changes with much of DG Development being absorbed into the new European External Action Service (EEAS) (Gavas and Koeb 2010) and development and trade policy being brought together with other aspects of external policy, including foreign policy under the EEAS, at least on paper. Equally significant is the greater role for the European Parliament (EP) that now has co-decision-making (ordinary legislative procedure) powers for all trade legislation. This means that EU legislation implementing unilateral trade measures such as General System of Preferences (GSP) now requires the assent of the EP and the Parliament must give its consent to all preferential and multilateral trade agreements (Woolcock 2012).

EU policy is also likely to be influenced by the varied *interests of DCs* themselves. The extent to which the EU considers the position of its DC trading partners will clearly shape the reciprocity versus development equation and is central to the differentiation debate. The ability of the EU's DC partners will also vary according to their negotiating capacity and general position on trade. The major emerging country markets have more supply capacity, more negotiating capacity and more market power, thanks to their market size.

The *policies of other developed WTO members* can also be expected to shape EU policy on PTAs. Competition from such countries in negotiating PTAs has been a key factor in the shift towards a more active EU policy from the middle of the 2000s onwards (Dür 2007, Woolcock 2007, Baccini and Dür 2011). This can be expected to take the form of the EU seeking to match the scope and depth of PTAs negotiated by its main competitors, such as the USA and Japan, in order to ensure EU interests are not prejudiced. A major 'competitor' in the PTA business is the USA. During much of the 2000s the USA did not pursue an active trade policy, although it had already opted for a 'competitive liberalisation' strategy in the last 1990s (Evenett and Meier 2008). But from 2011 the USA began to engage more actively in trade policy and most of this has been pursued through PTAs.

Finally, there are the *international legal commitments* entered into by the EU, such as the WTO agreements that constrain, to a greater or lesser degree, the scope of action for the EU. Bound most favoured nation (MFN) tariffs, existing agreements on a range of non-tariffs measures, such as safeguards, technical barriers to trade (TBT) and sanitary and phytosanitary (SPS) measures as well as the General Agreement on Tariffs and Trade (1994) (GATT) and General Agreement on Trade in Services (GATS) provisions on preferential agreements limit the scope of EU policy. GATT Art XXIV has of course been presented by the Commission as limiting the scope for EU flexibility in the EPA negotiations.

Assessing the above factors shaping EU policy on PTAs it is possible to suggest the following hypotheses. Shifts in the general balance of growth, the PTA policies of competitors and the desire of key sectors to gain matching access to emerging, relatively protected growth markets can be expected to drive the reciprocity agenda. This applies to market access because of the relatively high rates of bound MFN tariffs and limited services commitments of most emerging markets compared to the EU. It also applies to non-tariff and regulatory barriers where the creation of the Single European Market and WTO commitments have liberalised the EU while such rules related barriers to trade remain relatively untouched by binding commitments by DCs. Compared to these commercial pressures, norms such as sustainable development or even regional integration are likely to have less influence on EU policy.

At the other end of the spectrum, EU policy towards LDCs appears to be shaped more by normative factors, such as the EU debate on trade or policy space, as well as institutional factors that shape the balance of this debate by shifting the locus of EU policy-making between DG Trade and Development or the EP. Normative issues shape market access as well as trade rules in the sense that commitments on the latter are seen either as reducing policy space or facilitating investment and development by ensuring good trade governance (i.e. transparency, rule of law and property rights). Commercial factors are less likely to drive EU policy because the commercial interests are generally small as the figures above suggest, although this does not mean that there are no sector interests.

In the middle of the development spectrum the picture can be expected to be more complex. Some high-income DCs may well offer significant markets and competing PTAs will then also be a factor, as for example, in the cases of Mexico and Chile in the past (Dür 2007). The influence of commercial and normative interests may also be more balanced, as in the case of countries that offer potential markets but also pose normative challenges in the shape of inadequate labour or environmental standards. With these hypotheses in mind, the focus of the article now moves to the content of EU PTAs.

Provisions in EU PTAs

The treaty provisions

The core aims of EU trade policy (Common Commercial Policy (CCP)) are set out in Art 206 of the TFEU, which states that the EU shall 'contribute, in the common interest, to the harmonious development of world trade, the progressive abolition of restrictions on international trade and on foreign direct investment, and the lowering of customs and other barriers'. The CCP must also conform to the general external aims of the EU as set out in Art 21 the Treaty on EU. These include general normative aims, such as promoting democracy, rule of law and human rights, the preservation of peace and good governance and – with more specific reference to trade and investment – the 'foster(ing of) sustainable economic, social and environmental development of developing countries with the aim or eradicating poverty' and 'encourag(ing) of the integration of all countries into the world economy, including through the progressive abolition of restrictions on international trade' (TFEU Art 21 (d) and (e)).[2] These objectives clearly provide wide scope for interpretation. Reference to the harmonious development of the 'world economy' would seem to be consistent with an approach that is less multilateral provided it does not constitute aggressive forms of preferential or discriminatory trade policy. The reference to the progressive abolition of barriers to trade provides the basis for the EU's comprehensive approach covering market access and non-tariff or rules issues. Although there is no reference to reciprocity in the treaties, the trading system has, since 1948, been largely determined by reciprocal trade negotiations that have thus shaped EU trade policy thinking. The question is how broad or narrow to define reciprocity given that the treaty refers to the aim of promoting a 'progressive and gradual integration' of DCs into the world economy.

This section provides an initial analysis of how the EU has applied differentiation in practice. It looks first at the aims and principles as set out in each PTA before assessing the substance of PTAs. It is based on analysis of the detail of the text of the EPA with the East African Community (EAC),[3] as an example of an agreement with a region that contains developing as well as

LDCs; the comprehensive EPA with the Cariforum[4] as an example of an agreement with a range of lower to middle-income DCs; the EU–Colombia–Peru Free Trade Agreement (FTA),[5] an example of a PTA with non-ACP middle-income DCs and the EU–Korea FTA[6] as an example of a PTA with a country at or near the developed end of the spectrum.[7] Given that these agreements are very recent it is not possible to assess the important question of how they are applied.

General objectives

In all the four PTAs considered, the objective is a progressive liberalisation process, but the wording varies between the agreements. The text of the EPA with the EAC and the comprehensive EPA with Cariforum refers to the gradual integration of these economies into the world economy. In the case of these two PTAs with ACP regions there is also reference to respecting the policy choices and development priorities of the EU's partners (Art 2 (c) EAC and Art 1(c) Cariforum). The agreement with Colombia–Peru refers to 'progressive, gradual liberalisation' in conformity with the GATT Art XXIV (which provides the general exception from the GATT Art I commitment to MFN for all customs unions and preferential agreements).[8] The EU–Korea agreement refers to 'progressive and reciprocal liberalisation' (Art 2.1). So there is already differentiation in objectives, with the agreements with the ACP states recognising development priorities and the EU–Korea agreement stressing reciprocity.

Trade in goods[9]

With regard to *tariffs* the EU has accepted asymmetric commitments from DCs. Although the EPAs are negotiated with the substantially all trade requirements of GATT Art XXIV in mind and thus more reciprocal than the unilateral preferences under Lomé or Cotonou they still provide a degree of asymmetry. The EU has generally committed to 98% plus liberalisation with short transition periods – if at all – for a very limited number of sensitive sectors but accepted lower commitments from DC trading partners.[10] For example, the EAC text excludes slightly more than 17% of EAC imports by value from any liberalisation commitment, while the EU commits to more or less full liberalisation. EAC tariff reductions would also be phased in with no tariff liberalisation for seven years.[11] The bulk of EAC liberalisation is envisaged for years 7–13 after entry into force of the agreement, and some sensitive products (between 2% and 3% of tariff lines) would be liberalised over a period of up to 25 years.

In the case of the Cariforum EPA the picture is complicated by the variation between the tariff commitments of the Cariforum states. Broadly speaking, the larger more developed states are to liberalise more tariff lines sooner than the smaller states with higher tariffs. The transition period for liberalisation extends up to 25 years, but most of the major liberalisation will also be in an interim period between years 5 and 15 when the more important tariffs (of more than 20% will be liberalised). Cariforum does not yet have a common external tariff and tariffs are still applied on intra-regional trade (ODI 2008) but the EPA allows these intra-Cariforum tariffs to remain for a decade. Most Cariforum states have excluded a number of sensitive sectors from liberalisation such as food and animals as well as chemicals. Access to the EU is DFQF but liberalisation also means a loss of price guarantees for Cariforum sugar producers. As for the EAC, the EU is expecting ACP liberalisation but offering little or nothing in terms of new access to the EU because it already offered duty-free access under the Cotonou Agreement. The EPAs offer only secure, legally binding access and thus generally reduce the degree of asymmetry favouring the ACP states.

In terms of EU imports, much the same applies for the PTA with Colombia–Peru. Imports from these countries were already zero for the vast majority of products under the EU's GSP scheme. The PTA provides only additional – but not DFQF – access for Colombia–Peru in sectors like bananas and some other food products. This PTA has therefore also made trade more reciprocal, with the benefits for Colombia and Peru coming in the form of guaranteed access to the EU market. Moving up the scale, the EU–Korea PTA provides for more or less complete and quicker tariff liberalisation by both parties, with the EU achieving tariff-free access to the Korean market for 91% of tariff lines on entry into force of the agreement (many of these tariff lines already had a zero MFN rate), 95% in three years, and nearly 100% within seven years, with only rice as an exception. The EU also agreed to more or less complete tariff liberalisation. Differentiation between Colombia–Peru and the EPAs took the form of a greater coverage of liberalisation for Colombia–Peru with far fewer sectors excluded from liberalisation and shorter 11-year transition period.

Recent PTAs therefore require more reciprocity than under Cotonou for the ACP or other countries under the GSP, but retain differentiation in the shape of asymmetry favouring the LDCs and DC, while more developed country partners face demands for full reciprocity.

Rules of origin (RoO) are important because compliance with complex rules can add to trade costs and constrain the development of regional supply chains when there is no provision for cumulation.[12] High compliance costs with RoO can be the cause of low utilisation of tariff preferences. The EU has reformed its RoO by first harmonising rules on the Pan-Euro system. Previously rules varied from one PTA to the next. The Pan-Euro system, however, still uses different 'rules' (change of tariff heading, value content added and technical requirements) to determine origin of different products or sectors that add to complexity and thus the costs of compliance especially for DC exporters. For the ACP states, the Cotonou RoO are applied. These take the form of specific rules for each product. More recently, the EU has introduced a number of changes to RoO for its GSP schemes that adopt a simple value content rule. To date, these reformed RoO have been limited to the GSP with PTAs, including the EPAs continuing to apply the more complex 'Cotonou-plus' rules. The intension is to progressively introduce more simplified rules that take account of the development needs of the ACP states (see, for example, Art 12 of the EU-EAC text). For the EPA with Cariforum, there is a specific commitment to review the RoO provisions after five years with a view to simplifying them (Protocol 1 on RoO). The EU–Cariforum EPA also reformed RoO in textiles, which should facilitate exports from Cariforum. The progressive reform of RoO in the interests of DCs is to take the form of negotiations on simplified rules for sectors that are of particular importance for DC exporters. The RoO used with regard to the EU–Korea agreement are the full set of specific rules.

Cumulation of origin is also important for DCs especially when the development of supply capacity rests in part on regional value chains. The EU provided cumulation for the whole of the ACP under the Cotonou Agreement. This is extended to countries that sign interim EPAs. Equally cumulation is envisaged for regions in which there are various EU PTAs. Thus the EU agreement with Colombia–Peru envisages extending diagonal cumulation to other countries that negotiate PTAs with the EU (Art 4 of Annex II EU Colombia–Peru).[13] On RoO, therefore, the EU is moving slowly to accommodate DC interests in simplified rules and is ready to extend diagonal cumulation to DCs that have concluded PTAs with the EU with the same RoO protocols.[14]

Whilst tariffs remain important for many DCs, especially LDCs *TBT and SPS* have grown in relative importance. For DCs that still rely heavily on the export of agricultural products, SPS measures can constitute a major barrier to market access in the EU by hampering efforts to move up the value chain and export higher value-added products. There is limited evidence on the impact of provisions on standards in PTAs. What – very limited – research has been done seems to suggest that the introduction of common standards facilitates trade (Chen *et al.* 2006). But there is anecdotal evidence that EU SPS measures in particular sectors have restricted DC exports.

EU policy on PTAs is in line with the WTO rules and requires national treatment for regulatory standards and conformance assessment. Special and differential treatment for DCs then takes the form of technical assistance to help develop national capacity to ensure compliance (see Chapters 6 and 7 of the EU–Cariforum text, for example). Under the WTO TBT and SPS agreements, DCs can be given a longer period to comply with new regulations or standards. As the EU PTAs refer to the WTO provisions, this presumably applies to the DC parties in EU PTAs, but there is no specific reference to it. EU PTAs promote the use of agreed international standards. This should have positive network externalities for DCs in complying with common international standards.

Meeting DC interests in TBT and SPS therefore takes the form of (generally non-binding) technical assistance by the EU. The EU provides more assistance than most developed WTO members for capacity building in this area. Specialist bilateral committees established by PTAs also provide a channel for technical assistance and cooperation on a permanent basis. Differentiation can also be found in the formal requirements of PTAs. At the LDC end of the spectrum, the EAC EPA text only provides a *rendezvous* clause for TBT and SPS issues, in other words it will be returned to sometime in the future. The Cariforum EPA reaffirms the WTO agreements and EU commitments to enhance Cariforum capacity to ensure compliance with international standards for goods and promote intra-regional cooperation within Cariforum with a view to achieving recognition of equivalence with EU SPS requirements (Art 53 Cariforum text). The EU–Colombia–Peru PTA follows the model set by the earlier EU–Chile PTA by including strong procedural measures to promote cooperation in subcommittees for both TBT and SPS. In the case of SPS, this means procedural measures to promote the application of principles set out in the WTO agreement such as recognition of disease and pest free products (see EU–Colombia–Peru Chapters 4 and 5 and Annex VI on the SPS cooperation). In the case of Korea, EU exporters argued that the removal of tariffs, for automobiles, for example, would have no effect unless TBTs were addressed. The EU–Korea FTA therefore sets a precedent by establishing sector specific committees to monitor the application of the national treatment and non-discrimination obligations of Korea in automobiles, machinery and chemicals.

On TBT and SPS issues therefore differentiation ranges from no provisions (in addition to the existing rather weak WTO rules), to technical support for capacity building in DCs in order to enable exporters from these countries to meet EU or international standards. For middle-income countries the approach has been to intensify cooperation. And for the emerging/developed economies the aim has been to push for more extensive means of ensuring that TBTs do not become or remain barriers to trade for the EU exporters.

All trade agreements include scope for the use of commercial instruments, such as *safeguard measures* and anti-dumping provisions. Generally speaking, the EU follows the existing GATT provisions in Art XIX and Art VI, respectively. EU PTAs also include bilateral safeguard provisions. In these, the EU has provided some degree of asymmetry favouring DC partners. For example, EAC and Cariforum texts include provisions that enable safeguard actions when imports 'cause or threaten to cause disturbances to an infant industry'. Normally, and in trade with developed economies, bilateral safeguards are only permitted when an import surge threatens serious injury to an existing industry. There is no reference to infant industries. Safeguards to protect infant industries can be taken by the EAC or Cariforum states for periods of up to 4 years and renewable for a further 4 years, but only during the first 10 years of the agreement (EU–Cariforum Art 25 (5) (b): EAC EPA text Art 21(5)(b)). Neither the EU–Colombia–Peru nor the EU–Korea agreements include such an infant industry clause, and neither allow for a bilateral safeguard to extend for a period of more than four years in total.

Services and investment

Services liberalisation in certain sectors, such as those that provide general inputs into the rest of DC economies, has been argued to be in the interests of development. But the ACP states have opposed inclusion of services in the EPAs, arguing that this is not required under the Cotonou Agreement or in order to comply with WTO obligations. Some DCs have offensive interests in services. Indeed, services trade is significant for LDCs (due to transport and tourism) accounting for 15% of gross domestic product (GDP) compared to less than 9% for middle-income DCs. Services trade in India is equivalent to 12% of GDP.

The EU has offensive interests in service especially vis-à-vis the emerging markets, but practices differentiation. In the EPAs with less developed states or regions, there is merely a reference to services in the *rendezvous* clause (e.g. for the EAC EPA). The agreement with Cariforum, on the other hand, includes a comprehensive agreement on investment, trade in services and electronic commerce that is clearly GATS-plus. There are extensive sectoral chapters covering regulation in sectors such as telecommunications and financial services. Flexibility takes the form of positive listing of coverage, so the Cariforum parties were still able to exclude sensitive sectors. There is also a general 'right to regulate clause' (Art 60(6) EU–Cariforum EPA) and a safeguard clause to enable capital controls that are otherwise caught by a requirement for free movement of capital. The Cariforum states have made commitments covering between 60% and 75% of service sectors compared to 90% for the EU. As for other provisions based on scheduling such as tariffs and government procurement, a full assessment of the degree of asymmetry requires a detailed analysis of the schedules that is not possible here. The EU seeks commitments in sectors such as telecommunications and financial services, while the ACP states favour sectors in which mode 4 is prevalent, because with lower labour costs these are the sectors in which the DCs have a comparative advantage. EU liberalisation in mode 4 has, however, been limited to key personnel.

The EU–Colombia–Peru agreement generally follows the approach of the EU's EPA with Cariforum in that there is significantly GATS-plus with coverage extending to commitments in 10 major sectors for Colombia and 8 for Peru in modes 1 and 2 compared to less than 4 for Colombia under the GATS (of 1994) and none for Peru. There are also provisions covering regulation in specific sectors, such as computer and postal services, telecommunications and financial services as well as electronic commerce. Hybrid listing (a mixture of positive and negative) means that Colombia and Peru were able to exclude sensitive sectors such as utility services (power, gas and water) as well as the air and sea transport. In mode 4, there are the same limitations on access to the EU markets as for the GATS and other agreements, with access limited to temporary presence of key personnel, graduate trainees and other business people.

The EU–Korea agreement is an example of where the EU was after matching and ideally improving on the commitments made by Korea in the KORUS agreement with the USA. Broadly speaking the EU was able to achieve this aim, with some KORUS-plus provisions in financial and legal services as well as certain other sectors. The EU–Korea services commitments were however based on positive listing so provided the scope for greater flexibility than with the negative listing approach of KORUS.

The position with regard to *investment, and thus establishment* under mode 3 in services is broadly similar to that for cross-border supply of services. The EAC EPA text includes investment only in a *rendezvous* clause. To date only Cariforum has accepted investment provisions among the ACP regions. The use of positive listing means that sensitive sectors could be excluded by the Cariforum partners. But Chapter 5 of the Cariforum EPA includes the same sector specific disciplines for establishment as for cross-border supply of services. There are specific exclusions from the EU–Colombia–Peru agreement that permit policies promoting the interests of indigenous peoples or cultural heritage in Columbia and Peru. Broadly speaking, these countries have made commitments to the EU that are broadly equivalent to those made to the USA in PTAs. So here is another example of where competition with other countries has clearly shaped EU policy. The one area in which the EU has not broadly matched US PTAs is that of investment protection. This has been due to the lack of EU competence in the field of FDI before the adoption of the Lisbon Treaty. The EPA with Cariforum and the EU–Colombia–Peru and EU–Korea agreements were negotiated before the adoption of the Lisbon Treaty, even if they were provisionally adopted after it applied.

Government procurement and sustainable development

Government procurement is another of the so-called Singapore issues the EU seeks to promote in its comprehensive rules agenda. It is an area of some controversy concerning the costs and benefits for DCs. On the one hand, more transparency and competition in public contracts that account for large percentages of public expenditure in LDCs can improve the efficiency of public funds and limit corruption. On the other, DCs (apart from the emerging economies) have little capacity to supply EU public markets and as smaller economies tend to have more open procurement markets.

There are no multilateral rules governing public procurement, but a plurilateral Government Procurement Agreement (GPA), which in its latest revised version of 2011 includes in Article V provision for special and differential treatment for DCs. Under this developed country participants are to take account of DC interests and provide technical assistance. There are also specific provisions that allow for exemptions for DCs. But this asymmetric coverage must be negotiated, which means the asymmetric power still favours the developed countries.

EU PTA policy differentiates in procurement in that there are only *rendezvous* clauses on procurement in most EPAs, such as in the EAC EPA text. The EU–Cariforum text constitutes the next stage with provisions on transparency, and MFN for locally established affiliates, but no 'liberalisation' commitments included in the agreement. 'Liberalisation' in the form of schedules of purchasing entities committed to comply with national treatment and other provisions are to be agreed subsequently (by consensus) by the EU–Cariforum Joint Trade Committee. The EU offers asymmetric access to the EU procurement markets by offering more or less full GPA 'liberalisation', although this of course raises the question of whether the Cariforum states have the supply capacity to compete on the EU markets concerned. The EU–Columbia–Peru PTA provides the next, more comprehensive and 'liberal' model in that Colombia and Peru commit to more or less full GPA framework provisions and 'liberalisation' commitments for central and local government entities. Again the EU offers asymmetric access by offering Colombia and Peru more or less full GPA equivalent commitments, while those of Columbia and Peru are much less extensive. The top end of the differentiation is then represented by the EU–Korea FTA that provides full GPA commitments as both the EU and the Republic of Korea are signatories to the plurilateral GPA. Indeed, the EU–Korea PTA went beyond the GPA coverage by including build and operate contracts that were then subsequently included in the general extension of the liberalisation commitments of GPA signatories in December 2011. Procurement also offers a taste of how the EU may approach the major emerging markets in that a 2012 proposal from the European Commission called for a narrow definition of reciprocity vis-à-vis major markets that do not agree to open state or state-owned enterprise dominated procurement within the context of the GPA negotiations (European Commission 2012b).

Finally with regard to *sustainable development and human rights*, all EU preferential agreements or the accompanying cooperation agreements, now include a human rights clause and provisions on sustainable development. There has been some discussion as to whether these are enforceable. Certainly there is no specific enforcement provision for the human rights clause, although there is probably scope for parties to take 'appropriate measures' in the case of non-compliance with the human rights provisions. This has been interpreted as the power to suspend any obligations under (for example Article 8 (2) of the EU–Colombia FTA) (European Parliament 2012). Such clauses are a source of tension in relations with countries as diverse as Canada, which failed to see why it should agree to human rights clause, and various ACP states given the presence of non-execution clauses that would enable the EU to effectively sanction a country for gross violation of human rights.

The sustainable development provisions that the EU now include in its PTAs require compliance with certain core ILO Conventions and a set of multilateral environment agreements. Given the role of the EP in ratifying the agreements the EU negotiates, it likely that all future PTAs will include some sustainable development provisions. The question is how they will be enforced. The EU agreements favour a soft law approach with peer review and cooperation.

This brief discussion of the content of policy suggests that, within an overall reciprocity-based approach to trade, differentiation provisions are built into the detail of the trade and investment provisions of EU PTAs in the form of either progressive commitments, technical assistance, special treatment for DCs or asymmetric commitments. There are, in addition, development chapters in the EPA agreements and the provision of development finance in parallel with the EPAs and for some other PTAs. Differentiation means that the EU clearly looks for reciprocity in relations with more or less developed economies, such as Korea and no doubt increasingly with countries like China, India or Brazil. Non-ACP DCs appear to be asked to make greater commitments than the middle-income ACP states (e.g. Cariforum), which in turn have been asked to make greater commitments in the comprehensive EPAs than the less advanced ACP states, such as the EAC.

Some refined hypotheses on the factors shaping EU policy

The analysis above has focused on the concrete substance of a selection of EU PTAs rather than the factors shaping EU policy. All that can be offered is therefore a refined set of hypotheses concerning the shaping factors. The first point to make is that the relative importance of factors shaping EU PTA policy can be expected to vary from case to case. For PTAs with emerging market economies and perhaps some larger developing economies, reciprocity can be expected to predominate. These are potentially large markets for EU manufacturing and service sectors that have relatively high bound MFN tariffs compared to the EU and in which domestic regulation and other non-tariff barriers mean their markets are still relatively closed compared to the EU. Competitive PTAs concluded by the USA or Japan are also likely to play a relatively important role given that first mover advantages gained through PTAs may shape long-term competition. Norms, such as sustainable development or the promotion of regional integration, can be expected to play a far less important role. This hypothesis is clearly born out in the case of Korea, although as noted above this is not the best proxy for an emerging market.

For middle-income DCs commercial interests in terms of offensive, market access interests seem likely to play less of a role, which provides scope for more asymmetry of commitments. The competitive policies of other state's PTAs do however appear to be important for this group of countries. Thus the EU moved to conclude agreements with Colombia and Peru and Central America to match US PTA policy towards these countries, but was willing to accept a degree of asymmetry. Competition has also shaped EU policy in other cases not covered here, such as Mexico and Chile, as well as in efforts to conclude bilateral PTAs with Association of South East Asian Nations (ASEAN) states in advance of a broader EU–ASEAN agreement. Normative factors also appear to have been more important in shaping the PTAs with Colombia–Peru and Central America, such as in the shape of the debate over sustainable development and human rights in Colombia. Equally, the promotion of regional integration retained a more important role in the PTAs with Cariforum, Central America and Colombia–Peru.

For LDCs, commercial interests do not appear to have been so important, or have at least not prevented more favourable differentiation. As suggested in the introduction this would seem to rest on the fact that the commercial benefits are either only in relatively long term or uncertain except for a few limited sectors. Competition from other PTAs has been less important. Neither the USA nor Japan is competing to conclude PTAs with most of the ACP states. EU policy is therefore more influenced by the normative debate within the EU on the balance between trade and policy space, reciprocity and liberalisation. In this context institutional factors, such as the shift of negotiating competence for the EPAs from DG Trade and out of DG Development, play a role because these tend to reflect competing normative positions.

A comparison of the case studies carried out for this article suggests that path dependence also needs to be included in any framework for assessing the factors shaping policy. While the number of PTAs being concluded looks daunting at first glance, a closer look reveals standard patterns. This goes for the EU as well as USA and Japanese PTAs (Heydon and Woolcock 2013). Although the EU may be more 'flexible' in accommodating the interests of its trading partners than the USA, precedents set for one partner or for one level of development will probably shape agreements with equivalent countries. This raises the question of whether any differentiation is really just the evolution of EU PTA policy rather than a coherent policy. This can only be addressed by an analysis of more EU PTAs over a longer time period.

Finally, it has been questioned whether differentiation in EU policy reflects objective criteria on the part of the EU or simply the negotiating clout or capacity of the EU's partners. The broad range of cases studied here suggests that there is no straightforward answer to this question. On the one hand, the negotiating clout of the larger emerging markets by virtue of their market size and relatively good growth prospects is likely to shape EU preferences if not policy in favour of reciprocity rather than policy space. On the other hand, differentiation favouring more policy space has been adopted for LDCs despite their lack of market power and negotiating capacity.

Conclusions

This article set out to assess how the EU applies differentiation within the context of what are generally seen as reciprocity-based PTAs and identify which factors are likely to be the most important in shaping policy. The broad picture that emerges is one in which PTAs are shaping trade and investment policy more than multilateral negotiations or autonomous trade policies. EU PTA policy provides for differentiation. There is a distinction between EU trade policy vis-à-vis the emerging markets (more reciprocity-based) and LDCs (more development-based). The analysis of the case studies covered suggests there is also differentiation between LDCs and middle-income DCs. This differentiation applies across all policy areas, market access and rules. Seen from a broader multilateral perspective, if differentiation lies at the root of the difficulties in multilateral negotiations, as is argued here, EU policy in PTAs will be of considerable importance to future trade relations, as will the policies of other major players. This is particularly the case given that it is highly unlikely that overarching country-by-country criterion for assessing development and thus the 'suitable' level of commitment of DCs members of the WTO will be found. How differentiation is applied in each policy area in the PTAs therefore seems likely to determine future outcomes. More work assessing the EU and other countries approaches to PTAs is therefore necessary.

Acknowledgements

The author would like to thank Maurizio Carbone and Jan Orbie as well as all the contributors to the special edition and four reviewers for their helpful insights and comments.

Notes

1. This remains the case despite the agreement reached at the 9th WTO Ministerial Meeting in Bali in December 2013 on trade facilitation, aspects of agricultural trade and some special and differential treatment questions.
2. For an English text of the treaties see, for example, *Official Journal C* 115 of 9 May 2008.
3. See http://ec.europa.eu/trade/policy/countries-and-regions/regions/eac/ [accessed 10 November 2013].
4. See http://eur-lex.europa.eu/LexUriServ/LexUriServ.do?uri=OJ:L:2008:289:0003:1955:EN:PDF [accessed 10 November 2013].
5. See http://ec.europa.eu/trade/policy/countries-and-regions/regions/andean-community/ [accessed 10 November 2013].
6. See http://ec.europa.eu/trade/policy/countries-and-regions/countries/south-korea/ [accessed 10 November 2013].
7. A better test of EU policy vis-à-vis emerging markets would of course be a PTA with India or Mercosur (Brazil), but neither of these had been concluded at the time of writing. A further PTA would be the EU–Central America agreement, which constitutes a region-to-region agreement. In many respects the EU–Central America text is the same as that for Colombia and Peru however.
8. GATT Art XXIV refers to a 'reasonable period of time' to achieve liberalization, which has been generally interpreted by WTO members to mean anything between 7 and 15 years or even up to (or beyond) 25 years in some recent PTAs.
9. This generally includes agricultural products, such as in the discussion of tariff liberalisation in PTAs. The EU has not entertained any debate on subsidies in PTAs. It has however made some commitments to phase out export subsidies for products covered by the tariff liberalisation schedules in the CARIFORUM EPA (Art 28 EU-CARIFORUM EPA).
10. The EU has interpreted Art XXIV of the GATT to apply to north–south FTAs and the 'substantially all trade' provisions to mean 90% of trade and tariff lines. DCs have challenged this arguing that north–south PTAs should be covered by the enabling clause or some new interpretation of Art XXIV.
11. Some 65% of EAC MFN tariffs are already zero, so the initial commitments would not remove any tariffs.
12. Cumulation is the method by which the working of a product in more than one country can contribute to that produce acquiring originating status and thus qualifying for preferential treatment under a PTA.
13. For example, this would apply to an EU-Mercosur FTA with common rules of origin to those used in the Colombia–Peru PTAs.
14. The condition that parties must adopt the same (EU defined) RoO is problematic in that there are competing systems of RoO such as the NAFTA system. This means DCs must comply with different rules when exporting the EU or the USA. The current negotiations with Canada are important in this respect in that the aim is to agree to a mutual recognition of RoO, this could set a precedent for other agreements and dispense with the requirement to have common rules.

References

Agawal, V. and Fogarty, A.E., 2004. *EU trade strategies between regionalism and globalism*. New York: Palgrave.

Baccini, L. and Dür, A., 2011. The new regionalism and policy interdependence. *British Journal of Political Science*, 42 (1), 57–79.

Chen, M.X., Otsuki, T. and Wilson, J.S., 2006. *Do standards matter for export success?* World Bank Working Paper No. 3809. Washington, DC: The World Bank.

De Ville, F. and Orbie, J., 2014. The European Commission's neoliberal trade discourse since the crisis: legitimising continuity through subtle change. *British Journal of Politics and International Relations*, 16 (1), 149–167.

Di Caprio, A. and Trommer, S., 2010. Bilateral graduation: the impact of EPAs on LDC trade space. *Journal of Development Studies*, 46 (9), 1607–1627.

Dür, A., 2007. EU trade policy as protection for exporters: the agreements with Mexico and Chile. *Journal of Common Market Studies*, 45 (4), 833–855.

European Commission, 2006. *Global Europe: competing in the world*. COM (2006), 567, 10 May. Brussels: European Commission.

European Commission, 2010. *Trade growth and world affairs*. COM (2010) 612, 9 November. Brussels: European Commission.

European Commission, 2012a. *Trade, growth and development*. COM (2012) 22, 27 January. Brussels: European Commission.

European Commission, 2012b. *Proposal for a regulation of the European Parliament and of the Council on access to third-country goods and services to the Union's internal market in public procurement*. COM (2012) 124. Brussels: European Commission.

European Parliament, 2012. *European Union: Free Trade Agreement with Colombia and Peru*. Directorate General for External Policies, INTA PE 433.865.

Evenett, S. and Meier, M., 2008. An interim assessment of the US trade policy of 'competitive liberalization'. *The World Economy*, 31 (1), 31–66.

Gavas, M. and Koeb, E., 2010. *Setting up the European External Action Services: building a comprehensive approach*. ODI Background Note, April. London: Overseas Development Institute.

Gavas, M. and Maxwell, S., 2009. *Options for architectural reform in European development cooperation*. ODI Background Note, August London: Overseas Development Institute.

Heron, T. and Siles-Brügge, G., 2012. Comparative liberalisation and the 'Global Europe' services and investment agenda: locating the commercial drivers of the EU-ACP economic partnership agreements. *Journal of Common Market Studies*, 50 (2), 250–266.

Heydon, K. and Woolcock, S., 2013. *Comparing trade policies: EU, EFTA, US and Japanese FTAs*. European Parliament, Directorate-General for External Policies.

Meunier, S. and Nicolaidis, K., 2006. The European Union as a conflicted trade power. *Journal of European Public Policy*, 13 (6), 905–926.

ODI (2008) *Analysis of contents of the CARIFORUM and Pacific ACP Economic Partnership Agreements and challenges ahead*. Overseas Development Institute for the Commonwealth Secretariat. Available from: www.thecommonwealth.org/files/185769/FileName/CFTC-EAD-BCWG-208Final Report.pdf [accessed 10 November 2013].

Woolcock, S., 2007. *The EU approach to Free Trade Agreements*. ECIPE Working Paper 3. Brussels: ECIPE.

Woolcock, S., 2012. *European Union economic diplomacy: the role of the EU in external economic relations*. Farnham: Ashgate.

World Trade Organisation (WTO) 2013. *The future of trade: the challenges of convergence*. Report of the Panel on Defining the Future of Trade convened by WTO Director General Pascal Lamy. Available from: www.wto.org/english/res_e/publications_e/future_of_trade_e.htm [accessed 10 November 2013].

EU trade and development policy beyond the ACP: subordinating developmental to commercial imperatives in the reform of GSP

Gabriel Siles-Brügge

Politics, School of Social Sciences, University of Manchester, UK

Following the stagnation of negotiations with the African, Caribbean and Pacific states, the centrepiece of the European Union's (EU's) trade and development strategy has been a reform of the Generalised System of Preferences. Although policy-makers in the Commission's Directorate General for Trade have argued they are 'refocusing' these preferences on the 'neediest', by rendering a significant proportion of emerging economies' exports ineligible for the scheme, this article argues that the reform is actually part of a broader 'reciprocity' agenda being pursued in the context of the current economic crisis. This is about ensuring the EU possesses sufficient offensive *leverage* in ongoing free trade agreement negotiations, rather than representing any mercantilist move towards greater domestic protection. In arguing that the EU's developmental trade agenda is increasingly subordinated to commercial imperatives, this article adds to a literature that has situated the study of EU trade and development policy within the field of political economy.

Introduction

The European Union (EU) is the world's single largest market for goods from developing countries (Woolcock 2012, p. 149), with imports totalling 845 billion euro in 2012 (Eurostat 2013). As a result, the decision to introduce a series of changes to its Generalised System of Preferences (GSP) has significant global consequences. Originally authorised by a meeting of the contracting parties of the General Agreement on Tariffs and Trade (GATT) in 1968, GSP was seen as the key component of the 'special and differential treatment' offered to developing countries in the context of calls for a New International Economic Order (see White 1975, pp. 547–548, Whalley 1990, pp. 1319–1321). By way of derogation from the Most-Favoured-Nation (MFN) principle – authorised by the 1979 Enabling Clause of the GATT – the idea was for developed economies to (unilaterally) offer preferential duty rates to any developing country in order to assist in their development. In the case of the EU, however, GSP has not lived up to its full potential because it was seen as secondary to the scheme of preferences for African, Caribbean and Pacific (ACP) states under the Lomé Conventions (Heron 2013, Chapter 2). In this vein, the EU's recent self-professed attempts to 'refocus' GSP preferences 'on those countries most in need' (Commission 2012, p. 2) – while its negotiations with ACP countries on a successor arrangement to Lomé have stagnated – can be read as a rebalancing of EU's priorities in the direction of GSP.

That being said, in this article I challenge the view that these changes (which kick in from January 2014) represent a boon for developing countries. Under the GSP reform *all* high- and upper-middle-income countries will lose eligibility for preferences, while a whole host of products (mostly from emerging economies) will also be graduated (i.e. no longer eligible for preferential treatment). Although the European Commission's Directorate General for Trade has justified these changes in terms of providing the poorest (Least Developed Countries [LDCs] and the so-called 'vulnerable' economies) with the space to develop their export markets, the fact remains that the alleged benefits for these economies are far from certain. What is more, it is rather odd that the Commission is seeking to develop a model of poverty reduction based on non-reciprocal trade preferences when it chose to abandon such a model in the case of the ACP group in favour of reciprocal trade deals, the so-called Economic Partnership Agreements (EPAs) (see note 7). Although the idea of 'differentiating' between developing countries is not entirely new to EU trade policy, the lack of a coherent development rationale for the recent GSP reform begs two important questions. Firstly, what is driving these changes to the scheme and, secondly, what does this reform say about the broader 'trade-development' nexus in EU policy that authors have begun explicitly writing about (Young and Peterson 2013)?

In response to the first question, I situate the GSP reform within the broader crisis landscape, where policy-makers in DG Trade are increasingly concerned with showing that trade (liberalisation) 'works'. In this vein, their policy discourse of late has been rife with an emphasis on 'reciprocity'. This may seem at first like a turn to mercantilism (understood here as a concern with maximising net exports) and consequently also the interests of protectionists. However, a closer reading of EU policy as well as interviews with Commission officials and interest group representatives[1] suggest that the references to reciprocity actually betray a strong desire to enhance the EU's trade negotiating *leverage*. I interpret the GSP reform as just one (albeit significant) attempt to recapture lost leverage with emerging economies with which the EU has been negotiating flagship free trade agreements (FTAs) following the 2006 *Global Europe* communication.

This finding naturally raises broader implications for the study of the 'trade-development' nexus; the GSP reform appears to be driven by commercial interests to which developmental considerations have been subordinated. As a result, one of the broader contributions of this article is to challenge the idea of a uniquely 'normative power Europe' intent on exporting its progressive values and which acts in a development-friendly fashion (Manners 2008). Indeed, and echoing the sentiments of this literature, policy-makers have been keen to stress the differences between supposedly 'developmental' and 'commercial' trade policy-making, where agreements of the former type (e.g. with the ACP) are said to be driven by distinct imperatives when compared to agreements of the latter type (say with emerging markets) (Commission 2009, p. 1). Such views have also been implicitly supported by the scholarly literature on the trade-development nexus; this has tended to focus on institutional conflicts between bureaucracies within the Commission – especially between DG Trade and DG Development – which allegedly embody these distinct imperatives (see Holland and Doidge 2012).

In contrast, I argue that there is evidence to suggest that EU's external economic diplomacy is not much unlike that of its allegedly more hard-nosed rivals (e.g. the USA or China). In doing so, I align myself with a number of authors who have sought to move beyond the institutional determinants of EU external policy-making and begun to situate its study within the wider discipline of political economy (see De Bièvre and Poletti 2014). What has mattered to such scholars in particular, following a voluminous literature in the field, is how the balance of domestic-societal interests is an important determinant of trade policy outcomes, with exporters seen as key drivers of the EU's offensive trade agenda embodied by *Global Europe* (Heron and Siles-Brügge 2012).[2] In this article, I also find that the influence of political economic interests has been an important determinant of the GSP reform, with exporters being key drivers of the EU's recent *leverage* agenda. Indeed, the notion of 'reciprocity' is understood to be a key underlying feature in the political economy literature on international trade negotiations, often seen as necessary to mobilise exporters in favour of trade liberalisation and thus offset protectionist interests (Gilligan 1997).

The remainder of the article is structured as follows. In the next section, I provide an overview of the evolution of EU trade and development policy since the start of the crisis, before discussing the specifics of the GSP reform. The third section challenges the Commission's rationale for the reform, arguing that the new regulation has to be interpreted as a move to subordinate developmental policy objectives to the needs of enhancing trade negotiating leverage. The fourth section then turns to the interest group politics behind the drafting and approval of the GSP reform, finding that the views of exporters were privileged over those of importers, import-competing sectors and development-minded Non-Governmental Organisations (NGOs). The final section concludes, offering some thoughts on the exposure of EU development policy to commercial imperatives.

Reforming the GSP scheme[3]

Since the start of the crisis, there has been a move towards consolidating the EU's offensive FTA agenda. This had been initiated earlier – in the context of the stagnation of the Doha Round of multilateral trade talks – by the 2006 *Global Europe* communication written under Trade Commissioner Peter Mandelson. Specifically, *Global Europe* argued for the need to target the emerging economies of South and East Asia and led to the initiation of FTA talks with these countries (Commission 2006).[4] In this vein, the *Trade, growth and world affairs* strategy – which replaces *Global Europe* as the guiding document for EU trade policy and was authored under the leadership of Karel De Gucht, who took over as Trade Commissioner in February 2010 – has stuck to the ambitious liberalisation agenda set back in 2006 (Commission 2010c).

The only variation in the new communication with respect to *Global Europe* was the latter's emphasis on 'reciprocity'. The argument was that 'for an open trade policy in Europe to succeed politically, others – including both our developed and emerging partners – must match our efforts, in a spirit of reciprocity and mutual benefit' (Commission 2010d, p. 4). The reference to reciprocity, however, betrays a concern with ensuring the EU possesses sufficient *leverage* in ongoing trade negotiations, rather than representing any mercantilist move towards greater domestic protection as some may have concluded (see De Ville and Orbie 2014). The problem from DG Trade's perspective is that there is now even more pressure to deliver tangible liberalisation gains (for exporters) to boost growth and counter protectionist sentiment, but fewer negotiating chips to accomplish this with, especially vis-à-vis emerging economies; the EU market is perceived to be less attractive due to comparatively lower rates of growth and it is already largely open to the world – with the obvious exception of agriculture where the EU has little room to negotiate trade concessions (Young 2011, p. 726, Siles-Brügge 2014, Chapter 6). Moreover, given the increasing macroeconomic policy constraints imposed by austerity packages within the EU, De Gucht (2013, p. 3) has eagerly noted that trade liberalisation 'is the cheapest stimulus package you can imagine'.

In this context, the Commission announced a new trade and development strategy in January 2012. The aim of *Trade, growth and development: tailoring trade and investment policy for those countries most in need* was to 'propose[...] concrete ways to enhance synergies between trade and development policies' (Commission 2012, p. 2, emphasis omitted). Crucially, the communication 'stresse[d] the need to increasingly differentiate among developing countries to focus on those most in need' (Commission 2012, p. 2), with trade preferences seen as a crucial instrument in the fight against poverty. This is, of course, not an entirely new sentiment. Differentiation between developing countries in the area of trade has featured prominently in the

EU's policy discourse for a number of years, particularly in the context of the Doha Round (see Mandelson 2005, p. 13, Woolcock 2014). The communication, however, has not only reiterated this point, but rather taken it beyond any previous initiatives: the communication's flagship policy announcement – a proposal for a reformed GSP scheme – appears to offer the prospect of differentiation without a particularly coherent developmental rationale. This is a point I return to below, after having considered the design of this new regulation.

'Income' and 'product' graduation

The new GSP regulation was adopted in October 2012 and is due to enter into force in January 2014. It largely reflects the Commission's original proposal from May 2011 (Commission 2011a), introducing three key changes with respect to the previous scheme (for details on the minor changes introduced by the European Parliament [EP] and Council of Ministers, see the fourth section below). Firstly, the Commission successfully changed the eligibility criteria for GSP so that *all* high-income and upper-middle-income countries – in other words, those which meet the appropriate World Bank definitional criteria for the most recent three consecutive years – are no longer entitled to preferences (this is referred to as 'income graduation' in a study from the Overseas Development Institute, ODI 2011). Secondly, it would also remove those countries and territories with a trade agreement with the EU 'which provides the same tariff preferences as the scheme, or better, for substantially all trade' from the list of beneficiaries of the scheme (Regulation [EU] No 978/2012, Article 4). According to the Commission, these changes reduce the pool of eligible countries and territories from 177 (in essence almost all countries or territories self-classifying under WTO rules as 'developing') to 90 (Commission 2013, p. 4).

The final key innovation is a series of changes to the graduation principle for GSP imports. Under the old regulation, products were grouped into 21 so-called 'sections' (or groups of products). If any country's exports under GSP for a particular product section exceeded the so-called 'graduation threshold' – 15% of the total EU GSP imports for a particular section (12.5% for textiles) – they were no longer eligible for GSP (on the basis that such products were competitive enough to establish a foothold in the EU market). In this respect, the new GSP regulation makes it easier for products to be graduated ('product graduation', again to use the term from ODI 2011) for two reasons. Firstly, even though the relevant threshold values will be increased to 17.5% and 14.5% for textiles, the number of product categories will expand to 32 (meaning smaller categories). Secondly, the value of total imports used to calculate market share (the so-called 'denominator') will decrease, given the significant reduction in the number GSP beneficiaries. As a result of the increased ease with which imports could, therefore, surpass thresholds, 5.3 billion euro worth of trade (2009 data) – spread among six countries (China, India, Indonesia, Nigeria, Thailand and Ukraine) – was originally estimated by the Commission to no longer be eligible for GSP treatment (Commission 2011a, p. 115). The tariff lines on which these estimates were based quite closely corresponded to the first list of products graduated under the new regulation (for the years 2014–2016) (Commission Implementing Regulation [EU] No. 1213/2012). Moreover, an ODI study from 2011 found that there was significant potential for an additional two countries (Iraq and Vietnam) to lose preferences from product graduation (ODI 2011, p. 7).

Interrogating the commission's rationale: the GSP changes as an instrument of leverage[5]

As noted in the framing communication on *Trade, growth and development*, the Commission and its officials have maintained that the reform is intended to 'focus the GSP preferences on the countries most in need' (Commission 2011a, p. 2). These are, in their eyes, LDCs and the so-called 'vulnerable economies' (those lacking product diversification and being poorly integrated into the world economy; see Commission 2011b, p. 11), the respective recipients of the 'Everything But Arms' (EBA) and GSP+ schemes.[6] Based on the analysis of a study it had commissioned, the Commission has argued that the main beneficiaries of GSP, prior to the reform, were in fact emerging economies with increasingly competitive sectors, at the expense of countries in greater need of preferences (Commission 2011b, pp. 11–13). New eligibility criteria were needed so that GSP preferences could be targeted on poorer countries, while the new graduation mechanism would serve to 'weed out the more competitive product sections' among those economies that remained eligible for the scheme (Commission 2011b, p. 24).

There are, however, significant reasons for doubting the Commission's stated rationale. Firstly, it would be using the tools of a development model premised on non-reciprocal preferences which it has explicitly rejected since the 1996 *Green Paper on EU-ACP relations* (Commission 1996). This brought to an end the era of one-way trade preferences under Lomé and laid the foundations for the Commission's current agenda of EPAs.[7] Not only is the Commission trying to sign EPAs with LDCs already in receipt of EBA (albeit unsurprisingly without much success) but, similarly, out of 14 GSP+ recipients it has signed FTAs with 8 – Peru, Columbia, Costa Rica, El Salvador, Guatemala, Honduras, Nicaragua and Panama – and has previously also sought an agreement with two others (Bolivia and Ecuador) before talks broke down. Thus, the Commission's claim that it is aiming to improve the value of non-reciprocal preferences for those 'most in need' – LDCs and 'vulnerable economies' in receipt of GSP+ – is not entirely consistent with its general preference for contractually enshrined free trade.[8]

A second challenge to the Commission's development-based argument can be found in the aforementioned ODI report on the GSP changes. This argues that '[p]roduct and income graduation [as found in the new regulation] is not an effective way of helping poor, uncompetitive states' (ODI 2011, p. iii). Firstly, it finds that many of the goods for which there will be graduation are not ones that lower-income countries export. Moreover, even if a lower-income country does export an affected product, the preference margin afforded by GSP may be insufficient to counter a graduating country's existing export competitiveness. Finally, even where the preference margins are significant, other, higher-income countries are likely to be the biggest beneficiaries of the GSP changes. The report finds that even for products where poorer countries account for at least 5% of EU imports – products in which such states could potentially establish a foothold in the EU market and which could thus contribute to poverty reduction – high-income and upper-middle-income countries currently account for almost two-thirds of EU imports (ODI 2011, pp. 12–13). Very similar findings are echoed in another recent study of the GSP scheme undertaken by the Centre for the Analysis of Regional Integration at Sussex (CARIS) (Gasiorek *et al.* 2010, p. 8). Although this does not rule out any beneficial effects for lower-income countries, and is based on static analysis that neglects the potential dynamic effects of changing export patterns (as noted by one Commission official) – it does suggest that large-scale benefits of the GSP proposals for this group of states are far from certain, in contrast to more predictable gains from trade diversion for higher-income countries. In this vein, the CARIS study of the GSP scheme found that 'there is little evidence that the EU's preference regimes have led to a diversification of exports into new products' (Gasiorek *et al.* 2010, p. 8). More generally, EU preference schemes (such as EBA) have been criticised precisely because LDCs (in particular) lack the 'governance' and 'economic' 'capacity' to exploit them (Faber and Orbie 2009, p. 769).

As a result, I argue that these changes to the supposedly 'developmental' side of EU trade policy have to be situated within the wider context of the EU's commercial trade policy – where they are more likely to have a discernible impact than in contributing to poverty reduction.

More specifically, the reform of GSP has to be seen as part of the move towards improving leverage in ongoing trade negotiations as a means of delivering on the *Global Europe* objectives of access to emerging country markets. Indeed, the impact of the changes will be most strongly felt by the FTA partners identified in the *Global Europe* communication that the EU is currently negotiating with or seeking to open talks with. This is unsurprising if we consider that in 2008 these countries accounted for 7 of the top 11 sources of GSP imports to the EU (Commission 2010a). They are listed in Table 1.

It becomes clear from this that the exports of many of the EU's *Global Europe* FTA partners are *significantly* and *negatively* affected by the new regulation. Table 1 shows that the most significant 'income graduated' *Global Europe* FTA partners, which will be completely excluded from the scheme, stand to lose preferences on a significant proportion of their total exports: the ODI study's estimates (based on average trade data from 2008–2010) suggest that it could be as much as 7.31% in the case of Argentina; 8.96% in the case of Brazil and 12.2% in the case of Malaysia. The same may be said of 'product graduation' for those which remain within GSP. India, for example, is estimated to lose preferences on 2.37% of its total exports and Vietnam on 4.13% (Table 1). Moreover, these changes potentially affect exports that would have benefitted substantially from GSP. In India's case, the ODI study estimated that almost half (44.8%) face MFN tariffs of 5% or more, while the equivalent figures are 27.6% for Thailand and a whopping 76.1 for Vietnam (ODI 2011, p. 10; see also Table 1)! In sum, the countries and products likely to be excluded from GSP are consistent with the objective of boosting the EU's leverage as they significantly impact on the exports of emerging economies the EU is currently negotiating FTAs with (e.g. India and a number of ASEAN Member States). In contrast, the

Table 1. The likely effects of the reform on the top GSP exporters[a] to the EU: enhancing the EU's negotiating leverage.

Global Europe trading partner	Status of FTA talks with EU	Net graduation of GSP imports from partner as a percentage of total EU imports (2008–2010 average)[b]	Net graduation of GSP exports to EU as a percentage of partner's total exports (2008–2010 average)[b]	Product (P) or Income (I) graduation?	Percentage of affected GSP exports facing MFN tariffs >5%[b]
India	In progress	0.29	2.37	P	44.8
ASEAN	Suspended				
Indonesia	Sought by EU	0.06	0.88	P	25.7
Malaysia	In progress	1.15	12.20	I	11.6
Thailand	In progress	0.03	0.36	P	27.6
Vietnam	In progress	0.13	4.13	P	76.1
Mercosur	In progress				
Argentina	As part of Mercosur	0.26	7.31	I	23.1
Brazil	As part of Mercosur	0.89	8.96	I	11.2
Other major GSP exporters					
China	N/A	0.21	0.29	P	26.7
Russia	N/A	8.31	45.50	I	N/A
Ukraine	N/A	0.06	1.86	P	0.2

Sources: Eurostat (2013), IMF (2013), and ODI (2011).
[a]Top 11 GSP exporters to the EU in 2008, excluding Saudi Arabia (for which data was deficient).
[b]Calculated from ODI estimates.

GSP reform's relatively small impact on EU imports suggests that the reform has less to do with protecting EU producers (more on which in the following section). For most of the countries depicted in Table 1 (which provides data on almost all of the top GSP exporters to the EU), affected GSP imports represented less than 1% of total EU imports – including for that persistent bugbear of import-competing sectors, China. Moreover, in all cases affected GSP trade accounted for a more significant proportion of a trading partner's exports than of EU imports.

In assessing the GSP changes, DG Trade emphasised that these 'ha[d] nothing to do with other [commercial] trade negotiations'. On the same page, however, it also noted that they 'might still have the unintended consequence of providing more advanced developing countries with a greater incentive to enter into and conclude reciprocal trade negotiations with the EU' (Commission 2011b, p. 15). In this respect, DG Trade has consistently singled out India (whose exports, as I noted above, rely heavily on GSP and which stands to lose considerably from graduation); the concern is that while it

> enjoys relatively good market access for goods to the EU under the GSP [. . .] [it also] maintains fairly high tariffs and some peaks in areas particularly important to EU industry (such as cars, wines and spirits) and significant non-tariff barriers in other sectors important to EU exporters. (Commission 2010d, p. 8)

By scrapping or limiting preferences for emerging economies the Commission hopes to put free trade on a contractual (and reciprocal) footing with such countries – as De Gucht (2011, p. 2) explicitly recognised in a speech launching the proposals in May 2011. This sentiment also informed the specific proposal to scrap GSP for those in receipt of preferences under an FTA. As illustratively noted by a Commission official, there are no countries that stand to lose GSP that are not already in advanced FTA negotiations with the EU; the crux of their argument was that such countries, therefore, had the option of maintaining their access to the EU market. In this vein, the press has reported the EU's Ambassador to Thailand lobbying that government to start FTA negotiations in the light of the GSP reform (Pratruangkrai 2012). This strategy, moreover, has also begun to bear fruit. Several sources have since noted that the reform has been a key factor in driving Thailand to agree to start FTA negotiations with the EU in March 2013 (the EU's GSP scheme covered 3.58% of Thailand's total exports). Thai policy-makers were allegedly keen to complete the trade talks before GSP preferences run out (Foreign and Commonwealth Office 2013).

What about protectionists? The interest group politics of the reform[9]

Having provided an overview of the GSP changes and shown how they serve the objective of enhancing the EU's negotiating leverage, my aim in this section is to offer an overview of the interest group politics behind the reform. I argue that this not only played an important role in shaping the initial Commission proposal and final regulation, but also helps to underscore my argument that this is about EU leverage rather than protectionism. While my findings in the previous section suggest that the GSP reform will have a greater impact on emerging countries' *exports* than EU imports (accounting for a far more significant share of the former), the fact remains that the GSP reform still restricts imports. According to some, this can be seen to indicate the growing influence of protectionists in trade policy following the Financial Crisis (Nowakowska 2010). The reduction of preference margins for some products of interest to retailers and other importers – such as textiles and clothing (see Gasiorek *et al.* 2010, p. 8) – could, in particular, be said to be a sign of the marginalisation of such groups at the expense of protectionists, as has happened on other occasions in the EU (De Bièvre and Eckhardt 2011). In contrast, I find that while importers may well have been marginalised, the new regulation reflects, to a large extent, the interests of *exporters* rather than protectionists.

Exporters made their views most apparent to the Commission during a stakeholder consultation exercise held from March to May 2010. The main concern for such businesses was the issue of leverage in negotiations, particularly with India (which, as became apparent above, was also the bugbear of DG Trade officials). As one such organisation representing pan-European business interests was to note: 'GSP undermines the EU's negotiating position in bilateral and especially multilateral trade negotiations because partners already have preferential access to the EU market or they are concerned about preference erosion' (Commission 2010b, p. 4). More broadly, exporters consistently stressed two things during this consultation. Firstly, they underscored the need to restrict eligibility by excluding higher (and even, in some cases, middle-income countries) from the scheme and, secondly, they requested facilitating the graduation of imports by allowing for the graduation of individual products (Table 2). Although the Commission's initial proposal and the regulation were slightly more moderate than this – excluding only high-income and higher-middle-income countries and increasing the number of product sections rather than allowing for individual product graduation – exporting interests expressed surprise in interviews at the degree to which their requests were reproduced in the Commission's proposal. Moreover, the Commission appears to have privileged their views over the wishes not only of importers (in particular retailers) and European development NGOs but also import-competing interests (notably textile, clothing and leather producers, which were particularly sensitive, given the significance of preference margins under GSP, see Gasiorek *et al.* 2010, p. 8). Their requests for, respectively, a more open (and less variable) scheme; a maintenance of the existing system and a very restrictive (and extremely responsive) graduation were not significantly reflected in the Commission proposal. As a result, and in contrast to exporters, import-competing sectors and importers were not completely satisfied with the Commission's May 2011 proposals – even if they were inclined to see, respectively, the benefits of the proposed regulation in terms of restricting imports and providing for greater simplicity and predictability in the EU's import regime. NGOs, for their part, were generally dissatisfied with a regulation they saw as undermining poverty reduction efforts (Table 2).

It is naturally difficult to determine to what extent exporters are responsible for the content of the Commission proposal, beyond highlighting the similarity of their requests to the final regulation. There is, however, additional evidence to suggest that their influence was not negligible. Firstly, the views of the Commission appeared to shift after its 2010 consultation of business groups. Indeed, if we examine the previous state of Commission thinking on the matter under both Peter Mandelson and Pascal Lamy, we find an interesting contrast to the current reform. Although the Commission was proposing back in July 2004 to amend the GSP regulation to better '[t]arget the GSP on the countries that most need it', and doing so by tinkering with product graduation (Commission 2004, p. 7) it also wanted to avoid graduating entire sections on the basis of only a few products (Commission 2004, p. 9). The 'substance' of the 2005 GSP scheme that came out of these proposals was not altered with the 2008 GSP scheme (Commission 2007, p. 3), but was clearly quite different to the emphasis placed in the most recent reform on creating a greater number of product sections. Indeed, the Commission – echoing the views of business on the matter (Commission 2010b) – highlighted that under the previous system 'graduation has been barely used' and was therefore 'insufficiently responsive' to the competitiveness of product sections. This, it said, justified the more disaggregated approach to graduation taken in the latest reform (Commission 2011b, p. 16). Similarly, while earlier GSP schemes had practised some income graduation this only applied to high-income countries that were 'sufficiently diversified in their exports' (i.e. where the top five GSP sections accounted for less than 75% of total GSP exports), leaving several such states (as well as all upper-middle-income countries) on the GSP beneficiary list (Council Regulation [EC] No. 980/2005, Council Regulation [EC] No. 732/2008).[10] Although this does suggest that the idea

Table 2. Interest group requests for reform of the GSP.

	Exporters	Import-competitors	Importers	Development NGOs
Key groups (EU-level 'sector' and 'cross-sectoral' organisations; Greenwood 2011, pp. 75–92, 131)	BUSINESSEUROPE (cross-sectoral, representing national business federations from across Europe; broadly represents exporter interests, see Siles-Brügge 2014, Chapter 3)	The European Apparel and Textile Confederation (EURATEX) and the Confederation of National Associations of Tanners and Dressers of the European Community (COTANCE)	EuroCommerce (representing national federations of retailers and wholesalers); the Foreign Trade Association (representing assorted retailers and importers) and the European Branded Clothing Alliance	European Confederation of Relief and Development NGOs (CONCORD)
Summary of requests (largely derived from submissions to the consultation and groups' position papers)	1. Exclude high- (and, at times, middle-) income countries from scheme 2. Graduate individual product lines (Commission 2010b, pp. 4, 9–12, 18–20, 86, 147, 157, 204, 207–210, BUSINESSEUROPE 2011, Quick and Schmülling 2011)	1. Extend the sectors to be covered by special safeguards 2. Institute an extremely rapid withdrawal of GSP benefits 3. A product graduation criterion based on global rather than EU market share (Commission 2010b, pp. 12, 164, 211, EURATEX 2012, p. 16)	1. Maintain the two-tiered system of classifying developing countries (developing and 'least developed') 2. Higher thresholds for product graduation (especially for textiles and clothing) 3. Decrease the frequency of graduation (Commission 2010b, pp. 184, 217, 227, 234, EuroCommerce 2010, p. 2, Foreign Trade Association 2010, pp. 2–3)	1. Maintain the existing system of unilateral preferences 2. Focus on the developmental impact of preferences (Commission 2010b, pp. 34, 49, 52, 57, 96–97).
Are the groups satisfied with the Commission's initial (May 2010) proposals?	Yes. Illustrative example: 'BUSINESSEUROPE has welcomed the European Commission proposal [...]' (BUSINESSEUROPE 2011, p. 1)	Only partly. Illustrative example: EURATEX (2012, p. 16) sees the 'reduction in the beneficiary countries' as 'positive', but is worried about the lack of graduation in GSP+	Only partly. Illustrative example: '[The proposal's] main elements maintain the improvements made to the GSP in the past decade: no more annual graduation, simpler product classification, only one special incentive regime (GSP+), and enough time for importers to prepare' but the new system needs to '[f]ocus on its target group' of 'importers' (EuroCommerce 2011, p. 1)	No. Illustrative example: CONCORD (2011, p. 1) 'is particularly concerned by the proposed new eligibility criteria which will see more than half of current GSP beneficiaries removed. [. . .] CONCORD believes that it will [. . .] undermine progress towards poverty reduction through trade'

Sources: Commission (2010b); BUSINESSEUROPE (2011); EURATEX (2012); EuroCommerce (2010); Foreign Trade Association (2010); CONCORD (2011); Quick and Schmülling (2011).

of graduation in the context of GSP is not entirely novel – as I have noted above – it also points to the fact that, following the lobbying efforts of exporters, it has taken on an entirely new dimension.

When it came to lobbying the Council and EP over approval of the Commission's proposed changes to the GSP scheme, the impact of those groups that had been dissatisfied with the Commission's initial proposal was also minor. Both the Council and the EP were generally quite favourably inclined to the proposed changes in terms of 'income' and 'product' graduation (see Council 2012, p. 3, EP 2012a, pp. 31–33). Where revisions were sought by these two bodies these did not challenge either of these features of the original Commission proposal.[11] Although one amendment postponed its initial application until 2014 – and another included a transitional period for those countries having initialled but not yet ratified an FTA with the EU by November 2012 to prevent them from losing their market access under GSP – this can hardly be seen as a major concession to the interests of importers in facilitating market access under GSP. Much the same can be said for NGOs and the very modest increase in product coverage for GSP introduced by the EP and Council on developmental grounds. Import-competing interests appear, at first sight, to have been more successful. In line with their wishes, the regulation was amended to extend the special safeguards to include all textiles (and not just clothing); lower the threshold for this special safeguard and more generally strengthen safeguard provisions (on all these changes, see Council 2012, EP 2012a, Regulation [EU] No 978/2012).[12] It should be remembered, nevertheless, that safeguard clauses are rarely used by the EU, given more burdensome requirements in establishing injury when compared to anti-dumping (Siles-Brügge 2014, pp. 121–122).

Notwithstanding their relatively minor impact, these amendments broadly satisfied protectionist interests in the Council and EP – as well as those concerned about the 'predictability' of EU market access arrangements for importers and the developmental impact of the regulation (EP 2012b). The amended regulation was, therefore, approved without much controversy at a 'first reading' of the EP in June 2012 and subsequently by Member States in October (d'Imécourt 2012). It is consequently fair to say that the lack of serious opposition from protectionists (or indeed importers and NGOs) was a factor in facilitating the relatively smooth passage of the proposed legislation through the Council and the EP – although the content ultimately reflected a concern with accommodating the interests of exporters.

Conclusion

My aim in this article has been to situate the EU's supposedly 'developmental' trade policy in the case of the GSP reform within the wider context of its exporter-driven trade agenda. The reform, although justified in developmental terms as an effort to improve the value of preferences for the 'neediest', is in fact part of the effort to improve the EU's leverage in negotiations with emerging economies. In support of this argument, I showed how the supposed benefits of 'income' and 'product' graduation for the 'intended' LDCs and 'vulnerable' economies are far from certain. Moreover, the 'targeting' of non-reciprocal trade preferences (and indeed their broader reinvigoration) as an instrument of poverty reduction is not entirely consistent with the move away from non-reciprocity in the EU's other trade relations with developing economies – where FTAs are seen as the preferred option by Commission policy-makers. In contrast, the GSP reform has a noticeable impact on the exports of emerging economies the EU is currently negotiating FTAs with. Similarly, rather than representing a move towards greater protection at a time of economic crisis, the GSP changes will have little impact on total EU imports, with policy-makers in DG Trade ultimately being more sympathetic to the arguments of exporters than import-competitors (or indeed any other lobbyists).

Taken more broadly, my empirical findings challenge the common EU policy-maker narrative that trade and development policy are driven by distinct imperatives or that the EU is a uniquely 'normative power' (see Manners 2008). Rather, I have shown that the political economic forces shaping trade policies in other entities play an important role in the EU as well, adding to a literature which seeks to situate the study of EU external economic diplomacy within the wider political economy of trade (which has long been attuned to 'reciprocity' as a tool for serving exporters and offsetting protectionist pressures). In a short article such as this, there is of course no space to fully explore the implications of such a development – but it does raise questions as to the desirability of the current trade-development nexus. If the EU's primary concern in trade policy is to establish liberal markets which its firms can compete in, to what extent can it contribute to the economic development of developing countries, for which it is the most important global provider of market access? The GSP reform suggests that both objectives are not necessarily compatible as it serves the former much more clearly than the latter. It is thus a stark reminder of the problems associated with the entwinement of commercial and developmental trade policy already brought to the fore by the previous controversy surrounding the EPA negotiations, where critics accused the EU of restricting the policy space available to ACP countries (Hurt 2003, Langan 2014).

Acknowledgements

The author thanks the anonymous reviewers, Maurizio Carbone, Jan Orbie, Stephen Woolcock, Patrick Holden, Tony Heron, Alasdair Young, Peg Murray-Evans, Mark Langan, Stephen Hurt and several colleagues at Manchester for their insightful comments.

Funding

The author thanks the UK Economic and Social Research Council for funding some of the research behind this article.

Notes

1. Seven interviews were conducted in Brussels in May 2011 and January 2013. These have been anonymised at the request of the interviewees.
2. There is also an important ideational dimension in that the Commission subscribes to a neoliberal paradigm in trade that leads it to privilege exporter interests over other considerations. While consistent with my arguments here, a more detailed discussion of this dynamic is unfortunately beyond the more narrow scope of this article (see instead Siles-Brügge, 2014).
3. In this sub-section, I draw on interviews with Commission officials, 17 and 25 May 2011 and 25 January 2013.
4. As a result, the EU has signed FTAs with Korea and Singapore and is currently negotiating with India and some of the members of the Association of South East Asian Nations (ASEAN). It has also relaunched talks (originally initiated in 1999) with the Common Market of the Southern Cone (Mercosur).
5. In this section, I draw on interviews with Commission officials, 25 May 2011 and 25 January 2013.
6. GSP+ provides additional market access in addition to GSP to a series of countries qualifying as 'vulnerable', provided they sign up to a series of conventions on core human and labour rights, the environment and other 'good governance standards'. Under the new GSP regulation, recipients of GSP+ will not be subject to product graduation. Under EBA, the EU offers LDCs 'duty-free, quota-free' access to its market for almost all goods.
7. Although the EU was under WTO pressure to reform its scheme of non-reciprocal trade preferences vis-à-vis the ACP, there is evidence to suggest that the EU could have done more to resist this should it have wanted to (see Hurt 2003).

8. In this vein, while the 2001 EBA initiative may have institutionalised non-reciprocal preferences for LDCs, it has also been referred to as 'Everything But Development'; whereas its developmental impact has been modest it has been 'instrumental for some EU policy actors to steer' the EU into a more 'globalist-liberal' direction, among other things helping to reshape EU–ACP relations (undermining the cohesion of the ACP group) and winning over developing and developed countries to the EU position in the Doha Round (Faber and Orbie 2009, pp. 778–784).
9. In this section, I draw on interviews with interest group representatives, 20 and 26 May and 22 January 2013.
10. Similarly, while these earlier schemes also featured provisions for removing economies if they had an agreement with the EU offering equivalent market access to GSP, many states with preferential trading arrangements had remained on the list of beneficiaries (in contrast to the situation under the new regulation).
11. I should note at this juncture that the GSP reform proposals were also drafted with the need to balance Member State interests in mind (and to a lesser extent also Members of the EP). Discussing this is unfortunately beyond the scope of this article, which seeks to interrogate the underlying reason for the reform (which was initiated by the Commission and driven by its concern for exporter interests).
12. The final substantive change pushed for by the EP and Council was a limited duration of 10 years for the new regulation. The Commission had wanted it to be open-ended.

References

BUSINESSEUROPE, 2011. *Revision EU generalised system of preferences, policy briefing*. Available from: http://www.businesseurope.eu/content/default.asp?PageID=568&DocID=29337 [accessed 18 March 2013].

Commission, 1996. *Green paper on relations between the European Union and the ACP countries on the eve of the 21st century: challenges and options for a new partnership*. COM (96) 570 final. Brussels: European Commission.

Commission, 2004. *Developing countries, international trade and sustainable development: the function of the community's generalised system of preferences (GSP) for the ten-year period from 2006 to 2015*. COM (2004) 461 final. Brussels: European Commission.

Commission, 2006. *Global Europe: competing in the world*. COM (2006) 567 final. Brussels: European Commission.

Commission, 2007. *Proposal for a Council regulation applying a scheme of generalised tariff preferences*. COM (2007) 857 final. Brussels: European Commission.

Commission, 2009. *Introduction to the CARIFORUM-EC EPA*. Available from: http://trade.ec.europa.eu/doclib/docs/2010/march/tradoc_145879.pdf [accessed 27 July 2013].

Commission, 2010a. *GSP: 2008 statistics by country*. Available from: http://trade.ec.europa.eu/doclib/html/145945.htm [accessed 18 July 2011].

Commission, 2010b. *Public consultation on the EU generalised system of preferences (GSP): listing of answers received*. Available from: http://trade.ec.europa.eu/doclib/docs/2010/september/tradoc_146463.edited.pdf [accessed 18 July 2011].

Commission, 2010c. *Trade, growth and world affairs: trade as a core component of the EU's 2020 strategy*. COM (2010) 612 final. Brussels: European Commission.

Commission, 2010d. *Report on progress achieved on the global Europe strategy, 2006-2010: commission staff working document accompanying the commission's communication on 'trade, growth and world affairs'*. SEC (2010) 1268/2. Brussels: European Commission.

Commission, 2011a. *Proposal for a regulation of the European parliament and of the council applying a scheme of generalised tariff preferences*. COM (2011) 241 final. Brussels: European Commission.

Commission, 2011b. *Vol. I: commission staff working paper: impact assessment, accompanying the document for a proposal for a regulation of the European parliament and of the council applying a scheme of generalised tariff preferences*. SEC (2011) 536 final. Brussels: European Commission.

Commission, 2012. *Trade, growth and development: tailoring trade and investment policy for those countries most in need*. COM (2012) 22 final. Brussels: European Commission.

Commission, 2013. *The EU's new generalised system of preferences (GSP)*. Available from: http://trade.ec.europa.eu/doclib/docs/2013/september/tradoc_151705.%2013-07%20GSP%20InfoPack%20Update%20Final.pdf [accessed 24 October 2013].

CONCORD, 2011. *Recommendations by the CONCORD trade reference group for a development-centred reform of the EU's generalised system of preferences*. Available from: http://www.djei.ie/trade/marketaccess/euccp/concord_submission.pdf [accessed 18 March 2013].

Council, 2012. *Draft minutes: 3154th meeting of the council of the European Union (FOREIGN AFFAIRS) held in Brussels on 16 March 2012, 4 April*. Brussels: Council Secretariat.

De Bièvre, D. and Eckhardt, J., 2011. Interest groups and the failure of EU anti-dumping reform. *Journal of European Public Policy*, 18 (3), 338–359.

De Bièvre, D. and Poletti, A., 2014. The political science of European trade policy: a literature review with a research outlook. *Comparative European Politics*, 12 (1), 101–119.

De Gucht, K., 2011. *Remarks at the press conference on the review of the generalised system of preferences, speech delivered in Strasbourg, 10 May*. Available from: http://europa.eu/rapid/pressReleasesAction.do?reference=SPEECH/11/323&format=PDF&aged=0&language=EN&guiLanguage=en [accessed 18 July 2011].

De Gucht, K., 2013. *A European perspective on transatlantic free trade, speech delivered in Cambridge, MA, 2 March*. Available from: http://trade.ec.europa.eu/doclib/docs/2013/march/tradoc_150707.pdf [accessed 15 March 2013].

De Ville, F. and Orbie, J., 2014. The European commission's neoliberal trade discourse since the crisis: legitimising continuity through subtle discursive change. *British Journal of Politics and International Relations*, 16 (1), 149–167.

d'Imécourt, L.V., 2012. Council approves new GSP scheme. *Europolitics*, 4 October. Available from: http://www.europolitics.info/external-policies/council-approves-new-gsp-scheme-art343676-46.html [accessed 15 March 2013].

EP, 2012a. *Report on the proposal for a regulation of the European parliament and the council applying a scheme of generalised tariff preferences*. A7-0054/2012. Brussels: EP.

EP, 2012b. *Debates: Monday, 11 June 2012, Strasbourg*. Brussels: EP. Available from: http://www.europarl.europa.eu/sides/getDoc.do?type=CRE&reference=20120611&secondRef=ITEM-019&language=EN&ring=A7-2012-0054 [accessed 15 March 2013].

EURATEX, 2012. *Activities of the year: annual report 2011*. Available from: http://www.euratex.org/system/files/attached-files/Euratex+Annual+Report+-2011.pdf [accessed 15 March 2013].

EuroCommerce, 2010. *The GSP: importers need it simple, stable, predictable*. Available from: http://www.eurocommerce.be/media/7812/position-trade-gsp_consultation-20.05.2010.pdf [accessed 15 March 2013].

EuroCommerce, 2011. *Briefing: generalised system of preferences*. Available from: http://www.eurocommerce.be/media/11174/briefing-trade-gsp.pdf [accessed 15 March 2013].

Eurostat, 2013. *COMEXT database*. Brussels: Commission. Available from: http://epp.eurostat.ec.europa.eu/portal/page/portal/external_trade/data/database [accessed 26 July 2013].

Faber, G. and Orbie, J., 2009. Everything but arms: much more than appears at first sight. *Journal of Common Market Studies*, 47 (4), 767–787.

Foreign and Commonwealth Office, 2013. *Thailand/EU FTA: out of the starting blocs*. Bangkok: British Embassy Bangkok. Available from: http://opentoexport.com/article/thailand-eu-fta-out-of-the-starting-blocs-january-2013/ [accessed 15 March 2013].

Foreign Trade Association, 2010. *Position paper: the revision of the currently applicable generalized system of preferences from 1 January 2014 (at the latest)*. Available from: http://www.fta-u.org/doc/unp/opinion/en/Position%20Paper%20on%20GSP.pdf [accessed 15 March 2013].

Gasiorek, M. with Lopez Gonzalez, J., Holmes, P., Mendez Parra, M., Rollo, J., Wang, Z., Maliszewska, M., Paczynski, W., Cirera, X., Willenbockel, D., Robinson, S., Dawar, K., Foliano, F. and Olerreaga, M., 2010. *Mid-term evaluation of the EU's generalised system of preferences: Final Report*. Brighton: CARIS.

Gilligan, M., 1997. *Empowering exporters: reciprocity, delegation and collective action in American trade policy*. Ann Arbor, MI: Michigan University Press.

Greenwood, J., 2011. *Interest representation in the European Union*. 3rd ed. Basingstoke: Palgrave Macmillan.

Heron, T., 2013. *Pathways from preferential trade: the politics of trade adjustment in Africa, Caribbean and Pacific*. Basingstoke: Palgrave Macmillan.

Heron, T. and Siles-Brügge, G., 2012. Competitive liberalisation and the 'Global Europe' services and investment agenda: locating the commercial drivers of the EU-ACP economic partnership Agreements. *Journal of Common Market Studies*, 50 (2), 250–266.

Holland, M. and Doidge, M., 2012. *Development policy of the European Union*. Basingstoke: Palgrave Macmillan.
Hurt, S.R., 2003. Cooperation or coercion? The Cotonou agreement between the European Union and ACP states and the end of the Lomé convention. *Third World Quarterly*, 24 (1), 161–176.
IMF, 2013. *Direction of trade statistics (DOTS)*. Washington, DC: IMF. Available from: http://elibrary-data.imf.org/FindDataReports.aspx?d=33061&e=170921 [accessed 26 July 2013].
Langan, M., 2014. Decent work and indecent trade agendas: the European Union and ACP countries. *Contemporary Politics*, 20 (1), 23–35.
Mandelson, P., 2005. Trade at the service of development. Speech delivered at the London School of Economics, 4 February 2005. Available from: http://www2.lse.ac.uk/publicEvents/pdf/20050204-Mandelson.pdf [accessed 19 March 2013].
Manners, I., 2008. The normative ethics of the European Union. *International Affairs*, 84 (1), 45–60.
Nowakowska, M., 2010. Reform of the GSP regime and its potential impact on Sub-Saharan Africa. *In*: S.J. Evenett, ed. *Africa resists the protectionist temptation: the 5th GTA report*. London: Centre for Economic Policy Research, 113–135.
ODI, 2011. *The poverty impact of the proposed graduation threshold in the generalised system of preferences (GSP) trade scheme*. London: ODI.
Pratruangkrai, P., 2012. In view of GSP reform, EU pushes for trade talks. *The Nation*, 20 January. Available from: http://www.nationmultimedia.com/business/In-view-of-GSP-reform-EU-pushes-for-trade-talks-30174105.html [accessed 15 March 2013].
Quick, R. and Schmülling, U., 2011. A new approach to preferences: the review of the European GSP scheme. *Global Trade and Customs Journal*, 6 (1), 9–15.
Siles-Brügge, G., 2014. *Constructing European Union trade policy: a global idea of Europe*. Basingstoke: Palgrave Macmillan.
Whalley, J., 1990. Non-discriminatory discrimination: special and differential treatment under the GATT for developing countries. *The Economic Journal*, 100 (403), 1318–1328.
White, R.C.A., 1975. A new international economic order. *International and Comparative Law Quarterly*, 24 (3), 542–552.
Woolcock, S., 2012. *European Union economic diplomacy: the role of the EU in external economic relations*. Farnham: Ashgate.
Woolcock, S., 2014. Differentiation within reciprocity: the EU approach to preferential trade agreements. *Contemporary Politics*, 20 (1), 36–48.
Young, A.R., 2011. The rise (and fall?) of the EU's performance in the multilateral trading system. *Journal of European Integration*, 33 (6), 715–729.
Young, A.R. and Peterson, J., 2013. We care about you, but . . . : the politics of EU trade policy and development. *Cambridge Review of International Affairs*, 26 (3), 497–518.

Sanctions under the EU Generalised System of Preferences and foreign policy: coherence by accident?

Clara Portela[a] and Jan Orbie[b]

[a]*School of Social Sciences, Singapore Management University, Singapore;* [b]*Centre for EU Studies, Ghent University, Ghent, Belgium*

This article investigates the relationship between the European Union's withdrawal of trade benefits for developing countries under the Generalised System of Preferences (GSP) and its sanctions under the Common Foreign and Security Policy (CFSP). Our expectation is that GSP withdrawals and CFSP sanctions will not cohere. However, our research reveals that GSP suspension has been coherent with CFSP sanctions when the latter exist prior to the decision-making process on GSP sanctions *and* when the International Labour Organisation has set up a Commission of Inquiry condemning the country, as with Myanmar/Burma and Belarus. The presence of separate institutional frameworks explains the GSP suspension towards Sri Lanka in the absence of CFSP sanctions.

Introduction

The European Union (EU) produces different sets of foreign policies in two separate institutional arrangements: the supranational framework and the intergovernmental context of the Common Foreign and Security Policy (CFSP). The EU is often torn between the necessity to respect the co-existence of the specific tools and objectives under each institutional arrangement and a requirement that the different foreign policies cohere. Its policies towards developing countries illustrate this tension. Trade remains an exclusive EU competence, largely isolated from other policies. Development constitutes a shared competence between the EU and its member states. Foreign and security policy remains largely intergovernmental.

This article explores the relationship between trade, development, and foreign policy by analysing the withdrawal of trade preferences under the EU's Generalised System of Preferences (GSP). The 'stick and carrot' conditionality of the EU's GSP system constitutes the 'flagship' of trade initiatives aimed at supporting sustainable development and human rights (European Commission 2012a, p. 13). GSP preferences may be withdrawn in case of serious and persistent violations of core human and labour rights. To date, this only happened in the cases of Myanmar[1] and Belarus although it has been contemplated on various occasions. Also, Sri Lanka, a beneficiary of the so-called GSP+ scheme, saw its preferences downgraded.

The extent to which GSP withdrawals cohere with CFSP sanctions has not been researched yet. The aim of this article is to ascertain whether and why GSP and CFSP sanctions coincide, and which factors contribute to it. Given the lack of existing literature, the low number of cases, the complexity of the context surrounding sanctions decisions, and the extended time span of the study (1995–2013), we use an explorative and inductive approach. Although expectations on the incoherence between both types of sanctions are advanced, we refrain from using a predetermined theoretical framework. The research is based on an analysis of the GSP and CFSP sanctions decisions, a review of secondary literature, and a number of interviews.

We proceed in three steps. Firstly, we review the GSP conditionality system and posit why coherence between GSP withdrawals and CFSP sanctions cannot be expected. Secondly, we review cases where GSP preferences have been suspended (Myanmar, Belarus, and Sri Lanka) or where it has been contemplated but not effected (Pakistan, China, Russia, and India). Thirdly, we compare these different cases and find that GSP withdrawal coincides with some, but not all, cases of CFSP sanctions. In conclusion, we propose explanations for the unsuspected occurrence of coherence.

Expected incoherence between GSP and CFSP sanctions

Policy coherence can be defined as the absence of contradiction among different policies formulated by an actor, although some authors have gone beyond the sheer absence of contradiction to suggest the need for complementarity or even synergy of policies (Krenzler and Schneider 1997). In the case of the EU, incoherent outcomes are likely due to its fragmented legal–institutional structures. Two main dimensions of incoherence have been identified: vertical coherence refers to the lack of contradiction between policies formulated by the EU on the one hand and the member states on the other, while horizontal coherence, also called 'cross – or inter-pillar' coherence, is ensured when no contradiction exists between first-pillar policies adopted under the community method and the intergovernmental framework (Carbone 2008). The requirement of coherence was spelt out for the first time with the Single European Act (SEA) of 1986, bringing together two previously unconnected areas: the external policies of the community and the foreign policy co-operation among the member states. In the absence of a single executive, different actors of the EU have been granted coordinating powers in subsequent treaty revisions: the Presidency, the Council, the Commission, and recently also the High Representative for Foreign Affairs and Security Policy. In sum, the requirement of coherence aspires to hold together different policies whose formulation corresponds to different actors and institutions within the EU. It obliges all actors involved in European foreign policy to coordinate with a view to generating coherent outputs (Portela and Raube 2012). Yet, while the aspiration of coherence has been present since it was introduced in the treaties in 1986, it has been consistently criticised for its suboptimal design and insufficiency to bring about coherence (Smith 2004, Cremona 2011). While the Lisbon Treaty strengthens the coherence requirements, the trade sphere remains institutionally isolated within the Commission and the binding rules of the World Trade Organization (WTO) make it difficult to integrate foreign policy considerations into trade policies (Bossuyt *et al.* 2013). The issue of EU coherence has attracted particular attention from development scholarship due to the Organisation for Economic Co-operation and Development (OECD)'s commitment to the notion of 'policy coherence for development' since 2003. In essence, it recognises that development policy not only entails the transfer of financial resources, but also other economic tools such as trade preferences and foreign direct investment as well as political considerations such as the promotion of human rights and democracy assistance (Bourriche 2008, Carbone 2008). The need to make EU external policies, in particular trade and foreign policy, cohere with development policy objectives was recognised in the European Consensus on Development of 2005 as well as in the Lisbon Treaty.

The main preoccupation of the EU coherence literature so far has mainly consisted in assessing the adequacy of existing mechanisms to ensure coherence (Smith 2004, Bourriche 2008, Cremona 2011), exploring the fit or misfit between sets of policies produced under different frameworks (Carbone 2008). By contrast, in the present investigation, we depart from the premise that the withdrawal of GSP and the imposition of CFSP sanctions cannot be expected to coincide. Instead, we expect them to be applied to different targets. We justify this expectation on the basis of the differences in the grounds for adoption of each set of measures, the institutional procedures leading to adoption decisions, and finally, the absence of any provisions linking both sets of measures. Thus, we expect that GSP withdrawals and CFSP sanctions practice will not coincide, but will be applied against different targets and for different reasons. Contrary to our expectations, an empirical examination of the practice points to a coincidence of GSP withdrawals and CFSP sanctions, even though GSP withdrawal practice is minimal. The remainder of the article represents an attempt to solve this puzzle.

GSP withdrawals and CFSP sanctions: grounds for activation and procedure

The European Commission (EC)/EU[2] has given preferential market access to developing countries under the GSP since 1971. The GSP is implemented unilaterally by means of a Council regulation, which is revised periodically. Political conditionality made its appearance in the GSP in 1991, when the EU included a provision granting a number of Latin American countries more favourable access in reward for their efforts in fighting drugs production and trafficking. Negative political conditionality was first introduced in the 1994/1995 regulations which foresaw the temporary withdrawal of preferences in case of evidence of forced labour as defined in the Geneva Conventions (1926 and 1956) and International Labour Organisation (ILO) Conventions Nos 29 and 105.[3] It was applied for the first time to Myanmar in 1997. Complaints against alleged labour standard violations in Pakistan and China in 1997 in the same year did not result in investigations. The 1998 regulations introduce a social incentive system which allows developing countries to benefit from enhanced tariff preferences if they 'have adopted and actually apply domestic legal provisions incorporating the substance of' the ILO Conventions Nos 87 and 98 concerning freedom of trade unions and No 138 concerning child labour. The GSP revision of 2001 extended the legal basis of both the withdrawal and the incentive clause to correspond with all the eight fundamental Conventions of the ILO. This reflects an emerging consensus on fundamental labour rights recognised by virtually all states since the 1995 UN World Summit for Social Development in Copenhagen and the 1998 ILO Declaration on Fundamental Principles and Rights. According to this authoritative ILO Declaration, the rights enshrined in Conventions Nos 87 and 98 on 'Freedom of Association and Collective Bargaining'; No. 138 on 'Elimination of Exploitative Forms of Child Labour'; Nos 29 and 105 on the 'Prohibition of Forced Labour'; and Nos 100 and 111 on 'Non-Discrimination in Employment' constituted the core labour standards. Each of these principles is simultaneously considered as human rights law (Alston 2005). The EC started an investigation into violation of trade union rights in Belarus in 2003, which led to GSP withdrawal in 2006.

The 2005 revision was motivated by a decision by the WTO's Appellate Body declaring the GSP drugs incentive system discriminatory: in 2003/2004, India had successfully challenged the legality of the EU's drugs incentive system after the inclusion of Pakistan shortly after 9/11. According to the WTO, linking trade preferences with non-trade objectives was only admissible if it concerned a 'positive response' to an 'objective development, financial or trade need' (Bartels 2007). The reform broadened the list of international conventions relevant to the GSP+, going beyond the core labour conventions to encompass agreements related to sustainable development and human rights. All 'vulnerable' developing countries were now eligible for GSP+ incentives, provided that they 'ratified and effectively implemented' 16 human rights conventions, including the 8 fundamental ILO Conventions,[4] and at least 7 (out of 11) conventions on environment and governance[5] by the end of 2008. Withdrawal of GSP was allowed when beneficiaries perpetrated 'serious and systematic violations' of the principles laid down in the labour and human rights conventions. The 2005 regulation also mentions the possibility of downgrading GSP+ privileges to the general scheme, which was subsequently applied to Venezuela due to its failure to ratify the UN Convention against Corruption and to Sri Lanka because of human rights violations.[6] In 2012, the EU embarked on an overhaul of the GSP system (see Siles-Brügge, this volume) which entailed a slight modification of the conditionality system. The Apartheid Convention was removed, while the Climate Change Convention was added. Compared to the previous regulation that was criticised for focusing only on the ratification requirement rather than on the implementation of the conventions (Orbie and Tortell 2009), the new system puts more emphasis on guaranteeing compliance.

The suspension procedure, matured over subsequent regulations, provides that any EU member state or any natural or legal person which can show an interest in withdrawal can bring violations to the attention of the Commission, which is empowered to start an investigation. This investigation can last over one year. If the Commission concludes that withdrawal is advisable, it submits a proposal to the Council, which decides on suspension by qualified majority. Decisions to withdraw trade preferences should take into account 'available assessments, comments, decisions, recommendations, and conclusions of the relevant supervisory bodies' including the ILO. After the suspension has been decided upon, the beneficiary is given another six months to rectify the breach or to show its commitment to do so before the suspension takes effect.

The grounds and procedures for the imposition of CFSP sanctions are different. These sanctions – also called 'restrictive measures' – are imposed in pursuance of the CFSP objectives as defined by the Treaty. Originally introduced in the Maastricht Treaty, the objectives of the CFSP can be summarised as follows: to safeguard the common values, fundamental interests, independence, and integrity of the Union; to strengthen the security of the Union; to preserve peace and strengthen international security; to promote international co-operation; to promote democracy, rule of law, and respect for human rights and fundamental freedoms.[7] In addition, the Council declared in 2004 that it will impose sanctions to advance the fight against terrorism and the proliferation of weapons of mass destruction, and for upholding human rights, democracy, the rule of law, and good governance (Council 2004). The decision-making procedure to adopt CFSP sanctions has largely remained unaltered since the Maastricht Treaty. The Council agrees the imposition of sanctions regimes in the intergovernmental CFSP setting. Proposals for the imposition of sanctions can be tabled at the initiative of the High Representative or any of the member states. Any modifications to the sanctions regimes are decided by unanimity.

The comparison shows that GSP and CFSP sanctions cannot be expected to cohere. Firstly, they are designed to address different kinds of violations. CFSP sanctions are imposed in support of the objectives of the CFSP as stipulated by the treaty, in response to violations of international norms. They can be imposed in support of an ample pallet of broadly defined objectives from combating terrorism to upholding democratic principles. By contrast, the grounds for GSP withdrawal are much narrower: serious breaches of core human and labour rights as stipulated in a number of international conventions. Secondly, the decision-making processes differ considerably. The procedure leading to the suspension and reinstatement of trade preferences is a complex and lengthy process embedded in the (former) first pillar. It involves several EU institutions, has to be preceded by an investigation, can be triggered by non-state actors, and takes into account assessments by external agencies. It leaves ample discretion to the Commission, which is responsible for the launch of an investigation and the recommendation on withdrawal to the Council, which ultimately decides on suspension. The beneficiary at fault is invited to provide evidence, and international monitoring agencies (primarily the ILO) are given a major role. The 2012 GSP regulation has granted the European Parliament a role in the decision-making process: decisions on withdrawal are adopted by delegated acts, which can be revoked by the Parliament or Council anytime.[8] In contrast, CFSP sanctions and any alteration thereof have to be agreed by the Council by unanimity. Here, the Council enjoys considerable leeway: it decides on sanctions regimes in the absence of any requirement to consult any other EU institution or external actor. Thirdly, there are no mechanisms devoted to ensuring coherence between sanctions adopted under the CFSP and GSP withdrawals beyond the general requirement of coherence enshrined in the treaties since the SEA but effectively unaccompanied by measures allowing for enforcement (Portela and Raube 2012).

GSP sanctions as foreign policy tools?

GSP withdrawal of Myanmar, Belarus, and Sri Lanka

Myanmar

The investigation against Myanmar was triggered by a joint complaint filed by the European Trade Union Confederation (ETUC) and the International Confederation of Free Trade Unions (ICFTU) in 1995. The Commission did not obtain permission from Burmese authorities to dispatch a fact-finding mission. The investigation, which included hearings with non-governmental organisations (NGOs) and experts, pointed to the existence of forced labour. Ordinary civilians were compelled to work as labourers on infrastructure projects, often without salary. Civilians were also forced to support counter-insurgency operations as porters or as 'human minesweepers' (Howse and Genser 2008, p. 171). Burmese authorities contested the charges arguing that the practice was covered by an exception in the ILO Convention No. 29 allowing the population to carry out works as community service (art 2(2)), an interpretation that was challenged by the ILO. The Commission consulted representatives of the democratically elected government of Burma, which was favourable to the GSP withdrawal. Meanwhile, in 1996 also an ILO Commission of Inquiry had been established on forced labour in Burma. The EU regulation on withdrawal 'on account of the use of forced labour' was eventually approved by the Council in 1997. It stipulated that reinstatement of the trade preferences could be considered based on a Commission report which showed that the practices of forced labour in Myanmar no longer existed.[9] However, the provision on Myanmar's suspension was modified in subsequent GSP regulations. While the 2001 regulation remains silent on the reasons for the continuation of Burma's withdrawal, the 2005 and 2012 regulations state that it should be maintained 'due to the *political situation* in Myanmar' (italics added). This departs from the original stipulation that the suspension would be reversed once the condemned practices ceased.

Myanmar's GSP suspension followed the imposition of a broader range of restrictions that had started in 1990 (Table 1). The decision came only a few months after an EU Common Position condemning 'the absence of progress towards democratisation and at the continuing violation of human rights' in Myanmar, and deploring forced labour alongside arbitrary executions, political arrests, forced displacement of the population, and restrictions on the fundamental rights of freedom of speech, movement, and assembly. It confirmed earlier sanctions including an arms embargo and wielded visa bans for individuals associated with the ruling junta. Following the reform process initiated by President Thein Sein and its subsequent handover to a partially civilian government, the EU phased out sanctions in April 2012 and lifted them altogether in April 2013, with the only exception of the arms embargo (Bünte and Portela 2012). In this context, the Council indicated a readiness to work towards the reinstatement of the GSP to Myanmar, an intention that was quickly backed by the European Parliament. Because no procedure was foreseen in the regulation which installed the sanctions, the Commission chose to follow the ordinary legislative procedure, taking into account the enhanced role of

Table 1. Chronology of CFSP and GSP sanctions against Myanmar, Belarus and Sri Lanka.

	CFSP measures	GSP sanctions
Myanmar	• 1990 first imposition of sanctions • July 1996: Presidency statement • October 1996: Parliament resolution • October 1996: new sanctions	• June 1995: complaint received • January 1996: investigation launched • December 1996: withdrawal proposed • March 1997: adoption by Council
Belarus	• 2000 first imposition of sanctions • September 2004: new sanctions • April 2006: new sanctions • October 2006: new sanctions	• January 2003: complaint received • December 2003: investigation launched • August 2005: Commission report • June 2006: withdrawal proposed • December 2006: adoption by Council
Sri Lanka	No sanctions	• October 2008: investigation launched • October 2009: Commission report • February 2010: adoption by Council

Parliament by the Lisbon Treaty (European Commission 2012b). It also waited for the findings of an ILO report on forced labour in Myanmar (Reuters 2012). Reinstatement was completed in June 2013. Hence, GSP withdrawal followed CFSP sanctions, while reinstatement of GSP preferences followed the lifting of CFSP sanctions.

Belarus

In 2003, the Commission initiated an investigation against alleged violations of the ILO Conventions on freedom of association and the right to collective bargain, triggered by a joint request of the ICFTU, ETUC, and the World Confederation of Labour. In parallel to this process, the ILO appointed a Commission of Inquiry to investigate the freedom of trade unions in Belarus, which urged Belarusian authorities to implement 12 recommendations in July 2004. In June 2005, in view of the lack of implementation, the EC announced that it intended to submit a proposal for withdrawal to the Council unless Belarus 'made a commitment to take the measures necessary to conform with the principles referred to in the 1998 ILO Declaration on Fundamental Principles and Rights at Work' (European Commission 2006, p. 37). Belarusian authorities tried to create the impression of compliance on several occasions; however, all these attempts were assessed by the Commission as lacking any 'indication of effective implementation of ILO Conventions Nos 87 and 98' (European Commission 2006, p. 39). Trade Commissioner Peter Mandelson declared: 'Almost four years after the start of the withdrawal process ... Belarus has not taken any real, tangible measure to remedy the situation' (Mandelson 2006). In the absence of progress by Belarusian authorities in the six months that followed, the regulation entered into force in June 2007. It indicated that the preferences would be reinstated when the violations no longer prevailed.

Like in Myanmar, the procedure leading to GSP sanctions chronologically followed the adoption of restrictive measures under the CFSP (Table 1). In 2004, two Common Positions expressed the EU's concern about the violation of democratic principles and human rights in Belarus and upgraded existing sanctions.[10] Less than a year later, the Commission completed its report into violations of trade union rights in Belarus. The conclusions of the Commission's investigation and the Council's decision to withdraw GSP preferences followed the imposition of new CFSP sanctions. In subsequent years, CFSP sanctions continued to be extended several times before the EU eventually decided to withdraw GSP. CFSP and GSP sanctions were adopted in tandem.

Sri Lanka

Sri Lanka is the first – and so far the only – developing country that lost its GSP+ privileges for failure to effectively implement relevant conventions. It has been a beneficiary of the GSP+ scheme since 2004.[11] While Sri Lanka's compliance with labour standards was never challenged, in October 2008 the Commission launched an investigation into violations against the Covenant on Civil and Political Rights, the Convention against Torture, and the Convention on the Rights of Child. The Sri Lankan government was suspected of violating these conventions in the context of its offensive against the separatist group of the Tamil Tigers. Independent experts were tasked to conduct an investigation which included interviews with NGO representatives and officials of international organisations as well as a field visit to Sri Lanka. They concluded that the national legislation in Sri Lanka did not effectively implement these three human rights conventions and deplored the lack of co-operation from the Sri Lankan government (Hampson *et al.* 2009). On this basis, the Commission proposed to withdraw GSP+ preferences in October 2009. Since the regulation was to enter into force six months after its adoption, in June 2010 Commissioners De Gucht and Ashton communicated to the Sri Lankan government the corrective action to be taken for the Commission to reconsider its proposal to the Council. These included the cancellation of the state of emergency, the abolishment of the 'Prevention of Terrorism Act', and the implementation of the 17th Amendment to the Constitution. However, the government of Sri Lanka denounced these proposals as a breach of the country's national sovereignty. Thus, in August 2010 Sri Lanka reverted to standard GSP tariffs. The regulation states that withdrawal will last 'until it is decided that the reasons justifying the temporary withdrawal no longer prevail'. Unlike the cases of Myanmar and Belarus, GSP+ withdrawal was neither preceded nor accompanied by CFSP sanctions.

Beneficiaries which came close to withdrawal: Pakistan, India, China, and Russia

The examination of GSP withdrawal practice offers but meagre empirical evidence for our analysis. Thus, the article now turns to instances in which GSP sanctions were contemplated but ultimatly aborted. On the one hand, this 'almost' GSP withdrawal helps us palliate the minimalistic character of GSP withdrawal practice, as it allow us to consider cases which incited EU actors to push for withdrawals. At the same time, these instances provide a basis for comparison, offering interesting insights regarding the criteria considered by Council and Commission in their decisions to adopt withdrawals.[12] A number of beneficiaries, Pakistan, India, China, and Russia, came close to withdrawal during the 1990s, but the EU ultimately fell short from suspending trade preferences. Shortly after the complaint against Myanmar, international trade unions filed a complaint regarding child labour practices in Pakistan, this time including the International Textile, Garment and Leather Workers' Federation. After it was rejected, the complaint was resubmitted in 1998 with charges of massive forced and child labour, especially in the carpet industry. The complaint was supported by the EU's Economic and Social Committee. This time the Commission launched an investigation. In contrast to the Burmese case, the Pakistani authorities supplied information on the internal legislation to combat forced labour and requested assistance from the Commission to address the problem (Clapham and Martignioni 2006). Nevertheless, an ILO assessment which the Commission took into consideration during the investigation concluded that the Pakistani government had made practically no effort to ascertain the scale of the problem, prevent it or provide for penalties. Eventually, a negative opinion on the appropriateness of withdrawal was enacted (Fierro 2003, p. 375). According to the Commission, the reasons for the negative decision were of a technical–legal nature: Art 9 of the GSP regulation referred to 'forced labour' and not to 'child labour' as such. Indeed, when the EU received a complaint alleging the use of child labour in the country in 1997, ILO committees had not commented on Pakistan's observance of child labour conventions because it had not ratified any of those conventions and was thus not bound by them. Therefore, the complaint had to be worded as 'forced labour'. In the absence of formal condemnation of Pakistan by the ILO, the EU was unable to make reference to any formal decisions by supervisory bodies (Orbie and Tortell 2009, p. 676). Brandtner and Rosas (1998) argue that international rules on the subject of child labour were 'less than clear' (p. 5). Further arguments put forward by the Commission was that Pakistan had already committed to take effective steps to reverse the practice of child labour, and that the suspension of trade preferences would predictably aggravate the problem (Lerch 2004).

In 1997, the European Parliament called on the Commission to open investigations into forced and prison labour in China (European Parliament 1997). At the time, China was one of the main GSP beneficiaries, and evidence of practices contrary to the labour standards embedded in the GSP regulation existed, such as forced prison labour (Lerch 2004). However, the Commission rejected the complaint given that, according to procedural requirements at the time, only a member state or a natural or legal person showing interest in the complaint were legitimised to trigger the investigation. Also, evidence of the presence of forced labour in China necessary to support the complaint was difficult to obtain because it takes place primarily in prisons. In addition, this practice only represents a violation of ILO Convention No. 29 if the produced goods are exported (Lerch 2004).

In the case of India, the EU considered the suspension of GSP in condemnation of the nuclear tests conducted in May 1998. In response to the Indian tests, the Council instructed the Commission to reconsider India's eligibility for the GSP. Following the tests conducted by Pakistan shortly after, the Council temporarily postponed the conclusion of the impending Partnership and Co-operation Agreement with Islamabad. Yet, the CFSP Common Position issued the following October did not make any reference to those measures.[13] Instead, it announced a package of incentives supportive of non-proliferation as well as the provision of technical assistance in the implementation of export controls (Portela 2003).

Finally, in the context of the war in Chechnya, the European Council denounced human rights violations by Russian security forces in late 1999 and mandated the suspension of some provisions of the Partnership and Co-operation Agreement (PCA); the transfer of some Technical Aid to the Commonwealth of Independent States (TACIS) funds towards humanitarian assistance; and the limitation of TACIS funds for the year 2000 to priority areas (European Council 1999). These instructions were to be subsequently concretised by the Council. The formulation used by the European Council allowed sufficient flexibility to limit the scope of the measures to be decided by the Council. The Council considered the suspension of GSP privileges, which affected 10% of Russian exports to the EU, and the suspension of the Most-Favoured Nation (MFN) status that Russia enjoyed under the PCA. However, it eventually decided on milder measures, including, among others, the prohibition to extend GSP privileges to products not yet covered (Portela 2010). Commissioner Patten questioned the use of cutting off financial assistance which may 'provoke a political backlash against the international community in the run-up to the Duma elections' (Patten 1999). Eventually, GSP were only affected in the sense that Russia's application for GSP remained frozen for a few months (Lerch 2004).

Explaining unexpected coherence

The findings show more coherence between trade and CFSP sanctions than initially expected. Trade sanctions against Burma and Belarus, the two most severely sanctioned countries under the EU's GSP, constituted the tail of a whole range of CFSP sanctions. Table 1 shows that in both cases the imposition of CFSP sanctions pre-dated the withdrawal of GSP. The reference to the 'political situation' in Myanmar in the 2005 GSP regulation constitutes the clearest indication of a connection between CFSP sanctions and GSP withdrawal: 'Due to the political situation in Myanmar, temporary withdrawal of all tariff preferences in respect of imports of products originating in Myanmar should remain in force' (point 18 of preamble). Similarly, the 2012 regulation stipulates that 'due to the political situation in Burma/Myanmar and in Belarus', the withdrawal of all tariff preferences should be maintained. These provisions contradict the conditions for lifting in the original regulation withdrawing Burma's GSP in 1997, which stipulated that preferences will be reinstated when practices of forced labour disappear, rather than when the political situation changes. This reformulation makes the reinstatement of GSP conditional on the fulfilment of the objectives of the CFSP Common Position. Although the complete withdrawal from GSP has always followed foreign policy sanctions, the inverse relationship does not apply. Most countries under CFSP sanctions do not face GSP withdrawals, even if these measures were considered as in the cases of China, India, and Russia. Thus, CFSP sanctions seem to be a necessary but not a sufficient condition for GSP withdrawal. Then, under which circumstances can foreign policy sanctions can be expected to coincide with GSP sanctions? The answer appears to lie in a combination of three factors.

Firstly, an authoritative condemnation by the ILO facilitates the imposition of GSP sanctions. What Myanmar and Belarus have in common is that both had reached the highest level of condemnation by the relevant ILO instance, the Commission of Inquiry, which was established for each of these countries in parallel to the EU procedure leading to GSP withdrawal (Table 2). No ILO Commission of Inquiry was established for Pakistan, in spite of ILO criticisms of practices of forced and child labour in this country, nor for Sri Lanka, China, Russia, or India.[14] As argued by Orbie and Tortell,

> the EU would only take such drastic steps as the withdrawal of trade preferences for breach of labour standards in cases in which the ILO has unambiguously held that such breach has not only occurred but has been persistent and serious. (2009, p. 679)

Burma in particular reached an unprecedented level of ILO condemnation when in 2000 the ILO adopting a resolution under article 33 of its constitution for the first time in its history (Howse and Genser 2008, p. 172).

Table 2. GSP beneficiaries at fault.

Name of beneficiary	Previous CFSP sanctions	ILO Commission of Inquiry	Type of (alleged) violation	Type of suspension
Myanmar	Yes	Yes (1996 established, report in 1998); art 33 in 2000	Core labour standard	GSP withdrawal
Pakistan	No	No	Core labour standard	None
China	No[a]	No	Core labour standard	None
India	No	No	Non-proliferation	None
Russia	No	No	HR/humanitarian law	None
Belarus	Yes	Yes (2003 established, report in 2004)	Core labour standard	GSP withdrawal
Sri Lanka	No	No	HR/humanitarian law	GSP+ to GSP
Zimbabwe	Yes	Yes (2008 established, report in 2010)	Core labour standards	None

Source: Own elaboration based on European Commission (2013), Portela (2010), and Orbie and Tortell (2009).
[a]The arms embargo on China is not a CFSP sanction (see Portela 2010).

GSP sanctions follow the ILO's level of condemnation as an objective benchmark, in line with the EU's commitment to taking into account multilateral institutions' assessment. Thus, even though the Commission's behaviour is not formally bound to any external agency, withdrawal practice shows that the EU tends to rely on ILO assessments. ILO condemnations in the cases of Burma and Belarus also make it easier for the EU to document violations. By contrast, the breaches detected in China were difficult to document, and the relevance of child labour practices in Pakistan to the ILO conventions appears not to have been sufficiently clear-cut. It should also be considered that a high level of ILO condemnation implies that there is a wide consensus in the international trade union movement on the violations of labour standards, because trade unions are actively involved in the ILO's tripartite structure. In turn, the existence of ILO condemnations makes it easier for trade unions to file a complaint under the EU's GSP system. Because the filing entity has to furnish evidence of the violation, the preparation of the complaint dossier is burdensome. Recent practice suggests that the EU also tends to rely on ILO assessments: the re-establishment of Burma's trade preferences in July 2013 only took place after a favourable ILO report.

Secondly, condemnations of the CFSP have not led to GSP sanctions when considerable commercial or strategic EU interests were at stake in the target countries due to resistance by a 'blocking minority' in the Council. Even if the Commission had proposed withdrawal in the above-mentioned instances where this step was contemplated, a minority of member states could have blocked the decision in the Council. The case of Pakistan illustrates how the prioritisation of geopolitical interests made the EU reluctant to impose sanctions. An official from one of the international trade unions which prepared the complaint observed that 'the Pakistani government was very active in lobbying member states and the Commission' (interview 2000). The EU's failure to suspend Pakistan's GSP preferences was criticised as motivated by the interests of certain member states reluctant to imperil the ongoing negotiation of a co-operation agreement with Pakistan (Greven 2005, p. 22). Illustratively, the Council's decision to extend the drugs incentive scheme to Pakistan in October 2001 caused India to successfully challenge its legality at the WTO. The extension of preferences represented a barely veiled attempt to reward Pakistan for its role in the fight against terrorism. Indeed, the Commission justified the move with reference to the response to 9/11:

> As a consequence of the events of 11 September, Pakistan is facing [serious] problems [. . .] The international community acknowledged this by agreeing on a number of programs and actions providing special assistance to this country. The European Union is called upon to join these efforts.

Further attempts by the EU to offer Pakistan better tariffs, e.g. through a 'humanitarian' measure following the floods of 2010, proved highly controversial (Van Elsuwege and Orbie forthcoming). The 2012 regulation has relaxed the vulnerability criterion for the GSP+ from 1% to 2%, making Pakistan eligible.

Also in the India/Pakistan nuclear tests case, disagreements within the Council softened the EU's approach. In the case of China, the EU was wary of jeopardising relations with this important partner, as exemplified by Commissioner Lamy's rejection of calls for the activation of the withdrawal procedure with China on account of the Commission's 'incentitative approach by strengthening of the GSP social incentive scheme'.[15] Tougher sanctions against Russia were dismissed by the Council due to its geopolitical importance and for fear of obstructing Russia's democratic course. By contrast, impoverished Myanmar counted few friends in the Council, and even though the UK reportedly opposed suspension, the weak relationship Yangon entertained with the EU did not allow for an anti-suspension coalition to crystallise. In the case of Belarus, there was some opposition to suspension by some members, including Poland, Lithuania, and Latvia. Eventually, 'horse trading' solved the stalemate in the Council: Italy, Greece, and Cyprus gave up their opposition to withdrawal in exchange for British, German, and Swedish agreement to antidumping measures against Chinese footwear (*EUObserver* 2006). Against this backdrop, international trade unions lost interest in filing complaints against strategically or commercially important countries. As explained by an international trade unionist involved in the Myanmar complaint: 'after our experience with Pakistan, we did not start with [...] China, India, Bolivia, Peru or Brazil . . . partly because of a lack of encouragement that we would be successful' (interview 2000).

Thirdly, the EU is wary of withdrawing GSP unless the connection between the violation at hand and government action is manifest. Kryvoi posits that the responsibility of the government in labour rights violations is central to triggering penalties. While elsewhere labour rights violations are often committed by the private sector, in Myanmar and Belarus these were perpetrated by the authorities themselves (Kryvoi 2008). The same applies to the Sri Lankan case. Conversely, this factor would account for the lack of suspension of Pakistan, which did not engage in proscribed labour practices but failed to enforce the ban against them. In contrast to the above-mentioned cases, Pakistani authorities co-operated with the EU investigation.

However, GSP withdrawals have not invariably followed CFSP sanctions. Sri Lanka constitutes an exception to the general picture of coherence between foreign policy and GSP withdrawals. In a departure from the pattern of CFSP sanctions pre-dating GSP withdrawal, the EU suspended Sri Lanka's GSP+ preferences in the absence of CFSP sanctions. The isolation of the GSP sanctions against Sri Lanka from other foreign policy measures remains puzzling. In addition, the choice of the instruments appears to be out of keeping with the nature of the situation addressed, namely actions affecting non-combatants protected under humanitarian law. While the GSP+ suspension is warranted from a legal vantage point, CFSP measures appear as a better fit for breaches committed in armed conflict. How can this outcome be explained?

CFSP sanctions were contemplated in response to the human rights violations perpetrated by the armed forces against the Tamil Tigers. However, these never materialised due to opposition by certain member states. Some of them opposed suspension on account of their close ties to Sri Lanka, while others were reluctant to issue a stronger condemnation of government actions in the fight against separatist group (interview 2013). Then, why were GSP suspended in the face of this opposition? GSP+ withdrawal is decided by Qualified Majority Voting (QMV), which might have prevented the wielding of a veto by a small number of Council members. In addition, Sri Lanka clearly is of only relative strategic or commercial importance for the EU, especially when compared to Russia, China, India, or even Pakistan. Perhaps as importantly, officials suggest that failure to suspend GSP+ in the face of overwhelming evidence of human rights violations reported by independent experts would have seriously damaged the credibility of the GSP+ system (interviews 2011).[16] Interestingly, the extensive procedural requirements for GSP withdrawal, which include an independent investigation involving consultations with various actors, limit the EU's options. In contrast, CFSP decision-making on sanctions depends directly on the political constellation in the Council.

Conclusions

The expectation that GSP and foreign policy sanctions would not cohere has been invalidated in our exploratory analysis. On the contrary, CFSP sanctions co-existed, and even pre-dated, GSP withdrawal in the two cases that constitute our extremely small sample. Yet, the presence of CFSP sanctions does not suffice to account for the decision to withdraw GSP. GSP suspension seems to come about when CFSP sanctions are in place *and* the ILO has set up a Commission of Inquiry that has condemned the beneficiary for failure to apply core standards. In the absence of both factors, the EU refrained from suspending GSP. The EU's manifest reluctance to apply GSP sanctions is only overcome when *both* conditions are met.

On the other hand, the design of the procedure for GSP withdrawals largely explains why GSP sanctions, but not CFSP sanctions, were adopted against Sri Lanka. Initiated following a complaint by human rights organisations, the elaborate procedure took into account an independent expert report whose findings ultimately made it difficult for the Council to maintain special preferences. By contrast, decision-making in the CFSP framework is manifestly politically driven, lacking any obligation to consider independent assessments. Nevertheless, these examples also show that in a setting of institutional fragmentation, certain outcomes can come about despite dissimilar member states' interests thanks to the presence of authoritative assessments on human and labour rights violations. These enhanced the likelihood of GSP withdrawal, illustrating the influence of multilateral organisations such as the ILO and of independent assessments on EU responses to human rights violations.

Our enquiry into the EU's GSP sanctions reveals some useful insights that depart from the conventional assumptions about incoherence in EU foreign policy and merit further research. Perhaps one of the most evident findings from the point of view of sanctions theory is that coherence between CFSP and GSP sanctions is not a forcibly desirable outcome. In Myanmar and Belarus, GSP withdrawal became subsumed into the CFSP sanctions regime. Illustratively, the GSP regulations stipulate that only a change in the 'political situation' – rather than the observance of the relevant labour conventions – justifies reinstatement of trade preferences. The linkage between both measures reduces the incentives for the target to correct violations of labour standards, since he cannot expect GSP benefits to be reinstated until the political situation is altered. Besides, the policy implications of linking trade and foreign policy sanctions can be negative. The impact of foreign policy objectives on trade policy has already proven controversial at the WTO, as witnessed notably with the now defunct drugs incentive scheme. In coming years, conflicts between both spheres are likely to proliferate given the growing role of the European Parliament in EU trade policy, the stronger coherence requirements in the Lisbon Treaty, and the growing securitisation of international trade politics.

Acknowledgements

The authors thank Alasdair Young, Lorand Bartels, Maurizio Carbone, and three anonymous reviewers for their helpful comments on earlier versions of this article; Alan Winters, Ann Van Aaken, Tony Heron, and Gabriel Siles-Brügge for their input and Stefanie Proost for providing access to her interview material.

Notes

1. The historical name of Burma and the official name of Myanmar are used interchangeably throughout the article.
2. Throughout the article, we refer to the 'EU' even when the former European (Economic) Community is meant.
3. Council Regulation No. 3281/94 of 24 March 1997.
4. In addition to the eight fundamental ILO Conventions: International Covenant on Civil and Political Rights; International Covenant on Economic Social and Cultural Rights; International Convention on the Elimination of All Forms of Racial Discrimination; Convention on the Elimination of All Forms of Discrimination against Women; Convention against Torture and other Cruel, Inhuman or Degrading Treatment or Punishment; Convention on the Rights of the Child; Convention on the Prevention and Punishment of the Crime of Genocide; and International Convention on the Suppression and Punishment of the Crime of Apartheid.

5. Montreal Protocol on Substances that Deplete the Ozone Layer; Basel Convention on the Control of Transboundary Movements of Hazardous Wastes and Their Disposal; Stockholm Convention on Persistent Organic Pollutants; Convention on International Trade in Endangered Species; Convention on Biological Diversity; Cartagena Protocol on Biosafety; Kyoto Protocol; UN Single Convention on Narcotic Drugs; UN Convention on Psychotropic Substances; UN Convention against Illicit Traffic in Narcotic Drugs and Psychotropic Substances; and UN Convention against Corruption.
6. The 2008 GSP reform did no alter the conditionality system.
7. This summary is based on art 11 Treaty on European Union (TEU) of 1992. The Lisbon Treaty subsumes these objectives into an expanded list (art 21). However, the withdrawal cases discussed here were considered in the pre-Lisbon era.
8. See Regulation (EU) No. 978/2012, Art 19(10).
9. See Council Regulation No. 552/97 of 24 March 1997 (supra fn 2).
10. See Common Position 2004/848/CFSP and Common Position 2004/661/CFSP.
11. See Council Regulation No. 2342/2003 of 29 December 2003.
12. The list is not exhaustive as no official record exists.
13. 98/606/CFSP, 26 October 1998.
14. An ILO Commission of Inquiry was also created for Zimbabwe. However, Zimbabwe is not a GSP beneficiary.
15. Answer to the question by Bernard Poignant (*Parti Socialiste Européen* (PSE)) to the Commission, 21 February 2002 (E-0384).
16. Interview material collected by Stefanie Proost.

References

Alston, P., 2005. Labour rights as human rights: the not so happy state of the art. *In*: P. Alston, ed. *Labour rights as human rights*. Oxford: OUP, 1–24.

Bartels, L., 2007. The WTO legality of the EU's GSP + arrangement. *Journal of International Economic Law*, 10 (4), 865–886.

Brandtner, B. and Rosas, A., 1998. Human rights and the external relations of the European community: An analysis of the doctrine and practice. *European Journal of International Law*, 9 (3): 468–90.

Bossuyt, F., Drieghe, L. and Orbie, J., 2013. Living apart together: EU comprehensive security from a trade perspective. *European Foreign Affairs Review*, 18 (5), 63–82.

Bourriche, M., 2008. La cohérence de la politique européenne de coopération au développement. *In*: M. Dony and L.S. Rossi, eds. *Démocratie, cohérence et transparence. Vers une constitutionnalisation de l'Union européenne?* Bruxelles: Université de Bruxelles, 249–263.

Bünte, M. and Portela, C., 2012. Myanmar: the beginning of reforms and the end of sanctions. *GIGA Focus International*, 3, 1–8.

Carbone, M., 2008. Mission impossible: the European Union and policy coherence for development. *Journal of European Integration*, 30 (3), 323–342.

Clapham, A. and Martignoni, J.B., 2006. Are we there yet? In search of a coherent European Union strategy on labour rights and external trade. *In*: V.A. Leary and D. Warner, eds. *Social issues, globalisation and international institutions: labour rights and the EU, ILO, OECD and WTO*. Boston, MA: Martinus Nijhoff, 233–310.

Council of the European Union, 2004. *Basic principles for the use of restrictive measures*, Council Doc. 10198/1/04 REV 1 Brussels, 7 June 2004.

Cremona, M., 2011. Coherence in foreign policy – the legal dimension. *In*: P. Koutrakos, ed. *European foreign policy: legal and political perspectives*. Cheltenham: Edward Elgar, 15–54.

EUobserver, 2006. EU "horse trading" links Belarus and Chinese shoes. 29 September.

European Commission, 2006. *Proposal for a council regulation temporarily withdrawing access to the generalised tariff preferences from the Republic of Belarus*. COM (2006)0438 final.

European Commission, 2012a. *Trade, growth and development: tailoring trade and investment policy for those countries most in need*. SEC (2012)87.

European Commission, 2012b. *European Commission proposes to reinstate trade preferences to Myanmar/ Burma*. Available from: http://trade.ec.europa.eu/doclib/press/index.cfm?id=831 [accessed 26 October 2013].

European Commission, 2013. *Restrictive measures (sanctions) in force*. Available from: http://eeas.europa.eu/cfsp/sanctions/docs/measures_en.pdf [accessed 26 October 2013].

European Council, 1999. *Presidency conclusions*. Helsinki, 10–11 December.

European Parliament, 1997. *On the Communication from the Commission on a long term policy for China–Europe relations* (COM(95)0279 – C4-0288/95), Committee on Foreign Affairs, Security and Defence Policy, Rapporteur: Mr Edward McMillan-Scott, A4-0198/97.

Fierro, E., 2003. *The EU's approach to human rights conditionality in practice*. The Hague: Martinus Nijhoff.

Greven, T., 2005. Social standards in bilateral and regional trade and investment agreements. *Friedrich Ebert Stiftung Occasional Papers*, 16, 1–56.

Hampson, F., Sevón, L. and Wieruszewski, R., 2009. *The implementation of certain human rights conventions in Sri Lanka*. Report for the European Commission, 30 September.

Howse, R. and Genser, J., 2008. Are EU trade sanctions on Burma compatible with WTO law? *Michigan Journal of International Law*, 29 (165), 165–196.

Krenzler, H.G. and Schneider, H.C., 1997. The question of consistency. *In*: E. Regelsberger, P. de Schoutheete and W. Wessel, eds. *Foreign policy of the European Union: From EPC to CFSP and beyond*. Boulder, CO: Lynne Rienner, 133–151.

Kryvoi, Y., 2008. Why European Union trade sanctions do not work. *Minnesota Journal of International Law*, 12 (2), 209–246.

Lerch, M., 2004. *Menschenrechte und Europäische Aussenpolitik*. Wiesbaden: VS Verlag für Sozialwissenschaften.

Mandelson, P., 2006. Trade policy and decent work intervention. Speech at *EU Decent Work Conference*, Brussels, 5 December.

Orbie, J. and Tortell, L., 2009. The new GSP + Beneficiaries: ticking the box or truly consistent with ILO findings? *European Foreign Affairs Review*, 14 (5), 663–681.

Patten, C., 1999. Declaration on Chechnya. Speech at *the European Parliament,* Strasbourg, 17 November.

Portela, C., 2003. The EU's role in the non-proliferation of weapons of mass destruction. *PRIF Report*, 65, 1–39.

Portela, C., 2010. *European Union sanctions and foreign policy*. Routledge: London.

Portela, C. and Raube, K., 2012. The EU polity and foreign policy coherence. *Journal of Contemporary European Research*, 8 (1), 1–20.

Reuters, 2012. EU says won't be pushed into lifting Myanmar sanctions. *Reuters*, 30 March.

Siles-Brügge, G. 2014. EU trade and development policy beyond the ACP: subordinating developmental to commercial imperatives in the reform of GSP. *Contemporary Politics*, 20 (1), 49–62.

Smith, M.E., 2004. *Europe's foreign and security policy*. Cambridge: Cambridge University Press.

Van Elsuwege, P. and Orbie, J., forthcoming. The EU's humanitarian aid policy after Lisbon: implications of a new treaty basis. *In*: I. Govaere and S. Poli, eds. *EU governance of global emergencies*. Leiden: Brill.

Challenging the European Union: the rising powers and the USA in the Doha Round

Anders Ahnlid[a] and Ole Elgström[b]

[a]*Permanent Delegation of Sweden to the European Union, Brussels, Belgium;* [b]*Department of Political Science, Lund University, Lund, Sweden*

In this article, the challenges posed to the European Union's (EU) role in trade policy and its implications for development policy during the World Trade Organization's Doha Development Agenda, also known as the Doha round, are highlighted. The authors argue that transformed power relations have created a situation characterized by *role uncertainty*, for the emerging powers but also for the EU. Priorities among multiple possible roles – in the existing trade regime, in relation to the global South and in the ongoing negotiations – become subject to redefinition. For the EU, heavily wedded to a multilateralist and reformist mission because of its own history, this process is particularly difficult. The EU's traditional role conceptions as a leader and a benign partner to developing countries have been challenged and partly replaced by a more realist approach.

Introduction

It is a commonplace to argue that a new global order is emerging, in which the rise of new major actors, in particular China, India and Brazil, challenges the United States' (US) hegemonic position and the prominent, multilateralist role of the European Union (EU). New constellations of power create novel patterns of interaction and new alliances. They also create an uncertain and ambiguous environment, where the international roles of major actors are challenged and have to be reconsidered.

In this article, we highlight the challenges posed to the EU's role in trade policy and its implications for development policy during the World Trade Organization's (WTO) Doha Development Agenda (DDA), also known as the Doha round. Many scholars have looked at internal explanations for EU role incoherence (cf. McGuire and Lindeque 2010, Poletti 2012), whereas this article points at role change and incoherence as a result of external transformations. We argue that transformed power relations have created a situation characterized by *role uncertainty*, not only for the emerging powers but also for the EU. Priorities among multiple possible roles – in the existing trade regime, in relation to the global South and in the ongoing negotiations – become subject to redefinition. For the EU, heavily wedded to a multilateralist and reformist mission because of its own history, but simultaneously constrained by internal protectionist vested interests, this process is particularly difficult. The challenge of rising powers is, in the words of Smith (2013, p. 654), 'existential … penetrating to the heart of perceptions of the EU as an international actor'.

We start by clarifying the relationship between changes in the global distribution of power and role uncertainty, emphasizing the possible existence of multiple roles and of role competition. We also discuss various layers and types of role conceptions that may be encountered in the context of WTO negotiations and briefly delineate what roles the EU played at the end of the 1990s, before the rise of the emerging powers. In the empirical part, we first give an account of the changing status of these powers, and of the Western powers, in WTO negotiations, focusing on their role in decision-making structures.[1] Thereafter, we delve into the positions, coalition patterns and roles of the EU, the USA, Brazil, China and India in the actual DDA-negotiations, with a focus on three key areas of conflict. We highlight how these actors have interacted with the EU and emphasize how the EU's roles have changed in the course of the Round. In the concluding discussion, we pinpoint trends in the global trade and development regime and what challenges these may bring for EU role conceptions.

Power change, role uncertainty and the rise of emerging powers

A role is, in the words of Harnisch (2011, p. 8), a 'social position that is constituted by ego and alter expectations regarding the purpose of an actor in an organized group'. The role concept is a cognitive construct, which evolves in dynamic interaction with other actors and in correspondence with images of self in social reality (Aggestam 2006, Elgström and Smith 2006). It predisposes an actor towards one set of purposive behaviour rather than another. A *role conception* is 'an actor's perception of his or her position vis-à-vis others ... and the perception of the role expectations of others as signalled through language and action' (Harnisch 2011, p. 8). It defines perceived responsibilities and obligations in foreign policy and includes policy-makers' perceptions of what functions their state should perform in the international system or in regional subsystems (Aggestam 2006). In exploring an actor's role in a certain context, for example, an international organization, it is important not only to study an actor's self-images, but also outsiders' perceptions and expectations of its appropriate foreign policy performance.

An actor may perform multiple foreign policy roles. These may reinforce each other but also result in *role competition*. The existence of several competing role conceptions may lead external actors to perceive the state's policy as incoherent. Breuning (2011) argues that the dynamics between multiple roles is one of the blind spots within role theory, especially when it comes to interpreting how and when role change takes place. Roles, like many other cognitive constructs, are generally believed to be change resistant, as they constitute key elements in actors' images of their status and position in the world. At times, however, decision-makers gradually reduce their emphasis on certain role conceptions and simultaneously increase the relative prominence of other role conceptions (Breuning 2011). Folz (2011) proposes three types of scope conditions under which change in the enactment of roles is more likely: uncertainty (when facing new situations), identification (when an actor identifies itself with another actor's role conception) and resonance (when changes in public opinion facilitate role change). In our view, uncertainty is the most prominent factor. We furthermore argue that changes in existing constellations of power in a certain area must be a key generator of uncertainty. We would, therefore, expect *role uncertainty* to occur in a situation where the relative power of key actors is under transformation or when new powers emerge. In such situations, actors are prone to reconsider what is the most appropriate way to behave and thus their relative prioritization of competing role conceptions. As the relative power positions of major trade actors have certainly undergone rapid change, we expect WTO negotiations to bear witness of role uncertainty and of fluid and at times incoherent role performance.

In this article, we are interested in three different layers of role conceptions. The first concerns what role or functions the actor seeks to perform in the *international trade system*.

Referring to the literature on the rise of emerging powers (see the section below), we distinguish between the roles of a supporter of the present system, of a revisionist actor and of a shirker, an actor that avoids responsibilities and obligations. From another perspective, an actor may entertain a multilateralist role conception or it may play a more unilateralist, or sovereignist, role. The second layer, which is particularly pertinent in a discussion of trade and its relation to development, refers to an actor's perceived *relation to the global South*. We imagine that rising powers, which geographically belong to the South, may, for example, act as leaders of the Third World, as loyal members of a Southern bloc, as regional leaders or as bridge-builders between North and South. The Western powers may also perceive themselves as bridge-builders but also, for example, as spokesmen for Third World interests or as competitors in a struggle for power and wealth. The third layer deals with roles in *actual negotiations*. According to the literature on the nature of multilateral negotiations (Zartmann 1994), the roles of leader, mediator and follower constantly and repeatedly appear and can indeed be seen as necessary elements of multilateral negotiations, as tools that render their striking complexity manageable.

Much of the existing literature on the rising powers is preoccupied with the consequences for the future international order. The fate of US hegemony and of the liberal world order are two major concerns (see, for example, Ikenberry 2008, Schweller 2011, Layne 2012). A key question is whether the emerging powers will be integrated into the Western liberal order or if they will oppose the ground rules of the existing order. Will they act as 'responsible stakeholders' or will they 'shy away from assuming significant global responsibilities', that is, act as shirkers (Patrick 2010)?

Turning to a brief, and admittedly sketchy, overview of the picture drawn of the roles of emerging powers, *India* has been seen as reluctant to take on the responsibilities of upholding the global order (Dormandy 2007) and as having occupied a rather confrontational and inflexible role in many international negotiations (Narlikar 2013). While some scholars maintain that *China* is a status quo power (Ikenberry 2008), others see it as a revisionist power, exhibiting 'deep ambivalence and dissatisfaction about elements of the existing international order' (Shambaugh 2013, p. 315). China has been reluctant to take on a leadership role in multilateral negotiations. *Brazil* is claimed to have demonstrated both international and regional leadership ambitions, wishing to be recognized as a leader of Southern coalitions. At the same time it has pursued the role of a bridge-builder between South and North in global negotiations (Burges 2013).

The *European Union* is a major stakeholder in the existing order. In the late 1990s – before the rise of the emerging powers – it was on the level of the international trading system portrayed as a committed multilateralist (van den Hoven 2006, Elgström 2007), but also as an active reformist, trying to regulate globalization through the introduction of stronger multilateral trade rules (Meunier 2007, Poletti 2012). In its relation with the global South, the EU presented itself as a benign, solidarist partner (van den Hoven 2006). This was demonstrated by its wholehearted support of the idea to launch a WTO development round and its use of a development discourse in its efforts to find allies among developing countries (van den Hoven 2004). On the level of actual negotiations, the EU was by external actors considered a powerful key player, and often but not necessarily as a leader; the latter because of its perceived policy incoherence (Elgström 2007).

The EU's diplomacy has over the years had as a predominant end the promotion of negotiated order, with a commitment to multilateralism, liberal regimes, integrative negotiations and the active pursuit of coalitions, 'since those are what has served the /EU/ project well through its half-century and more of existence' (Smith 2013, p. 659). This strong link to the EU's self-identification is why the rise of the emerging powers, with markedly different priorities from those espoused by the EU, poses a particular challenge to the Union. According to

Smith (2013, p. 670), the EU's power to ensure value-adding outcomes of negotiations, which it held in the 1990s, has disappeared as a result of this much less hospitable environment for the EU. Its leadership ambitions have arguably also been significantly thwarted. The EU's multilateralist role conception has always contained elements of insularity, as a consequence of internal bargaining, and this has given rise to accusations of incoherence. In recent years, its approach has increasingly also started to include minilateral and bilateral initiatives, leading to a questioning of its multilateralist ethos.

Changing status of power among new and old actors

Governance in the multilateral trading system, as embodied in the WTO, is performed through various formal and informal decision-making structures. Trade negotiations are conducted in layers of 'concentric circles' (Ahnlid 2012). At first the most powerful actors try to find common ground, where after a larger number of key partners are brought in, before consensus is ultimately sought with the participation of all. Changes in the status of power of major actors can be traced by mapping participation in the innermost concentric circle. The composition of this core group has changed considerably since the inception of the present multilateral trade regime in 1947.

The rise of the emerging powers is clearly manifested by their increasing weight in decision-making structures. The emerging powers have in fact become veto players: they can prevent any unsatisfactory outcome, but they cannot enforce the solutions they prefer (Schirm 2012, p. 212). This development constitutes a fundamental challenge to the EU, which it has to take into account.

During the heydays of its hegemony, the USA promoted trade liberalization in successive General Agreement on Tariffs and Trade (GATT) rounds. US relative decline led the EU to take on more of a leadership role during the Uruguay-round 1986–1994; first reluctantly, but gradually more assertively (Ahnlid 2005). The 'quad-group', to which Canada and Japan were added, embraced key proposals before they were taken up in a wider circle of countries, where the most important developing countries joined, including Brazil and India. The latter performed relatively active negotiating roles, often, but not always, as spoilers (Srinivasan 2000). As trade was increasingly recognized as an engine for growth and development, demands rose for a rectification of an alleged developed country bias. This was reflected in structural changes during the Doha Round.

It thus proved difficult to get real negotiations going in DDA before workable concentric circles were put in place. Dual EU–USA leadership was evidently no longer sufficient for progress; it could even become counterproductive. The quad-group had lost its importance since its '... exclusively rich-country membership seemed more anachronistic than ever at a time when large developing countries were growing by leaps and bounds in economic importance and assertiveness' (Blustein 2009, p. 183). The creation of the G-20[2] as a major player in the negotiations, with Brazil in the lead, and India as well as China as members, altered the balance of power in the WTO and reinforced the roles of Brazil and India as developing country leaders. According to McGuire and Lindeque (2010, p. 1341), 'the emergence of the G-20 as a relatively coherent bloc probably spells the end to American-European dominance of the final stages of WTO negotiating rounds'.

A new inner circle – the so-called Five Interested Parties (FIP: EU, USA, Brazil, India and Australia) – gained prominence in the preparation for a 2004 informal ministerial meeting. So far China had not been at the centre stage of DDA (Das 2004). On the one hand, China's considerable growth positioned it as a world leader in terms of the size of both its economy and its trade. On the other hand, China had not become a WTO member until 2001, and was a newcomer in the negotiations. Thus, China was a passive participant, arguing that it should not be required to make additional concessions in DDA due to its relatively far-reaching accession conditions. China, it was argued, needed more time for its '"peaceful rise" to Great-Power Status' (Zheng 2005).

This stance was not accepted by the old leaders. Then US Deputy Secretary of State Bob Zoellick argued that '/w/e need to urge China to become a *responsible stakeholder* in that system' (2005). While the EU according to Trade Commissioner Peter Mandelson stood ready to consider the requests of Brazil, China and India, it would ask the emerging powers ' ... to meet us, if not half way, then at least somewhere down the path to shared responsibility for, and shared contribution to, the global system we all need to sustain' (Mandelson 2006).

In the lead-up to the 2008 informal ministerial meeting – which constitutes the most serious attempt to date to bring the negotiations towards finalization – China was still not fully included in the inner circle. A new constellation – G-4 or the 'new quad', consisting of the EU, the USA, Brazil and India – met in order to prepare for the ministerial. After harsh negotiations, USTR Susan Schwab criticized India for not shouldering the responsibility that followed from being '... in the inner circle ... in a leadership position' (*Financial Times*, 22 June 2007). Acting upon their increasing negotiating leverage Brazil and India, on the other hand, found the offers by the EU and the USA to be insufficient.

The July 2008 ministerial meeting again changed the composition of the inner concentric circle as China was admitted to the elite table for the first time. G-7, consisting of Australia, Brazil, China, the EU, India, Japan and the USA, emerged as the core body. Concerning China it was noted that one could not ' ... yet say [that China] were a leader. But they were very engaged' (Amorim 2008), and that represented a considerable change compared to the previous phases of the DDA. The EU was now only one of several veto players.

Roles of leading actors in the DDA-negotiations

After failure at a meeting in Seattle in 1999, WTO-ministers launched the DDA, in Doha, Qatar, 2001 (Ahnlid 2005). The meaning of labelling DDA a 'development round' was debated from the outset. The notion was supported by the emerging powers who stressed the need to address anti-development asymmetries and for developed countries to open up their market for developing country products. Seeking a role as leader in the quest for development, the EU embraced the label, which was in conformity with EU's overarching positions on sustainable development and policy coherence for development. The USA, on the other hand, found the implications of a 'development round' unclear and questioned the use of the term.

The first phase of the Doha negotiations concentrated on consolidating the agenda, the most contentious issue being whether negotiations should proceed on the so-called Singapore issues (trade aspects of competition policy, investment, trade facilitation and government procurement). From its position as the lead advocate of a broad agenda, the EU argued that the Singapore issues were conducive to development. The USA held a more conservative view, prioritized market access over widened trade rules, and had only reluctantly agreed to inclusion of competition and investment on the agenda, not least due to fears of intrusion into domestic US jurisdiction. However, the main challenge of the EU view came from a large majority of developing countries, with India in the lead, that opposed negotiations on these issues, which were found hostile to development since they reduced national 'policy space'. When the EU, in response to this challenge from emerging powers and as a sign of leadership for the sake of the system as a whole, backed away from negotiations on three Singapore issues, keeping only trade facilitation as part of DDA, this represented a blow to its leadership ambitions, but also a step backwards for its role as an active regulatory reformist.

The DDA today covers about 20 topics negotiated in 8 separate bodies under the overall authority of the Trade Negotiating Committee, where any final deal covering all areas has to be struck in order to conclude the round. Early on it was recognized that the outcome of the round largely hinged upon results from the major actors relating to a 'triangle of issues' (Bridges 2006, Lamy 2006). Accordingly, the EU would have to offer meaningful reductions of agricultural tariffs, the USA would have to do likewise concerning domestic agricultural subsidies and the emerging powers would have to lower their tariffs on industrial products. Results in this triangle, it was argued, would pave the way for progress in other areas and, thereby, for a successful conclusion of the round. Much has already been written on the negotiations leading to the breakdown at the 2008 ministerial meeting (Bluestein 2009, Wolfe 2009, Ahnlid 2012), however, the roles of major actors in relation to the above triangle deserve further attention.

Agriculture

Despite representing a relatively small share of world trade, agriculture has remained at the centre of attention in the trading system. The protectionist EU Common Agricultural Policy has been the target of agricultural exporters for long. The USA led the charge in the 1980s and 1990s supported by the so-called Cairns-group of agricultural exporting countries, with Brazil as an important member.

A bilateral USA–EU deal on agriculture brought the Uruguay-round to a close. Unfinished business in agriculture, and the inability of the EU to move forward absent a broader round, largely explained the need for and launch of DDA. At this stage, protectionist agricultural policies were increasingly seen as an obstacle to development. In particular, EU export subsidies were heavily criticized for reducing room for domestic production in developing countries. EU willingness to phase out these subsidies was important for the acceptance by the Cairns-group and developing countries of the DDA negotiating mandate, and can be interpreted as an expression of leadership. A new farm bill in 2002, which increased US agricultural subsidies, turned the USA into a second major target for agricultural exporting and developing countries and made the US position more defensive.

A joint EU and US proposal on agriculture, in preparation for the Cancun ministerial meeting in 2003, was labelled 'ambitious' by EU Trade Commissioner Pascal Lamy, who also pointed out that the proposal had come about '... at the urgings of our partners ... ' and should be seen as a sign of EU willingness to contribute to agreement through '... a new approach in the treatment of development issues' (Lamy 2003). The emerging powers, however, rejected the EU interpretation and used the 'insufficient' EU–US proposal to spur the formation of G-20 whose counter-proposal '... emphasized agricultural subsidy reform and tariff reduction for developed countries with fewer demands on developing countries' (Hanrahan and Schnepf 2005, p. 3).

G-20 changed the power-constellation in the negotiation considerably by directly challenging EU and US supremacy. Cancun was, in the eyes of some observers, 'a watershed for international economic governance, as it laid bare the inability of Europe and the USA to force a settlement' (McGuire and Lindeque 2010, p. 1340). The G-20 challenged their joint ambition to lead the negotiations but also the EU's image as a partner for development. Arguably, the EU was to a certain extent surprised by the decisive rise of this coalition of emerging powers. According to Mortensen (2009, p. 86–87), it misjudged the 'new topography of global trade politics' and 'ignored the structural transformations in global trade'.

Previously, India and many other developing countries had turned to the EU for cooperation in agriculture due to similar defensive interests. Brazil on the other hand was a world leader in exports of several key agricultural commodities. Linking Brazil's offensive stance with India's defensive interests, which were shared by China, created uncertainty regarding the endurance of G-20. While the emerging powers agreed on the importance of fighting EU and US agricultural subsides, they held diverging views on the virtues of further liberalization of world agricultural markets. In addition to G-20, Cancun saw the birth of yet a developing country agricultural coalition; G-33, coordinated by Indonesia, but with both China and India as members. G-33 rallied around defensive developing country interests and stressed the need for protection for 'special products' of importance to large numbers of poor subsistence farmers.

Neither G-20 nor G-33 requests were met by the USA and the EU at Cancun, while the latter signalled more sympathy for G-33 interests than the former. The USA accused 'won't-do countries' in G-20 for the failure and deplored that Brazil declined to co-operate '... turning instead to India, which has never supported opening markets, so as to emphasise north-south division not global agricultural reform' (Zoellick 2003). The USA accused Brazil, India and others of 'overplaying their hand', and of pursuing 'tactics of confrontation'. A framework for negotiations was, however, agreed in July 2004 after a massive push from the USA, the EU and Brazil. The deal was largely hammered out by the FIP, with the USA as initiator, and on the basis of the EU dropping three of the Singapore issues.

In preparation for the 2005 Hong Kong ministerial meeting, the G-20 put forward the first formal proposal on agricultural modalities, which became the benchmark for evaluating developed country proposals (Hanrahan and Schnepf 2005), and now sought to align its interests with G-90, a group comprising the least developed and some other poor countries (Heydon 2006, p. 6). The EU offered to phase out export subsidies for agricultural goods by 2013 in an effort to save its image as a responsible leader.

At the opening of the ministerial meeting in 2008, the USA showed willingness to move forward by offering to cap domestic agricultural subsidies at 15 billion USD per year, down from 21 billion in the previous offer. For similar reasons, the EU offered to cut its farm tariffs by an average of 60%, compared to 54% previously. According to the EU, this was '... by far the highest farm tariff cut ever ... ' put forward in a multilateral trade negotiation (Mandelson 2008). Both improvements were conditional upon appropriate responses from other participants, and in particular so from the emerging powers on the third leg of the triangle of key issues.

However, the negotiations in G-7, now with China present, became difficult and confrontational. What roles the main actors would take was uncertain, as were their bottom-lines on key issues. Differences persisted with regard to the formulation of a Special Safeguard Mechanism (SSM) for developing countries in case of sudden hikes in food imports, promoted by India and G-33. Absent additional progress the chairman of the negotiations, WTO Director General Lamy, put forward a comprehensive compromise proposal to G-7. Under the compromise, the USA and the EU had to go a little bit further than in previous offers.

In G-7, Brazil announced its willingness to move on the basis of the compromise, as did the EU. The USA, China and India took more guarded positions. The USA initially seemed grudgingly willing to work on the basis of the proposed package. China did not directly object. India reportedly took the most negative position and frequently consulted the G-33 on the SSM, which India could not support in its present form. Simultaneously, support for the compromise grew among other developing countries, including the African group, who urged the G-7 to show leadership and bridge remaining differences.

In the last G-7 meetings, the USA and India maintained their unwillingness to agree on the SSM. Calling India a 'roadblock to success' (Wolfe 2009, p. 17), the USA rejected the compromise since it would make it possible for countries, including India and China, to raise tariffs above 'bound' levels for products that were important to the USA. India, on the other hand, refused to '... place the livelihoods of hundreds of millions of people at risk' (Blustein 2009, p. 266), and got backing from China and G-33 in rejecting the compromise version of SSM.

The EU sought to mediate and put forward compromise proposals. Brazil backed these efforts, took on a role as mediator and strongly urged India to agree. At the final phase of the meeting, the negotiating roles of the EU and Brazil had changed considerably compared to the roles previously pursued, and in relation to their former respective partners, the USA and India. The EU was now more a mediator than a leader. The USA–EU partnership was no longer fully upheld and G-20 loyalties were not strong enough to hold during the end-game of the meeting. The African group joined the proponents of the compromise, as did, albeit less vocally the African, Caribbean and Pacific (ACP) countries and the group of Least Developed Countries (LDC). But the efforts were in vain; the negotiations on agriculture broke down over the SSM-issue.

Industrial goods

The DDA-negotiations on industrial goods, or officially Non-Agriculture Market Access (NAMA) since they also cover raw materials and fisheries, were for quite some time secondary to the talks on Singapore issues and agriculture. Yet, it was clear from the outset that NAMA, representing about 90% of world trade, was indispensable to a successful conclusion of the round. The negotiating mandate called for reduction or elimination of tariffs, and in particular so on goods of interest to developing countries. The EU and the USA, who upheld relatively low levels of industrial tariffs, emerged as the key 'demandeurs' and emphasized the need to obtain gains in NAMA from the emerging powers, in which tariffs were substantially higher, in order to be able to reciprocate by concessions in agriculture. The EU and the USA stressed the development gains from successful NAMA negotiations but also the need for complementary elimination of tariffs in specific sectors. Emerging economies, on the other hand, stressed that development required continued tariff protection, sought 'flexibilities' and rejected sectoral tariff elimination.

As the 'triangle' of key issues took clearer shape in the lead-up to the ministerial meeting in Hong Kong 2005, NAMA negotiations became more detailed. Brazil, the EU, India and the USA (the 'new quad') failed to reach agreement on how to balance agriculture and NAMA in preparation for Hong Kong. An EU proposal, suggesting far-reaching formula tariff cuts for industrial goods from the emerging powers, triggered the formation of a group called NAMA-11, which consisted of developing countries with defensive NAMA interests. South Africa and Argentina were in the forefront of the group, but Brazil and India also joined.

After Hong Kong, G-6 (Australia, Brazil, the EU, India, Japan and the USA) sought to move the process forward without much success. While the developed G-6 members wanted far-reaching tariff reductions for industrial goods in countries such as Brazil and India, the latter argued for a 25% point difference in cuts between developed and developing countries (Ismail 2007). Even if Brazil and India participated in G-6 in their own capacity, they also performed as informal representatives of NAMA-11 and regularly reported back to the group.

China was so far conspicuously absent from the inner circle of negotiations. China's absence should be seen in light of China's wish to avoid further tariff reductions after its recent accession to the WTO and Brazil's and India's reluctance to lower tariffs in a way that would improve Chinas competitive position on their markets. The latter reason, no doubt, rendered negotiations more complex, and made attainment of EU and US objectives more difficult.

At the 2008 informal ministerial China was, however, brought into the innermost circle. G-7 negotiations on NAMA continued to be confrontational as Lamy puts forward his compromise proposal. The EU was reluctantly willing to accept the proposal, but not until after quite difficult internal deliberations, again showing willingness to respond to emerging powers, and safeguard the system, by accepting a compromise. This demonstrated its roles as a responsible protector of the existing system and as a bridge-builder between North and South. Brazil and India could also accept the 'Lamy-package' on NAMA. The USA manufacturing lobby, however, rejected the offer, which no doubt contributed to the pulling out of the USA from the overall negotiations. According to the USA, the formula did not produce sufficient new market access. China's strong objections to sectoral negotiations contributed to the US exit (Wolfe 2009, p. 10). It has been argued that the primary reason for failure of the 2008 ministerial was that the USA did not find the offer on manufacturing goods from Brazil, China and India satisfactory, rather than the SSM-issue (Blustein 2009, Ahnlid 2012). Regardless of the reason for collapse, the DDA has not recovered after 2008.

Other development issues

While the most important development gains from DDA in economic terms would most likely come from the triangle of key issues, the round also covered numerous other topics relating to development. An assessment of roles in these processes has to take into account that there has never been agreement in the WTO on the role of trade and trade policy for development (Wolfe 2009). Some argue that trade liberalization per se spurs development; others the opposite; that restrictions and exceptions from rules are necessary to achieve development goals in accordance with WTO provisions on 'special and differential treatment' for developing countries.

As part of its aspirations to be a leader on development, the EU proposed 'a Doha round for free' for the LDC, meaning that these countries would be asked neither to open up their markets nor to follow many rules (Blustein 2009, p. 184). In addition, the EU took the lead in advocating 'duty-free and quota-free' market access for exports from the LDCs to developed country markets on the basis of its own 'Everything-but-Arms-regulation', from 2001, which provided such treatment. The USA, on the other hand, accepted neither the notion of 'a round for free' nor full duty-free and quota-free access.

The EU also engaged with the LDC and ACP countries, gathered in G-90, to tackle concerns regarding 'preference erosion', which followed upon non-discriminatory liberalization of trade. G-90 had previously supported EU attempts to minimize its tariff reductions in agriculture in order to maintain a privileged position on the EU market. However, at the Hong Kong ministerial G-20 and G-90 joined forces, pressing jointly for developed country concessions. In July 2008, it became apparent that the cohesion of G-90 could not be maintained. The negotiations at this meeting also revealed cleavages within the LDC group as ACP members of the group sought long transition periods before they would lose their preferences on the EU market for textiles and other products. This, in turn, discriminated against Bangladesh, Nepal and Cambodia that did not benefit from the same kind of preferences.

While the EU sought to uphold a special relationship with G-90, it agreed with the USA that the emerging powers had to shoulder responsibility, liberalize their markets and, thereby, contribute to the development objectives of the round. It was pointed out that 70% of the tariffs paid by the poorest developing countries were paid to other developing countries, that the highest average tariffs were found in the developing world, and that increased 'south-south trade' would provide a considerable boost for development. Still, most developing countries, including the emerging powers, did not recognize EU leadership on development, and rejected the EU and US view of how the round would drive development.

Role-playing in the Doha Round

In this section, we summarize and discuss what roles the EU, the USA and the emerging powers have played, and how these have changed – if at all – in the course of the Doha Round. The focus is on how the EU has responded to the rise of the new powers. In the presentation, we follow our distinction between three layers of roles: in the global trading system, in relation to the global South and in actual negotiations.

All three emerging powers have been able to use the present *trade regime* to their advantage. At the same time, expectations, and certainly hopes, have been high in the Western world that they would take on the roles of system supporters and responsible stakeholders, not least by sharing the burden of maintaining the system. Despite this confluence of apparent self-interests and external role prescriptions, it is far from obvious that the emerging economies themselves ascribe to such role conceptions. *Brazil* has, as a leader of the G-20, used distributive bargaining tactics and a language of 'rebellion and substantive revision' in its statements (Narlikar 2013, p. 570), indicating a revisionist role conception. In the 2008 negotiations, however, its strong support for a compromise between North and South may indicate that it has realized that its status as an exporter of agriculture can only be advanced in a multilateral system and that it is increasingly adopting the role as a supporter of the present regime. If this is the case, the EU may in Brazil find an ally and a fellow-bridge-builder, rather than a challenger. *India* has continued to act as a staunch critic of the Western-led system, and its revisionist role has been manifested in confrontational language and tough bargaining behaviour. Outsiders conceive of *China's* role in the WTO mainly as a free rider that has been loath to take on leadership responsibilities. The fact that China is today part of the inner decision-making circles may, however, turn China into more of an active participant.

While the *USA* for natural reasons is a supporter of the present system as long as it serves its own interests, it is not perceived as a devoted multilateralist. The *EU* has played that role, especially in the period up to 2006 when it upheld a moratorium on new negotiations on bilateral agreements as a matter of principle. Things have changed, however, and the EU is today seeking to negotiate numerous bilateral and regional agreements, as does the USA, challenging outsiders' expectations that it will act as a defender of the multilateral regime. The ultimate step in this direction was the launch of the negotiations between the EU and the USA themselves on a Transatlantic Trade and Investment Partnership.

Brazil's role profile in *relation to the global South* is multifaceted. Its part in creating the G-20 reflects its role conception as a Third World leader. Furthermore, its assumption of a mediator role in Geneva 2008 mirrors another, potentially competing, role, namely that of a bridge-builder between North and South. *India's* coalition-building behaviour more distinctly reveals the pre-eminence of the role as 'prominent member of the Third World community'. It is an important spokesman for all developing countries in the WTO, despite the fact that its trade-related interests differ from most of the poorest countries. *China* is also double-hatted in both playing the role of a Third World country and of an emerging great power. Many poor countries have difficulties in seeing China as one of them, and growth economies (including Brazil and India) often perceive it as a competitor, rather than an ally.

While the *USA* was reluctant to the idea of having a WTO development round, the *EU* embraced this approach wholeheartedly. This reflects a difference in role conceptions: the EU sees itself as a partner in development, also in trade negotiations, while the USA wishes to keep trade separated from developmental concerns, or has a different conception of the relationship between trade and development. In its official policy, the European Union strives for 'policy coherence for development', indicating that its trade policies should take into account development policy objectives (Stocchetti 2013). This 'benign partner' view of the EU is, however, not always shared by the developing countries it negotiates with (cf. Sheahan *et al.* 2010).

In the 2008 negotiations, none of the players can be claimed to have pursued a leadership role. Both the USA and India contributed to the final negotiation failure, and can, therefore, be seen as spoilers while China stayed aloof from the most heated discussions, demonstrating its reluctance to assume leadership responsibilities. Brazil and the EU both took on the role of mediators and tried to convince other actors to accept the compromise proposal at hand. Arguably, the EU has in general reacted to the changing context by becoming more a mediator than a leader. The propensity of the emerging powers to portray themselves as part of a Southern coalition poses, however, a challenge to the EU and its attempts to act as a mediator have only been partly successful. Still, overtures such as those Brazil showed in Geneva might suggest possibilities for future constructive co-operation.

Conclusion: role uncertainty and challenges to the EU

Major changes in the distribution of power have taken place in multilateral trade negotiations. We have described how this has been reflected in the composition of the inner decision-making circle of the WTO, and in the emergence of rising powers as veto powers. We argue that this transformation has resulted in increasing gaps between role conceptions and others' role expectations. The emerging powers' unwillingness to take on leadership responsibilities has been confronted by the Western powers expectations that they should become 'responsible stakeholders'. The EU's leadership aspirations have been thwarted by the rise of powers with markedly divergent positions on many issues and with an image of the EU as a defender of Western interests, together with the USA. Its traditional role as a champion of multilateralism is challenged by trends of bilateralism and regionalism, which now, in a break with previous tradition, also involves negotiations on agreements between major powers.

We furthermore contend that such discrepancies result in *role uncertainty*. Regarding system-related roles, this is mirrored by the uncertainty surrounding the future roles of the rising powers: will they adopt a system-supporting role or will they turn into revisionists, either by trying to reform the present system or by trying to overthrow it? Uncertainty also reigns about how emerging powers will relate to the broader South. Up till now, they have attempted a precarious balancing act between roles as members – or leaders – of the Third World and roles as commercial great powers. Can such double roles be maintained in the face of increasingly divergent interests? Finally, uncertainty is also prevalent regarding roles in actual negotiations. Is anyone willing to assume a leadership role when negotiations reopen? Will Brazil and the EU continue to act as mediators? Will China take on a more active role in future negotiations? Are the USA and India prepared to once again act as spoilers if a new deal, supported by a global majority, seems to be in reach?

Pervasive role uncertainty creates a challenging environment. For the EU, which as a result of its own history has been heavily committed to integrative and value-creating negotiations and to multilateral solutions, the new environment is particularly challenging and arguably much less hospitable than the situation that existed before the rise of the new powers (Smith 2013). Its leadership ambitions and its aspiration to be a normative power are not part of others' role expectations and meet with resistance. Arguably, the EU is in a process of reviewing its objectives and adopting more 'realistic' role conceptions, as it has done in climate change negotiations (Bäckstrand and Elgström 2013). The current economic crisis, which tends to undermine external perceptions of EU power and weaken the EU's bargaining strength, makes such a prediction even more likely.

Notes

1. The empirical sections draw on existing accounts of the negotiations as well as the personal experiences of one of the authors (Ahnlid), who served as Sweden's member of the EU Trade Policy Committee 2005–2011. The views expressed in this article do not necessarily reflect the official opinion of the Swedish government.

2. By July 2008, the WTO G-20 had 23 members: Argentina, Bolivia, Brazil, Chile, China, Cuba, Ecuador, Egypt, Guatemala, India, Indonesia, Mexico, Nigeria, Pakistan, Paraguay, Peru, Philippines, South Africa, Tanzania, Thailand, Uruguay, Venezuela and Zimbabwe.

References

Aggestam, K., 2006. Role theory and European foreign policy: a framework of analysis. *In*: O. Elgström and M. Smith, eds. *The European Union's roles in international politics*. London: Routledge, 11–29.

Ahnlid, A., 2005. Setting the global trade agenda: the European Union and the launch of the Doha Round. *In*: O. Elgström and C. Jönsson, eds. *European Union negotiations: processes, networks and institutions*. London: Routledge, 130–147.

Ahnlid, A., 2012. Improving the effectiveness of multilateral trade negotiations: a practitioner's perspective on the 2008 WTO ministerial meeting. *International Negotiation*, 17 (1), 65–89.

Amorim, C., 2008. Too serious for trade ministers? Interview in *Newsweek Magazine*, 1 August.

Bäckstrand, K. and Elgström, O., 2013. The EU's role in climate change negotiations: from leader to 'leadiator'. *Journal of European Public Policy*, 20 (10), 1369–1386.

Blustein, P., 2009. *Misadventures of the most favored nations*. New York: Public Affairs.

Breuning, M., 2011. Role theory research in international relations: state of the art and blind spots. *In*: S. Harnisch, C. Frank and H.W. Maull, eds. *Role theory in international relations*. Abingdon: Routledge, 16–35.

Bridges Weekly Trade News Digest. 2006. Lamy sets end-June deadline for AG, NAMA modalities. 31 May, Vol. 10, No. 19.

Burges, S.W., 2013. Brazil as a bridge between old and new powers? *International Affairs*, 89 (3), 577–594.

Das, D., 2004. *Free-trade rhetoric and reality*. Munich: Ifo Institute, Center for Economic Studies. Forum 4.

Dormandy, X., 2007. Is India, or will it be, a responsible stakeholder? *Washington Quarterly*, 30 (3), 117–130.

Elgström, O., 2007. Outsiders' perception of the EU in international trade negotiations. *Journal of Common Market Studies*, 45 (4), 959–967.

Elgström, O. and Smith, M., 2006. Introduction. *In*: O. Elgström and M. Smith, eds. *The European Union's roles in international politics*. London: Routledge, 1–10.

Folz, R., 2011. Does membership matter? Convergence of Sweden's and Norway's role conceptions by interaction with the European Union. *In*: S. Harnisch, C. Frank and H.W. Maull, eds. *Role theory in international relations*. Abingdon: Routledge, 147–164.

Hanrahan, C. and Schnepf, R., 2005. *WTO Doha Round: agricultural negotiating proposals*. Congressional Research Service Report for Congress, Washington, DC, 9 November.

Harnisch, S., 2011. Role theory: operationalization of key concepts. *In*: S. Harnisch, C. Frank and H.W. Maull, eds. *Role theory in international relations*. Abingdon: Routledge, 7–15.

Heydon, K., 2006. *After the WTO Hong Kong ministerial meeting: what is at stake*. OECD Trade Policy Working Paper No. 27. Paris: OECD Publishing.

Ikenberry, G.J., 2008. The rise of China and the future of the West: can the liberal system survive? *Foreign Affairs*, 87 (1), 23–37.

Ismail, F., 2007. The G20 and NAMA 11: the role of developing countries in the WTO Doha Round. Lecture at the *Global Economic Governance Program Seminar Series on Making Globalization Work for Developing Countries*, Oxford, 23 November.

Lamy, P., 2003. *European Communities, Commission*. Statement by Mr. Pascal Lamy, Commissioner for Trade before the WTO ministerial conference in Cancun, 10 September, WT/MIN(03)ST/5.

Lamy, P., 2006. *Statement by Mr. Pascal Lamy, Commissioner for Trade, before the informal meeting of heads of delegation*. 24 July. Available from: http://www.wto.org/english/news_e/news06_e/tnc_dg_stat_24july06_e.htm

Layne, C., 2012. This time it's real: the end of unipolarity and the Pax Americana. *International Studies Quarterly*, 56 (1), 203–213.

Mandelson, P., 2006. *Brazil and the global economy*. Speech by EU Commissioner Mandelson, Sao Paulo, 11 September.

Mandelson, P., 2008. EU Trade Commissioner Peter Mandelson's Geneva blog, 21–29 July. Available from: http://www.trade.ec.europa.eu/doclib/docs/2008/august/tradoc_140024.pdf [accessed 5 October 2013].

McGuire, S. and Lindeque, J., 2010. The diminishing returns to trade policy in the European Union. *Journal of Common Market Studies*, 48 (5), 1329–1349.
Meunier, S., 2007. Managing globalization? The EU in international trade negotiations. *Journal of Common Market Studies*, 45 (4), 905–926.
Mortensen, J., 2009. The world trade organization and the European Union. *In*: K.-E. Jørgensen, ed. *The European Union and international organizations*. London: Routledge, 80–100.
Narlikar, A., 2013. India rising: responsible to whom? *International Affairs*, 89 (3), 595–614.
Patrick, S., 2010. Irresponsible stakeholders? The difficulty of integrating rising powers. *Foreign Affairs*, 89 (1), 44–53.
Poletti, A., 2012. *The European Union and multilateral trade governance*. London: Routledge.
Schirm, S., 2012. Leaders in need of followers: emerging powers in global governance. *In*: E. Fels, J.-F. Kremer and K. Kronenberg, eds. *Power in the 21th century: international security and international political economy in a changing world*. Heidelberg: Springer, 211–236.
Schweller, R., 2011. Emerging powers in an age of disorder. *Global Governance*, 17 (3), 285–297.
Shambaugh, D., 2013. *China goes global: The partial power*. Oxford: Oxford University Press.
Sheahan, L., Chaban, N., Elgström, O. and Holland, M., 2010. Economic partnership agreement negotiations between the European Union and the Pacific Islands. *European Foreign Affairs Review*, 15 (3), 347–366.
Smith, M., 2013. Beyond the comfort zone: internal crisis and external challenge in the European Union's response to rising powers. *International Affairs*, 89 (3), 653–672.
Srinivasan, T., 2000. *Developing countries and the multilateral trading system: from the GATT to the Uruguay Round and the future*. Boulder, CO: Westview Press.
Stocchetti, M., 2013. *Inside the European consensus on development and trade: analysing the EU's normative power and policy coherence for development in global governance*. Doctoral Dissertation, Department of Political and Economic Studies, University of Helsinki.
Van den Hoven, A., 2004. Assuming leadership in multilateral economic institutions. *West European Politics*, 27 (2), 256–283.
Van den Hoven, A., 2006. European Union regulatory capitalism and multilateral trade negotiations. *In*: S. Lucarelli and I. Manners, eds. *Values and principles in European Union foreign policy*. London: Routledge, 185–200.
Wolfe, R., 2009. *Sprinting during a marathon: Why the WTO ministerial failed in July 2008*. SciencesPo, Groupe d'Economie Mondiale, April.
Zartmann, I.W., ed., 1994. *International multilateral negotiation*. San Francisco, CA: Jossey-Bass.
Zheng, B., 2005. China's 'peaceful rise' to great-power status. *Foreign Affairs*, September/October.
Zoellick, R., 2003. America will not wait for the won't-do countries. *Financial Times*, 22 September.
Zoellick, R., 2005. *Whither China: from membership to responsibility?* Remarks to National Committee on US-China Relations, New York City, 21 September.

Tensions in the discourse and practice of the European Union's Aid for Trade

Patrick Holden

School of Government, Plymouth University, Plymouth, UK

The contemporary global Aid for Trade (AfT) agenda emerged out of world trade negotiations and it could have profound implications for the future of development aid, depending on how it is interpreted. The European Union (EU) has recontextualised this global agenda to suit its own approach to trade and development; specifically a focus on regional integration, and free market but 'pro-poor' development models. AfT is ascribed a variety of purposes in EU texts and its use continues to adapt as the EU's trade and development policy evolves. Institutionally the AfT framework has not strongly affected EU processes, organisational structures or methodology. A study of the use of EU aid for regional integration reveals dissonance between its development relationship and its trade policies while a focus on pro-poor AfT reveals a lack of capacity. Overall, there are tensions not just between discourse and practice but between different discourses of the EU.

Introduction

This article analyses the dynamics of the European Union's (EU's) trade and development policy in the twenty-first century through the prism of its Aid for Trade (AfT) policy. The concept of AfT came to global prominence with the launch of the Doha Development Round of World Trade Organization (WTO) talks in 2001. It is unclear what this concept represents in terms of international trade and development policy because the definition of AfT is very broad. It may be conceived of as an instrument to support trade agreements or a means of compensating for the iniquities of the global system. There are also uncertainties as to the AfT agenda's relationship to broader international development cooperation regimes and to aid policy norms. As a pioneer in combining trade and development, the EU might be expected to warmly embrace the global AfT initiative and this article explores how it has interpreted and implemented the agenda. In doing so it seeks to further light on the EU as a development actor and its relationship to global development governance.

While it is important in itself, a study of EU AfT policy can also shed light on our understanding of the EU's broader approach to trade and development. Of course, it should be noted that the trade–development nexus covers a wide range of policy areas (trade preferences, sustainability issues, policy space, human rights policy and so forth), and the aid–trade link is just one exemplar of how the two concepts interact. As implied above this article analyses how the global AfT initiative (which was the outcome of a compromise between different geoeconomic interests within the WTO) has been implemented by the EU. It asks whether the AfT agenda has changed EU aid and trade policy, and evaluates the coherence of the response of the EU system. This study is oriented around two themes or tensions within the AfT programme:

first, free trade-based neoliberalism versus a more 'interventionist' vision of development and, second, in regard to development aid policy, aid for export-led growth versus a human development/poverty reduction focus. The argument is based on a comprehensive analysis of policy documents and leaders' speeches; as well as 12 in-depth interviews with EU officials, other aid agencies and Non-Governmental Organisations (NGOs). The methodology is based on David Fairclough's critical discourse analysis (CDA) (Fairclough 2003) which analyses discourse (language) in the context of other actions, processes and 'facts' in general (the other elements of 'policy'). First the global AfT initiative, and the hopes and fears for this form of aid are explained. This is followed by an analysis of the political and policy discourse of the EU on AfT, which is then supplemented by a study of the institutional and funding changes, with special reference to the EU's declared speciality in regional integration and pro-poor aid.

The ambiguous AfT agenda and the role of the EU

The term AfT is broad and malleable precisely because it emerged as a result of (well-known) political disputes between the Global South and the Global North in the multilateral trading system. Developing countries felt that the General Agreement on Tariffs and Trade (GATT), and later the WTO, had marginalised their interests. They wanted to revisit aspects of the Uruguay Round (1994) and the push for new forms of trade liberalisation in the 1990s led to fierce opposition (Wilkinson 2006). It was clear that a sustained political and diplomatic campaign on the part of the wealthier states would be needed to gain any traction in the launch of a new round and AfT was a part of this. In the Doha declaration of 2001, AfT was cited as one area to be developed and as part of an effort to break a log-jam in negotiations a 'task force' – which included the EU and 12 other states and regional organisations, mostly developing states – was launched in 2005, to clarify the framework and guidelines for AfT. The Task Force defined the following as AfT (WTO 2006):

1. Technical assistance and capacity building for trade policy (to help countries negotiate and/or to implement trade agreements).
2. Trade development (assistance with trade promotion, market analysis and other forms of support for private sector businesses).
3. Assistance in dealing with trade-related adjustment costs.
4. Development of the productive capacities of the economy of the recipient state.
5. Development of trade-related infrastructure.
6. Other trade-related issues.

The WTO Secretariat and the DAC (Development Assistance Committee of the Organisation for Economic Cooperation and Development (OECD)) were given the task of promoting best practice and monitoring the adoption of AfT principles by aid donors (DAC 2009). This is challenging as the 'definition' is so broad that it includes many different forms of aid. There are a number of implicit purposes of AfT: to support growth, to help the poor in particular, to help the global economy, to compensate for the impact of trade agreements and to help negotiate and implement trade agreements (the original focus of donors). The general significance is that AfT, as defined here, goes beyond the latter to include more direct forms of development aid, for example, investment in infrastructure to enable countries to benefit from these agreements. Of course exactly what the priorities should be or what degree of intervention is required is left unclear as there was no agreement, and indeed probably could not be on the global scale (Page 2006). There are also potential tensions regarding the AfT agenda and development policy norms of poverty reduction and human development. Furthermore, there is a concern that AfT could be used by donor countries to skew their aid for their own economic interests, contrary to the official developmental norms especially in the wake of the global financial crisis (2008 on) which put pressure on western governments to use aid to support their own economies (Interview, NGOs in Dublin and Brussels March 2012/London November 2012).

To a significant degree, the AfT agenda was in line with the EU's own policies (Bilal and Rampa 2009, pp. 63–64). The EU was a pioneer in using development and trade relationships (Grilli 1993). One vital element of this was its complex series of trade preferences with various developing regions, notably with the Africa, Caribbean and Pacific (ACP) states. It also offered a General System of Preferences scheme for all developing countries. To this it added the Everything but Arms initiative for all least developed countries (LDCs) which was to grant them duty-free access to the EU market (Faber and Orbie 2009), for practically all products. Also, via its Policy Coherence for Development agenda the EU had committed to aligning its aid, trade and other policies for development (European Commission (EC) 2005). Its development aid was not always strongly focused on trade-related issues – at least not in the ACP, there had been a greater focus in Mediterranean and ex-Communist countries (Holden 2009) – but this had been changing since the Cotonou Agreement of 2001. Said agreement outlined its attempt to foster controversial Economic Partnership Agreements (EPAs) with its ACP partners. These were controversial because they involved reciprocal free trade rather than just offering them preferences and they were expansive in scope, going beyond trade in goods to other trade and regulatory themes (Curran et al. 2008). As a part of this process, the EU agreed to give substantial economic assistance to its prospective partners. Thus the AfT agenda could be easily translated into ongoing EU policy objectives but there were some challenging elements. The more expansive definition of AfT went beyond its tendency to define AfT as technical assistance. The greater voice of developing countries in regard to aid policy was ostensibly in line with EU values but potentially awkward, as, like other actors, it uses aid for its own particular agenda. The rest of this article analyses how the EU has adjusted to this new global aid initiative.

The meaning of the AfT initiative: a basic analytical and research framework

The AfT agenda has received much criticism from various perspectives. Some critique the expansive nature of the agenda and would prefer a more rigorous focus on technical assistance and impact evaluation (Hallaert 2013). Others argue that the funding has been insufficient (Stiglitz and Charlton 2012), while it is also critiqued as an effort to 'interlock aid and trade policies' in favour of the latter (Langan and Scott 2013, p. 8). This article contributes to these debates, and to global politics more generally, by focusing on how the global agenda has been interpreted by one donor, the EU. Two tensions have already been noted. First, aspects of AfT may challenge neoliberal theory, as in the doctrine of non-intervention in market dynamics (Hayek 1962, Friedman 2002). In terms of 'real world' policy choices, pro free-trade neoliberals such as Bhagwati (2004) would encourage AfT to support trade agreements and would not object to other aid, but the proposition that aid for infrastructure is a precondition for trade liberalisation sits uncomfortably with neoliberal precepts. This interpretation of the AfT agenda fits more with a range of interventionist approaches, which argue for a more strategic or 'managed' approach to international trade (Krugman 1986, Wade 2003, Stiglitz and Charlton 2006). A definitive argument on this point is beyond the scope of this article but they are two overarching paradigms which must inform any study. A second tension has also been noted between aid for export-led growth, and the mainstream consensus that development policy needed to focus less on aggregate economic growth and more on poverty reduction and human development (Ul Haq 1996). NGOs calling for AfT always stressed the need to focus it on the poor (Dóchas 2006, p. 10), but the task force report implied a strong focus on export-led growth. More generally, beyond development models, the global nature of the AfT regime is of note as it signifies a commitment to a universal development agenda as opposed to particularistic, and possibly competitive, statist and regional visions (Hynes and Holden 2013). Of course in practice, global norms and discourse are always recontextualised/adjusted when applied at different levels (Fairclough 2010). When we consider the EU's actual implementation, one must always consider its problematic coherence, in terms of its institutions and policies (Carbone 2008). In brief one would not expect this global agreement to be transplanted in total or to have effected a paradigmatic transformation of aid policy. On the other hand, one would expect such a high profile agreement to have at least some impact.

The approach adopted is based on CDA, which conceives of discourse (and specific *discourses:* coherent sets of vocabulary, logics, narratives and assumptions) as dialectically interlinked with reality. Thus, CDA involves an analysis of texts combined with a broader empirical analysis (Fairclough 2003, pp. 2–3). The first part of the discourse analysis is a standard qualitative study of the EU's language on AfT. This is applied to shed light on how the broader global AfT agenda has been implemented at the European level; in particular whether its conception of the link between trade and development aid has altered in the period in question and how this is affecting its behaviour. The linguistic analysis is informed by a factual analysis (of changes to aid structures, processes and funding priorities) in this period. Interviews were undertaken served both to explore in more depth the discourse and ideas of individual policy-makers and to supplement the factual research on funding and policy priorities. Although Fairclough uses CDA as a counter-hegemonic methodology to critique capitalist power structures, any sense of a monolithically hegemonic discourse is problematic in this case, given the fluidity of the term and its multiple ownership. While their theoretical approach is not adopted, the poststructuralist concept of a 'floating signifier' (Laclau and Mouffe 1985, pp. 113–141) has descriptive utility when it comes to understanding AfT. A floating signifier is a concept that has no fixed meaning, and its political utility flows from this variable and nebulous nature (it is always replete with possibilities and easily adaptable).

EU AfT discourse

The EU had always used the term 'trade-related assistance' (TRA) when referring to aid and trade issues. This denoted technical assistance/capacity building for reform of trade policy and involvement in trade negotiations, and trade development as well as other technical assistance: in other words Sections 1, 2 and 6 of the AfT Task Force categories. EU aid for infrastructure and private sector development was, of course, intended to support export-led growth but had not been described as AfT. Since the Doha ministerial and the Task Force report in particular the term AfT entered EU terminology. In 2007, the major policy response of the EU to this agreement emerged. The Commission released a communication on AfT in 2007 (EC 2007). It welcomed the report and the definition of the WTO Task Force but it retained its own terminology of TRA.[1] It also declared more substantial policy objectives. The Council of the EU effectively endorsed this AfT strategy later that year (Council 2007). This was a joint strategy of the EU and its member states.

This strategy document made some key commitments which reaffirmed the EU's role. Predictably the document argued that the EU's special focus in regard to AfT should be at the regional level and concerning the ACP countries in particular. In particular, it reaffirmed its interest in supporting regional integration. Thus, the general AfT agenda was recontextualised by the EU in terms of its own long-running interest in regional integration and its new ambitious inter-regional integration schemes for the ACP. The strategy document also committed to focus this form of EU aid more on poverty reduction. The poverty reduction discourse had entered the EU's (and other donor's) aid policy agenda as part of a recognition that a focus on aggregate economic growth has, even where successful, had limited impact on the poorest within developing societies. It is also often linked with a much broader non-utilitarian conception of development which goes beyond monetary income. There were implicit tensions here with the mainstream trade and regional integration focus of the document. AfT implies a focus on export-led growth, the full development of the stronger sectors of the economy, which will inevitably not involve the poorest. Also, aid for regional integration is not directed at the poor as a rule but rather at macro-level economic integration, either in regard to trade or functional sectors (see below). The strategy does not offer any hint of how these differing priorities might be realised.

The most high profile element of this strategy was a specific commitment to increase funding (from the EU aid funds as well as member states), however it should be noted that this commitment was made with regard to TRA, not AfT as a whole. TRA was to rise to €2 billion annually by 2010 (€1 billion from EU budget, €1 billion from EU states). Furthermore, the strategy re-emphasised the EU's role (the EC in particular) in monitoring; in helping to lead, and support developing country participation in the global review and in monitoring within the EU. It established an intra-EU monitoring mechanism via Annual AfT Monitoring Reports produced by the EC. This further consolidated the role the EC had established as leader of European development cooperation in general via involvement in other global development community initiatives (notably the UN-led Financing for Development initiative launched at Monterrey in 2002). The EC would integrate a report on European AfT into the annual EU Accountability Report on Financing for Development. These various reports and initiatives amount to an embryonic intra-European form of peer pressure and norm promotion, analogous to that which occurs within the DAC of the OECD (Pagani 2002).

This initial implementation of the AfT agenda took place in an era dominated by failing multilateral trade talks and increasingly acrimonious EPA negotiations. Most references to this form of aid took place in the context of discussions on EPAs. A major challenge put to the EU was that trade liberalisation between entities at such different levels of development would be detrimental to ACP countries. The EU's response was to offer transition periods, some exemptions and aid (Mandelson 2006, Ashton 2009). It emphasised the need for a comprehensive approach combining flexible legal arrangements, trade and investment as well as aid. The latter was vital in emphasising EU solidarity and trying to avoid the impression that it was engaged in an ideologically driven, free market-based initiative: 'While trade is an indispensable instrument for growth and poverty reduction, we all know that trade reforms do not automatically lead to sustainable and equitable Development' (Michel 2006). EU leaders also stressed the regional integration element of their AfT, as in supporting trade between ACP countries, separate from European interests. The general narrative put forward by the EU (since the 1990s) was that the pre-existing preferences for ACP countries had not worked, and that globalisation presented new opportunities, as well as challenges, for developing countries and the EU would help them make the best of this (EC 2002). Aid is understood as a vital force to help reform and also presented as an inducement to sign agreements.

A basic content analysis conducted of EU texts shows that AfT is ascribed a variety of similar, but distinctive, purposes. An analysis of 127 Commissioner speeches from 2004 to 2013 (sourced from the EC's Rapid database) showed that the primary objective of this form of aid is supporting *growth* (mentioned 41 times) while aid to adjust to trade liberalisation is the next most frequent, with 18 mentions. The purpose of achieving trade agreements/liberalisation is cited less often (9 times). When it comes to policy documents on trade and development growth is still the most common ascribed objective but poverty reduction is almost as prominent. As outlined below, new rationales for AfT also emerged over time.

Soon after the EU's official strategy was agreed we entered the era of economic crisis and global rebalancing which affected the EU and the global AfT agenda in several ways. The

Lisbon Treaty, ratified in 2009 also altered the legal basis for EU development policy but not in policy specific ways. The accelerated rise in the relative weight of emerging economic powers stimulated a new debate as to the future of development aid and the appropriate policies towards 'Middle Income Countries' (Koch 2012, pp. 3–12). The crisis and global rebalancing saw the EC (the Trade and Development Co-Operation directorates) outline new principles for development and trade and development policy (EC 2012a). In essence this involves refocusing trade preferences on poorer countries, 'leading on AfT' is discussed but aid is not the main focus. Despite some hints of protectionism and a more combative 'realist' approach the EU has retained, for the moment, a globalist attitude to trade policy which is also reflected in its conception of AfT (Orbie and De Ville 2011, Siles-Brügge 2011). At the AfT Policy Dialogue in 2013, Trade Commissioner Karel de Gucht, articulated the view that there is an inextricable link between global trade and development (citing in particular the role of trade in transnationalised production): 'Trade is now at the heart of the way goods are produced ... no economic strategy worth its salt can afford to ignore it' (De Gucht 2013). De Gucht here articulates a more comprehensive sense of AfT as a global public good to aid global development, North and South. In the face of the global recession which followed the financial crisis, this function of AfT began to emerge at the highest level, amidst general discussions of global stimulus. Notably the G-20 declaration at the Seoul Summit of 2010 included a commitment to maintain spending on AfT. In the same speech, the concern to make AfT more pro-poor is reiterated but (as outlined in the subsection below) the practical impact of this is debatable.

Apart from its explicit 'trade and development' policy the crisis also spurred the EU to reshape its development policy more generally. The Commission published the Agenda for Change in 2012 (EC 2011a). Here again the major focus was on 'differentiated development partnerships' and re-focussing aid on poorer countries (ibid., p. 9). AfT has a special role to play here, with a new determination to make it pro-poor, albeit with an unclear means of implementation (see details in later section). Involving the private sector more in AfT (planning, contributing and evaluating) is also a new focus although needless to add there are many concerns here about how this would work. Generally there is a sense that development policy is moving beyond aid. There are two key reasons for this: the increasing number of countries with development challenges but growing economies and healthy balance sheets (where a case can be made that financial assistance is not the primary need) and the acute budget constraints on the EU and its member states.

Thus the EU's response to the global AfT initiative reinforced its own regional integration project and its role as a norm promoter and monitor. It co-opted standard development policy 'poverty reduction' discourse but is dominated by free trade, export-led growth and regional integration considerations. This document remained the template for the EU's approach to AfT over the period in question. The EU has highlighted its importance as an AfT donor in relation to its role in global economic cooperation more generally. In the face of unprecedented economic challenges the EU's trade and development policies were reformulated and the importance of AfT was reiterated. However, the policy was not further specified, with no new initiatives planned and no major reformulation that would explain how AfT fits into the EU's new trade and development posture. Essentially the EU retained the ambiguity (as to the relative priorities of AfT) of the original initiative.

AfT in practice: institutions and funding

The Commission/EU aid apparatus has been frequently reformed and the most recent restructuring (in 2011) fused different policy and implementation bodies into one Development Cooperation Directorate General (DG Devco).[2] AfT is distributed through a large number of geographical and thematic aid instruments within this DG. One small unit in the DG Devco (C4) is responsible for specific 'horizontal' AfT policy matters (as well as support for the private sector and trade more generally). This gives advice on trade-related issues and produces the EU's official AfT material (notably the monitoring reports). However, the major flows of aid are managed according to the strategy, guidelines and culture of the various instruments (notably the European Development Fund (EDF), the Development Cooperation Instrument and the European Neighbourhood and Partnership Instrument). The AfT unit then translates this into 'AfT language' for reporting purposes. The general institutional structure, monitoring and evaluation processes continue as before. The new European External Action Service also has a role in aid management but its role will focus more on country/region strategies while the EC will play the main role in policy formulation (and it retains competence over trade matters and other relevant economic portfolios).

Not everyone agrees that the AfT agenda requires a re-haul of organisational structures; some view the AfT categories as primarily a means of tracing statistics (Interview OECD, September 2012). However, extending the definition of AfT to include broader categories of aid did imply a broader more holistic approach to using aid in support of trade. The problems of continuing with 'business as usual' in terms of structures and methodology are most apparent when it comes to the (crucial) issue of evaluation. There are considerable challenges in pinning down any kind of causality in terms of the impact of AfT on actual trade performance (OECD 2011). This is a perennial problem in aid but particularly so for AfT (given the many types of aid). It is significant that the EC, which completes on average 13 official aid evaluations per annum (from 2005 to 2012), has not ordered a general evaluation of its AfT. It has carried out evaluations on *specific forms* of AfT, notably TRA, private sector development, infrastructure support and regional integration, but there have been none on AfT as a whole for one country. The reluctance to evaluate AfT as a whole is contradictory given the EU's claims as to the importance of this aid and its use as encouragement to developing countries to sign trade agreements with it. The EU has supported the development of common indicators for topics such as private sector support but individuals within the Commission are much less enthusiastic about using these (Interview EC, 29 March to 30 March 2012). When it comes to programming the template for developing aid strategies requires only a minor analysis of the countries trading situation, with little on the potential.[3] Actual country and regional strategies vary widely in terms of the attention and detail which they pay to trade-related issues (apart from standard analyses related to regional integration and the EU's proposed EPAs). All of this implies that the impact of the AfT agenda – for better or worse – on the EU's organisation and methods has been limited. It is not the case that this agenda, and its guidelines, have affected the ideological character of EU aid (in terms of the degree of interventionism versus the uses of aid for free-market policies).

AfT is imperfectly aligned with the standard categories of aid (notably the DAC Creditor Reporting System/CRS) used for reporting and statistical purposes. The DAC developed a methodology to measure AfT levels by mapping the aid onto its standard categories but this can be problematic. For example, AfT category 4 (development of trade-related infrastructure) is measured by the assistance reported as aid for infrastructure (CRS category 21–23) but many would challenge whether all aid for infrastructure is really aid for *trade-related* infrastructure. Indeed, most of the policy-makers (from three different institutions) interviewed in the course of this research pointed out that the statistics on AfT were often disputed. With these caveats in mind let us turn to the EU's funding levels.

Within the EU institutions, the totemic element of the EU's commitment to AfT is the €2 billion target for TRA (Interviews EC and Parliament, April 2012). The Aid for Trade Monitoring Report (AfTMR) is the primary source of statistics on AfT and, as outlined in the 2011

AfTMR, the EU can demonstrate that it and its member states have kept this commitment. However, this TRA (for which the statistics are clear) was not the most important part of the AfT agenda for developing countries. There has also been a significant increase in EU and European AfT on the whole [4] (EC 2011b, p. 8). The EU and its member states as a whole committed nearly 10.7 billion in total in 2010; this amounts to approximately 32% of global AfT and more than any other single actor or cluster or grouping of donors. EU-managed AfT increased from €2.117 billion commitments in 2005 to €3.298 billion in 2009, but then dipped to 2.520 billion in 2010 (EC 2012b, p. 10). The largest increase is in the building productive capacity sector but this is the broadest and vaguest category of aid, and theoretically only those activities included as part of an agreed trade development strategy with aid recipients should be included but in practice donors include all of their funding within this CRS line. As Table 1 illustrates, aid classed as support for adjustment amounts to a tiny proportion of the overall total. While the EU can demonstrate an increase in AfT for Africa, the share of LDCs on the whole of EU-managed AfT remains very low: 22% in 2010 (EC 2012b, p. 29).[5] This is surprising when one considers the alleged importance of LDCs and poverty reduction in the WTO AfT agenda, and again implies that the EU's adoption of the global guidelines has been partial.

Regional and 'pro-poor' specialists?

The EU's special focus on regional AfT is intrinsically linked to its broader trade agenda, notably its efforts to reach inter-regional EPAs. The EU's explicit commitment to AfT does potentially give developing countries greater leverage to negotiate aid level and may in that sense advance development partnerships. Heron notes that a reason given by CARIFORUM (a Caribbean grouping of states) policy-makers for signing a full EPA was to acquire increased aid from the EU (Heron 2011, p. 331). These talks were occurring around the time of the '2 billion' announcement of the EU, which may have raised expectations. However, he also noted that:

> despite numerous references to 'development cooperation' in the text – 'development cooperation' and 'cooperation' appear in the text 13 times and 135 times respectively – the financial component of the CARIFORUM agreement remains almost entirely unbound. (Heron 2011, p. 331)

Other regions have been more circumspect and argued for more specific commitments. For example, in West Africa, the local organisations developed their own comprehensive EPA Development Programme (EPADP, often known by the French acronym PAPED) over 2007 and 2008. This outlined the local stakeholders' agreed priorities (and precise funding levels) for the European (EU and member state) assistance needed to accompany a putative free-trade agreement (ECDPM 2010). The EU Council offered a declaration in support of this (but this is still less than a legal commitment).

Table 1. A breakdown of EU-managed AfT (€ thousands).

	2009	2010	2011
1. Trade policy and regulation	315,655	145,111	320,332
2. Trade development	262,995	451,904	331,602
3. Trade-related infrastructure	1,103,032	950,198	967,446
4. Building productive capacity	1,535,414	1,108,553	973,297
5. Trade-related adjustment	11,312	16,580	30,594
6. Other trade-related needs	332,496	299,605	412,000
Total AfT	3,297,909	2,520,047	2,704,029

Note: The overall total does not include the figure for category 2 as this sum is included in the total for category 4.
Source: EC (2013, p. 72).

Regarding its specific regional aid, the EC divides it into three categories: aid to support regional trade and economic integration within the region (also linked to trade and integration with the EU), aid for functional integration within the region and aid for political institution building. There is no evidence that the AfT agenda affected this approach of the EU, but the first two categories do qualify as AfT. The EDF saw a substantial increase in the amount allocated for regional aid in EDF 10 (for the period 2007–2013). One notes a very large increase for certain areas such as West Africa, with funding of up to 1523 million from 624 million in the last round. This increase was a deliberate political signal to the EU's partners to encourage them to agree an EPA (Interview, EC 29 March 2012). However, very little of this money was spent in the time period intended due to procedural difficulties, which were not helped by political tensions created by the EPA agenda. In West Africa, for example, only 5% had even been committed by March 2012 (ibid.).

Indeed any discussion of aid relationships cannot ignore the broader political and diplomatic controversies of the EPA process. Notwithstanding the EU's elaborate justifications for EPAs, opposition has remained strong. This includes a vigorous civil society campaign (Del Felice 2012), but also resistance from governments (Olivier 2011), and only a limited number of interim agreements were signed in Africa. The EU decided to ratchet up the stakes by giving a deadline (in 2014) for countries to ratify their interim agreements or face a loss of preferences. This approach was condemned by a resolution of the 2012 ACP Council of Ministers, which also noted continue disagreements and mistrust over the developmental benefits of EPAs and the ever-increasing number of issues that the EU sought to include, including taxation and geographical indicators (ACP Council of Ministers 2012). Clearly the use of aid as a political incentive did not work. Officials admit that in some cases the mistrust over EPAs has spilled over into aid relationships (Interview, EC, 28 March 2012). Even where regional aid has been implemented, the fissile effect of the EU's tough economic diplomacy has had a greater impact than any integration assistance. For example, the EU's pressure on countries to sign EPAs has created serious splits in the regional institutions in Southern African and Central Africa, as only some countries have signed interim-EPAs the local customs unions (which should have a common external tariff) have been split (Chanda 2010, p. 20). Given this context, it is not surprising that, as recent EU documents admit, its aid for regional integration has been disappointing: 'We have dedicated substantial funding to regional integration, although results have often fallen short of expectations' (EC 2012a, p. 9).

Making AfT 'pro-poor' is not in itself an ideological position (although the greater targeting of the poor is itself a rejection of crude trickle-down growth strategies). It is, however, a vital part of contemporary development policy and of the EU's development discourse. As such it represents a commitment to a human-centred development project which is particularly significant given the concerns about the AfT agenda expressed previously. However, using AfT in a 'pro-poor' manner is intrinsically difficult as those companies with export potential are normally the larger more successful ones, while large scale infrastructure projects and other categories of AfT are not normally pro-poor in the sense understood by the development community; as in having direct benefits for the poorer elements of society.[6] The UK Department for International Development and the Swedish Ministry for Foreign Affairs funded a project by Overseas Development Institute (ODI 2010) on how to combine AfT with pro-poor/poverty reduction concerns. This provides a methodology for analysing and calculating the impact of AfT on different classes of society. The second phase of the project offers a methodology for programming AfT based on the concepts of disaggregated analysis and differentiated needs (Higgins and Prowse 2010). There is no sign of these methodologies being adapted as an EU standard. Likewise, the focus on regional integration sits uneasily with a declared poverty reduction priority for aid. A United Nations Development Programme report of 2011 recognised the traditional dissonance between regional integration and the pro-poor/human development agenda. It developed a framework for conceptualising and planning interventions to include poverty reduction considerations in support for regional integration (UNDP 2011). There is no sign of these, or equivalent, ideas being adopted by the EC. The EU's new development agenda reiterates the importance of pro-poor AfT as a part of a general package of support for 'small operators' (EC 2011b, p. 10), including reducing red-tape and support for cooperatives and fair-trade networks. Interviews with officials in the development units of the EC revealed no confidence in the institution's ability could translate this pro-poor ideal into reality.

Conclusion

The agreement on the global AfT agenda was a landmark event in the global governance of trade and development. A potentially important feature was the explicit recognition of the need for public financial assistance to help adjust to new trading regimes and to enable poorer states to benefit from these. However, notwithstanding its other achievements, the global AfT initiative is not specific enough to have a dramatic impact on aid policy, in the EU's case at least. The AfT agenda has been overshadowed by the evolution of EU's economic position and changes in its trade and development policy more generally. There are tensions, not just between discourse and practice but between different discourses of the EU, notably the global AfT discourse, the regional integration discourse and the pro-poor, human development centred discourse. Much of the EU's declared AfT is reconstructed by the EC from the spending in different regions and it would be a mistake to attribute any coherent global strategy let alone a comprehensive vision of trade and development to this aid. As such this study could not ascribe a specific change, made by the AfT agenda, to the ideology or the trade–development model of the EU. EU AfT policy continues to be characterised by a form of modified neoliberalism, in that it works primarily towards global free-market principles but recognises the need for various forms of public intervention. The AfT initiative has not resulted in a radical change in any direction and the conclusion is that AfT does not function as a hegemonic, monolithic, neoliberal discourse; it functions (in the case of the EU at least) more as a 'floating signifier', adaptable to different discursive and political contexts.

The defining shape of EU AfT policy is its support for regional and inter-regional integration through the EPAs. However, in practice the EU's controversial actions here have contradicted many of its declared objectives and its aid policy has been hampered by these political tensions. When it comes to the question of its actual pro-poor focus, while there is no evidence that EU AfT has led to a decreased focus on the poor neither is there evidence of EU discourse on pro-poor AfT being translated into actual policy and achievements. EU trade and development policy more generally is, as argued elsewhere in this volume, quite fragmented and this fragmentation is evident even in the relatively specific issue of AfT. Policy coherence, as an EU ideal, is as far away as ever and while it might be a laudable normative objective, it is hardly a realistic expectation. On the whole, its leadership role in the global AfT effort is not what one might expect and it has not developed a holistic AfT vision in terms of its institutional structures or programming and evaluation techniques. Clearly the EU's enthusiasm for a global conception of trade and development is not strong enough to over-ride its own institutional and geoeconomic dynamics. This is yet more evidence that the EU, as a development actor, retains its own particularistic agenda, distinct from global norms and the global development community. As such, this article has shown that the hopes *and* the fears the global AfT agenda inspired may thus far be misplaced. It has not, in the EU's case greatly affected its aid policy for better or worse. However, AfT will remain a prominent issue for the developing world, and the EU would do well to engage more fully with their perspectives on this concept. A universal, homogenous conception of AfT is not essential, but a greater level of trust is needed if the EU is to more effectively link its trade and development relationships.

Notes

1. Some highly debatable proposals are made here about reclassifying existing aid. For example, it argues that support for fiscal reforms could be classified as support for adjustment and hence AfT (ibid., p. 5). It is safe to assume that this is not what developing countries had in mind.
2. There is a small AfT programme managed by the Trade DG also.
3. This could be because aid strategies are supposed to be based on partners' trade–development strategies but trade may not be a high priority in some cases.
4. This refers to aid from the EU budget and the EDF although the report also covers member state spending.
5. This is still significantly higher than the EU member states (which averaged a proportion of 15% in this period).
6. In delineating the purpose of aid it is best to focus on immediate outputs and impact as otherwise any eventual outcome can be claimed, which makes any discussion meaningless.

References

ACP Council of Ministers, 2012. *Resolution of the 95th session of ACP council of ministers, Port Villas 13 June.* Available from: http://www.acp.int/content/decisions-resolutions-95th-session-acp-council-ministers-and-37th-session-acp-eu-council-min [accessed 19 November 2013].

Ashton, C., 2009. *Economic partnership agreements – remarks to European Parliament.* Speech/09/139. Available from: http://europa.eu/rapid/search.htm [accessed 19 March 2012].

Bhagwati, J., 2004. *In defence of globalization.* New York: Oxford University Press.

Bilal, S. and Rampa, F., 2009. What does the European experience tell us on aid for trade? *In*: P. De Lombaerde and L. Puri, eds. *Aid for trade: global and regional perspectives.* Bruges: UNU-CRI, 63–85.

Carbone, M., 2008. Mission impossible: the European Union and policy coherence for development. *Journal of European Integration*, 30 (3), 323–342.

Chanda, D., 2010. *Regional integration in southern Africa: focusing on the future of SADC and SACU.* Stellenbosch: Tralac.

Council of the European Union, 2007. *Adoption of an EU strategy on aid for trade.* Brussels 11 October. Available from: http://register.consilium.europa.eu/pdf/en/07/st13/st13070.en07.pdf [accessed 10 March 2012].

Curran, L., Nilsson, L. and Brew, D., 2008. The economic partnership agreements: rationale, misperceptions and non-trade aspects. *Development Policy Review*, 26 (5), 529–553.

DAC (Development Assistance Committee of the OECD), 2009. *Aid for trade at a glance 2009: maintaining momentum.* Paris: OECD.

DAC (Development Assistance Committee of the OECD), 2012. *Aid-for-trade data: creditor reporting system: explanatory note.* Available from: http://www.oecd.org/dataoecd/57/36/43234667.pdf [accessed 10 March 2013].

De Gucht, K., 2013. *Aid for trade: staying in for the long haul.* Speech/13/18, 16 January. Available from: http://europa.eu/rapid/press-release_SPEECH-13-18_en.htm [accessed 19 March 2012].

Del Felice, C., 2012. Power in discursive practices: the case of the STOP EPAs campaign. *European Journal of International Relations*, online first version June 14, 1–23. doi:10.1177/1354066112437769

Dóchas, 2006. *Aid for trade: Dóchas and Irish congress of trade unions submission to Irish aid.* Available from: http://www.dochas.ie/pages/resources/documents/Aid_for_Trade.pdf [accessed 17 February 2012].

EC (European Commission), 2002. *Trade and development: assisting countries to benefit from trade.* COM (2002) 513. Brussels: European Commission.

EC (European Commission), 2005. *Policy coherence for development – accelerating progress towards attaining the millennium development goals.* COM (2005) 134. Brussels: European Commission.

EC (European Commission), 2007. *Towards an EU aid for trade strategy – the Commission's contribution.* COM (2007) 163. Brussels: European Commission.

EC (European Commission), 2011a. *Increasing the impact of EU development policy: an agenda for change*. COM (2011a) 637. Brussels: European Commission.

EC (European Commission), 2011b. *Aid for trade monitoring report 2011 (Annex 6 of the EU Accountability Report 2011 on Financing for Development)*. SEC (2011b) 503. Brussels: European Commission.

EC (European Commission), 2012a. *Trade, growth and development: tailoring trade and investment policy for those countries most in need*. COM (2012a) 22. Brussels: European Commission.

EC (European Commission), 2012b. *Aid for trade monitoring report 2012 (Annex 6 of the EU Accountability Report 2012 on Financing for Development)*. SWD (2012b) 199. Brussels: European Commission.

EC (European Commission), 2013. *Aid for trade report 2013*. SWD (2013) 273. Brussels: European Commission.

ECDPM (European Centre for Development Policy Management), 2010. *The EU commitment to deliver aid for trade in West Africa and support the EPA development programme (PAPED), No. 96 May 2010*. Available from: http://www.ecdpm.org/Web_ECDPM/Web/Content/Download.nsf/0/F7D8B664ACE0F5ACC125771C002CAFBB/$FILE/10-96%20final%20may%2018.pdf [accessed 19 March 2012].

Faber, G. and Orbie, J., 2009. Everything but arms: much more than appears at first sight. *Journal of Common Market Studies*, 47 (4), 767–787.

Fairclough, N., 2003. *Analysing discourse: textual analysis for social research*. London: Routledge.

Fairclough, N., 2010. Discourse and 'transition' in Central and Eastern Europe. *In*: N. Fairclough, ed. *Critical discourse analysis: the critical study of language*. Harlow: Longman, 523–527.

Friedman, M., 2002. *Capitalism and freedom*. Chicago: University of Chicago Press.

Grilli, E., 1993. *The European community and developing countries*. Cambridge: Cambridge University Press.

Hallaert, J., 2013. The future of aid for trade: challenges and options. *World Trade Review*, 12 (4), 653–668.

Hayek, F., 1962. *The road to serfdom*. London: Routledge.

Heron, T., 2011. Asymmetric bargaining and development trade-offs in the CARIFORUM-European union economic partnership agreement. *Review of International Political Economy*, 18 (3), 328–357.

Higgins, K. and Prowse, S. 2010. *Trade, growth and poverty: making aid for trade work for inclusive growth and poverty reduction*. Working Paper 313. London: ODI.

Holden, P., 2009. *In search of structural power: EU aid policy as a global political instrument*. Aldershot: Ashgate.

Hynes, W. and Holden, P., 2013. *What future for the global aid for trade initiative? Towards a fair assessment of its achievements and limitations*. Discussion Paper for the OECD Policy Dialogue 2013/Institute for International Integration Studies Discussion Paper. Available from: http://www.tcd.ie/iiis/publications/discussion-papers.php [accessed 22 March 2012].

Koch, S., 2012. *From poverty reduction to mutual interests? The debate on differentiation in EU development policy*. Discussion Paper. Berlin: Deutsches Institut für Entwicklungspolitik.

Krugman, P., 1986. *Strategic trade policy and the new international economics*. Boston: MIT Press.

Laclau, E. and Mouffe, C., 1985. *Hegemony and socialist strategy. Towards a radical democratic politics*. 2nd ed. London and New York: Verso.

Langan, M. and Scott, J., 2013. The aid for trade charade. *Cooperation and Conflict*, online first version June 6, 1–19. doi:10.1177/0010836713482880

Mandelson, P., 2006. *The challenges and opportunities of the economic partnership agreements*. Speech/06/722. Available from: http://europa.eu/rapid/search.htm [accessed 18 April 2012].

Michel, L., 2006. *Setting a new course in co-operation between Europe and Africa*. Speech/06/129. Available from: http://europa.eu/rapid/search.htm [accessed 9 April 2012].

ODI (Overseas Development Institute), 2010. *Integrating poverty and social analysis into aid for trade programmes: trade policy and regulation*. ODI Brief 2. Available from: http://www.odi.org.uk/resources/docs/6208.pdf [accessed 24 February 2012].

OECD, 2011. *Strengthening accountability in aid for trade: the development dimension*. Paris: OECD.

Olivier, G., 2011. From colonialism to partnership in Africa–Europe relations? *The International Spectator*, 46 (1), 53–67.

Orbie, J. and De Ville, F., 2011. *The European Union's trade policy response to the crisis: paradigm lost or reinforced?* European Integration Online Papers 15. Available from: http://eiop.or.at/eiop/index.php/eiop/article/download/2011_002a/198 [accessed 19 March 2012].

Pagani, F., 2002. Peer review as a tool for co-operation and change. An analysis of an OECD working method. *African Security Review*, 11 (4), 15–24.
Page, S., ed., 2006. *Trade and aid: partners or rivals in development policy?* London: Cameron.
Siles-Brügge, G., 2011. Resisting protectionism after the crisis: strategic economic discourse and the EU–Korea free trade agreement. *New Political Economy*, 16 (5), 627–653.
Stiglitz, J. and Charlton, A., 2006. Aid for trade. *International Journal of Development Issues*, 5 (2), 1–41.
Stiglitz, J. and Charlton, A., 2012. *The right to trade: a report for the commonwealth secretariat on aid for trade*. Available from: http://unctad.org/meetings/en/Miscellaneous%20Documents/Right-to-Trade-Report.pdf [accessed 9 February 2013].
Ul Haq, M., 1996. *Reflections on human development*. Oxford: Oxford University Press.
UNDP (United Nations Development Programme), 2011. *Regional integration and human development: a pathway for Africa*, April. New York: UNDP.
Wade, R., 2003. What strategies are available for developing countries today, the World Trade Organization and the shrinking of development space. *Review of International Political Economy*, 10 (4), 621–644.
Wilkinson, R., 2006. *The WTO crisis and the governance of international trade*. London: Routledge.
World Trade Organization, 2006. *Aid for trade taskforce, recommendations*, 27 July. Available from: http://www.odi.org.uk/publications/4053-aid-trade [accessed 22 January 2014].

Much ado about nothing? The European Union and the global politics of untying aid

Maurizio Carbone

School of Social and Political Sciences, University of Glasgow, Glasgow, UK

This article has two main purposes. The first is that of providing a longitudinal analysis of the global politics of untying aid, by looking at a number of debates that have occurred within the Development Assistance Committee and in the context of a number of high-level forums on aid effectiveness. The second is that of proposing some explanations for the lack of significant progress in these contexts. The focus is on the European Union (EU), which has been widely perceived as one of the most fervent supporters of promoting the aid untying agenda. In all these debates, the EU's leadership aspirations have remained largely unfulfilled. Thus, the EU has failed to adopt a EU-wide vision on aid untying; persuade non-EU donors to untie their aid, even when it has played the reciprocity card; and promote a pro-poor use of foreign aid, by supporting local ownership and facilitating greater access of developing country firms to aid contracts.

Introduction

The practice of tying foreign aid to purchases of goods and services exclusively from firms based in the donor country not only hinders aid effectiveness but may also obstruct development in recipient countries (Jepma 1991, Clay *et al.* 2009, Ellmers 2011). Following 'long and divisive negotiations' (Lammersen 2001), in May 2001 the members of the Development Assistance Committee (DAC) agreed on a recommendation to substantially reduce their levels of tied aid. However, its impact was challenged by many, including the European Commission (2002), due to its limited geographic and thematic coverage: it included only a selected group of recipients – that is, least development countries (LDCs), and from May 2008 also heavily indebted poor countries (HIPCs) – and excluded areas that were strongly tied (that is, food aid and technical assistance). More than a decade later, and notwithstanding a number of prominent summits on foreign aid, progress has stalled. Unexpectedly, the DAC (2013) has talked of 'diminishing returns of further untying'. In fact, not only is a large portion of aid still formally tied, but the number and value of contracts awarded to firms in donor countries suggest that, informally, aid may be more tied than is generally acknowledged.

Against this background, this article has two main purposes. The first is that of providing a longitudinal account of the global politics of aid untying. It starts with the process that led to the adoption of the DAC Recommendation in 2001, and then covers the negotiations that took place in the context of three high-level forums on aid effectiveness (Paris in 2005, Accra in 2008, and Busan in 2011). The second is that of proposing some explanations for the lack of significant progress in these international contexts. The focus is on the European Union (EU), which apparently has been one of the most fervent supporters in pursuing the aid untying and, more generally, aid effectiveness agendas (Holland and Doidge 2012, Carbone 2013a). To be clear, this article does not address the domestic politics of (un)tying aid or variation in compliance of (European) donors with the DAC Recommendation. Rather, it seeks to shed some light on actors and processes, focusing on the role of the European Commission vis-à-vis the EU Member States and that of the EU vis-à-vis other international actors, and paying attention to both formal and informal practices. Surprisingly, these issues have been largely ignored by the academic literature on foreign aid, including relevant studies on tied aid and on donor performance (Moravcsik 1989, Easterly and Williamson 2011, Hall 2011, Knack et al. 2011), and by those on the EU's trade and development policies (Carbone 2007, Holland and Doidge 2012, Young and Peterson 2013).

Considering the nature of the discussions, this study relies not only on a meticulous analysis of primary and secondary sources – predominantly from the DAC, the EU, and non-governmental organisations (NGOs), together with various types of news sources – but, more importantly, it draws on 23 interviews conducted with officials from the DAC Secretariat, the European Commission, several EU Member States, some international NGOs, and four countries in sub-Saharan Africa.[1] Before the sections devoted to evolution and explanations, the next section first explores the concept of (un)tied aid and then briefly outlines some trends in formal and informal aid (un)tying.

Understanding tied and untied aid

Tied aid refers to the practice of a donor imposing restrictions on where a recipient can spend aid funds. Aid is *fully tied* when the purchase of goods and services is restricted to the donor country. It is *fully untied* when recipients have no limitations on where to procure goods and services. Multilateral aid, for instance, is subject to international competitive bidding and therefore is by nature fully untied. Aid is *partially tied* when goods and services may be procured from the donor country or from among a restricted group of other countries, which must substantially include all developing countries (DAC 2013). The EU's supranational programme, as will be seen below, falls under this category. Aid may be formally untied, yet it may prove difficult for firms outside the donor country to obtain a contract. *Informal tying* happens when, for example, donors choose to fund only projects in sectors for which their firms have a competitive advantage; impose bidding procedures that favour their firms (including advertising tender calls not easily accessible to bidders from developing countries); tie only a small component (or even none), but link present aid donations to larger purchases in the future; or select those companies that, having good access to credit markets, offer good prospects for the successful completion of the aid-funded project, thus often ruling out companies in developing countries (Jepma 1991, Morrissey 1993, White and Woestman 1994, Ellmers 2011).

Conventional wisdom suggests that tying aid reduces the value of aid, yet its costs are difficult to calculate. In the absence of effective competition, aid tying generally results in a higher price paid for goods and services. The most widely cited figures are still those estimated by Bhagwati (1967) and Jepma (1991), who, respectively, calculated the excess cost of tied aid to be in the range of 20–25% and 15–30%. Country-based studies have reached similar conclusions, with costs even higher for technical assistance and for food aid (Clay *et al.* 2009). Moreover, aid tying may result in the funding of projects requiring imports of capital-intensive goods (e.g. telecommunications and infrastructure) over smaller and more poverty-focused projects (e.g. rural development); in a significant increase of the administrative burden that recipients face from dealing with many donors; and even in the creation of further recipient dependency on donors, for maintenance and replacement parts, often at uncompetitive prices (Hendra 1987, Morrissey 1993, Jepma 1994). Thus, since the early 2000s, aid untying has become associated with the new agenda on aid effectiveness, and its two key pillars of (donor) coordination and (recipient) ownership (Knack and Smets 2013). Finally, by limiting international competition, tying aid is an impediment to free trade, which often results in the denial of commercial opportunities to firms in developing countries, thus impeding their economic development.

In spite of these costs, some donors resist attempts to end the practice of tying aid. The primary reason for this is that tied aid is believed to boost the donor's exports and contribute to improving its employment record. This use of tied aid as a trade policy instrument is a consequence of a number of restrictions imposed on more direct forms of export promotion, the growing interest in emerging markets, and the economic crisis faced by numerous western countries (Moravcsik 1989, Tajoli 1999, Hall 2011). Evidence of trade and employment generation through tied aid, however, is scarce. While some econometric studies have shown a positive correlation between aid flows and donor exports (Nilsson 1997), the vast majority of scholars have concluded that tied aid does not generate significant trade benefits to donors, not least because it accounts only for a small percentage of their exports (Tajoli 1999, Lloyd *et al.* 2000, Pettersson and Johansson 2013). Similarly, tied aid does not add significantly to the creation of new jobs, also because aid-financed procurements tend to be concentrated in capital-intensive industries, thus benefiting only a small number of firms (Jepma 1994, Clay *et al.* 2009). Thus, the case for tying aid is often more political than economic. Some argue that it is a way to preserve (political and cultural) relationships between countries. Others maintain that it helps to strengthen public support for foreign aid: particularly in cases of budget constraints, providing large shares of aid may be more acceptable if it is believed to generate significant returns for the donor. As with the economic cases, empirical evidence for these more political reasons is inconclusive (Morrissey 1993, Jepma 1994, Chinnock 1998, Clay *et al.* 2009). Finally, there is a recent claim that the costs of untying aid through international competitive bidding may exceed any potential cost savings (Knack and Smets 2013). However, evidence from case studies suggests that untied aid results in a much wider geographical sourcing of contractors than does tied aid (Clay *et al.* 2009).

Yearly fluctuations aside – which are often a reflection of improved reporting by individual donors – the share of formally untied aid has significantly increased. In 2010, it stood at 76% in respect to total bilateral aid, whereas in 2000 it was less than 40% – and in relation to aid covered from the DAC Recommendation the share was 88.7% (Table 1). Some variations between bilateral donors can be observed: in particular, a group of *untying champions,* mostly in northern Europe (e.g. Denmark, Ireland, Luxembourg, Netherlands, Sweden, and the UK), has significantly reduced their levels of tied aid. Conversely, a group of *untying laggards,* mostly in southern Europe (e.g. Greece, Italy, Portugal, and Spain), has not performed so well (DAC 2013). This positive assessment does not take into account that the share of technical cooperation and food aid is very high.

Perhaps more importantly, the distribution of contract awards raises doubts about the extent to which aid is untied in practice. Bearing in mind inconsistencies in reporting,[2] official DAC (2013) data show – with similar conclusions being reached by Clay *et al.* (2009) and Ellmers (2011) – that the share of contracts going back to the donor doubled over the period 2003–2010 (Figure 1), and stands at around 90% for a number of donors. Moreover, the gradual increase in contracts awarded to 'other developing countries' (including China and India) seems to mirror changing dynamics in global economic relations. Taking into account potential informal tying practices, three groups of donors can be identified (Table 2). In the first group (e.g. Denmark, Finland, Portugal, Sweden, the UK, as well as Australia, New Zealand, and

Table 1. Tying status of bilateral aid, 2002–2010 (% of total).

	Share untied, ODA covered by DAC Recommendation			Share untied, total bilateral ODA		Share untied, technical cooperation
	2010	2008	2002–2007	2010	2008	2010
Austria	94.7	96.2	89.7	54.5	72.3	31.1
Belgium	95.9	76.2	94.9	95.2	95.7	99.0
Denmark	94.6	96.8	87.7	97.4	98.6	100
Finland	95.7	98.7	98.7	85.3	93.3	86.7
France	99.4	99.4	96.6	95.0	84.7	91.9
Germany	99.7	99.9	99.8	74.7	77.2	47.8
Greece	–	92.0	57.9	39.5	12.8	27.5
Ireland	100	100	100	100	100	100
Italy	72.8	83.5	76.0	58.4	75.6	0.0
Luxembourg	100	100	92.0	99.2	99.9	100
Netherlands	100	97.2	94.3	91.1	93.7	–
Portugal	34.3	100	68.3	42.5	93.8	72.5
Spain	41.4	66.2	62.6	64.8	75.4	59.4
Sweden	100	100	98.9	94.5	80.6	0.1
UK	99.9	100	100	99.9	100	100
Australia	99.9	100	72.9	99.8	92.8	100
Japan	100	100	100	78.6	83.7	–
USA	84.7	92.8	84.2	68.4	72.9	16.9
Total DAC	88.7	73.9	77.1	76.0	71.2	53.9

Note: ODA, official development assistance.
Source: DAC (2013).

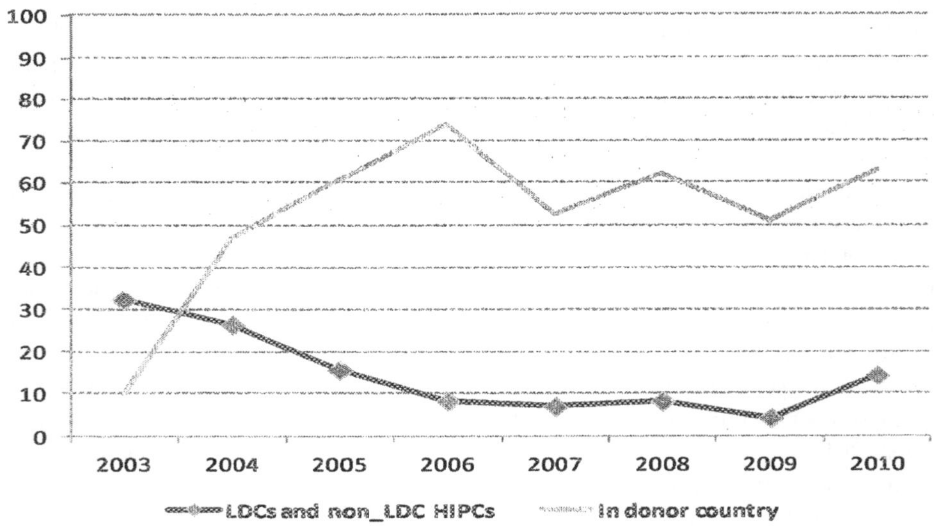

Figure 1. Distribution of contract awards from foreign aid, 2003–2010.

the USA), a large share of contracts is awarded to suppliers from the donor country. In the second group (e.g. Belgium, France, Germany, Luxembourg, as well as Japan), there is a more even pattern of contract awards across different categories of countries. A third group (e.g. Austria, Ireland, Italy, Netherlands, Spain, as well as Canada, Norway, and Switzerland) does not report on contract awards (DAC 2011). Of course no 'presumption of tying' can be made

Table 2. Distribution of contract awards from foreign aid, 2011 (% of total).

	Within donor country		Other OECD and non-DAC countries		LDCs and HIPCs		Other developing countries	
	Number	Value	Number	Value	Number	Value	Number	Value
Austria	97.4	87.5	1.6	12.5	0.8	4.1	0	0.0
Belgium	3.4	18.4	6.8	23.0	89.6	79.2	0	0.0
Denmark	79.9	70.0	18.0	28.9	0.4	0.8	1.4	0.4
Finland	100	100	0	0	0	0	0	0.0
France	22.5	11.9	53.0	7.5	36.1	4.9	36.0	75.5
Germany	43.3	28.9	13.3	22.8	35.4	46.3	7.9	1.8
Luxembourg	3.2	2.4	12.5	16.8	63.8	52.6	20.3	27.7
Portugal	30.6	41.7	0.7	0.0	63.6	46.1	4.9	12.0
UK	99.8	99.8	1.1	0.1	0	0	0	0.0
Japan	15.9	21.1	16.5	22.1	5.0	0.7	62.4	56.0
USA	70.4	90.9	2.3	0.1	3.5	6.1	23.6	2.7

Note: Donors not included in this table do not systematically report on contract awards. OECD, Organisation for Economic Co-operation and Development.
Source: DAC (2013).

(La Chimia 2013), and yet aid may de facto be more tied than it appears. At best, existing data reflect the difficulty that companies from LDCs have in winning contracts, particularly larger ones.

From the DAC Recommendation to the Busan high-level forum

Efforts to end tied aid date back to the early 1960s, but after some failed attempts in the 1970s, largely attributable to the economic crisis – with some countries even reinforcing aid as an instrument of trade promotion – a turning point was reached in 1991 with the adoption of the Helsinki Arrangement, a set of disciplines to limit the use of export credits to projects that were otherwise less commercially viable.[3] Attention then shifted to tied aid, but progress within the DAC halted until some important concessions were made to placate blocking countries: in April 1998, to limit the geographic coverage to the LDCs, and in May 1999, to exclude food aid and technical assistance from the recommendation under negotiation (DAC 2011). The reason behind these choices was that, in the first case, most developed countries have limited commercial interests in LDCs – hence the endorsement of the business community (Interviews, January–February 2004; *The Guardian*, 11 December 2000); in the second case, it was linked to the 'stubborn opposition' of the USA and Japan, which, respectively, had substantial food aid and technical assistance programmes (Interviews, January–February 2004; *Financial Times*, 12 May 2000, 14 June 2000).

In the final stages of the negotiations, the special case of EU's supranational aid programme – which did not make a distinction between LDCs and other developing – was singled out, mostly by Japan, as the key obstacle for the conclusion of an agreement. By opening tenders only to EU Member States and aid recipients, the EU was seen as preventing non-EU DAC members from competing for aid-related business (*Financial Times*, 19 June 2000, 26 June 2000; *The Guardian*, 23 June 2000). A solution to this impasse was eventually found: the European Commission committed to complying with the 'spirit' of the DAC Recommendation, proposing to untie all EU aid to the various developing regions and explore the possibility of including other DAC members (Carbone 2007). Moreover, the European Commission was instrumental in convincing Denmark and France to drop their reservations – but they demanded the inclusion of specific commitments on burden sharing, so that all those donors which allocated less aid to LDCs would 'pay their fair share' (*Financial Times*, 23 June 2000; Interviews, January–February 2004).

The DAC Recommendation, adopted in May 2001, established that aid to the LDCs would be practically untied in all areas except food aid and technical assistance and for contracts worth more than 700,000 special drawing rights (SDRs), or 130,000 SDRs for investment-related technical cooperation. It invited donors to make extra efforts to further untie aid 'to the greatest extent possible' and urged them not to reduce their aid flows to LDCs as a result of the implementation of the Recommendation. It called on donors to take steps so that aid would be 'both *de jure* and *de facto* untied', by informing the DAC Secretariat *ex ante* about tenders and *ex post* about contract awards, and by facilitating local and regional procurements in developing countries (DAC 2001). Despite its limited scope (only about one-tenth of total aid was expected to fall under the scope of the Recommendation), the adoption of an agreement, albeit voluntary, by all donors (or rather, those belonging to the DAC) marked the acceptance of the principle that aid tying represents a bad practice in international development.

After this, 'the European Union became the centre of the debates on untying of aid' (Interview, February 2004). There were, however, significant divisions between the Member States, who either questioned or supported the entrepreneurial role of the European Commission.[4] On the one hand, the *untying champions* (with the UK in the lead) wanted it to take initiatives with the view to extending the scope of the DAC Recommendation. On the other hand, the *untying laggards* cautioned it from embarking on any ambitious plan without having first complied with the DAC Recommendation (Interviews, January–February 2004). The *Financing for Development* (FfD) conference of March 2012, the first international attempt to agree on concrete actions to meet the Millennium Development Goals (MDGs), offered a new opportunity to address the issue of aid untying. Besides committing to boosting aid volumes, donors confirmed their intention 'to support and enhance recent efforts and initiatives such as untying aid'. In this context, the pledge made by EU Member States, with a leading role played by the European Commission, to boost their aid volumes was crucial because it reversed declining global trends in foreign aid, and because it showed that by acting as a single actor, the EU was able to influence the behaviour of other donors (Carbone 2007). Interestingly, a member of a European NGO conceded that, for the moment 'an agreement that boosts the volume of aid may be more important than an agreement to just untie aid' (Interview, January 2004).

The European Commission seized the opportunity emerging from the new confidence in foreign aid and in November 2002 it tabled what was perceived as a 'radical approach to aid untying' (Interview, February 2004). First, it proposed to broaden the scope of the DAC Recommendation, by extending the thematic (that is, include food aid and technical assistance) and geographic coverage (that is, include all developing countries) and by promoting a pro-poor agenda on aid procurements. Second, it recommended the full untying of the EU's supranational aid programme to all developing countries on a regional basis (in line with its region-based development policy) and open tenders to all DAC members on the basis of the principle of reciprocity (that is, the EU would not untie aid to other donors unless they reciprocated). Third, it promoted the idea of an EU-wide approach to aid untying, not least to avoid violations of EU legislation on competition policy and Single Market rules and prevent discriminations against contractors established in any of the EU Member States. The intense negotiations in the Council resulted in an undesirable outcome for the European Commission: the proposal on the EU's supranational programme was accepted with little hesitation, whereas that on the bilateral policies of the Member States was dismissed: the *untying laggards,* in fact, maintained that foreign aid was an area of mixed competence, not subject to EU rules (*Agence Europe*, 20 November 2002; Carbone 2007).

The adoption of two regulations in December 2005 on access to EU external assistance (superseded by new regulations in 2006) was still celebrated as going beyond what any other DAC donor had done.[5] For aid destined to the African, Caribbean, and Pacific (ACP) group through the European Development Fund (EDF), it was decided mainly to preserve the existing system, which established that only firms in EU Member States and ACP countries could bid for contracts[6] and that ACP countries would be guaranteed a price preference of 10–15%, depending on the value and type of contract, to promote local industries. The preservation of this arrangement was a consequence of significant pressure from ACP countries on the European Commission and several Member States (Interviews, January–February 2004; DAC 2007). For aid going to other developing countries through the EU budget, besides all beneficiary countries, it was decided to open it to other DAC members on the basis of the principle of reciprocity. The dual logic behind this choice was that of preventing other international donors from free riding while providing them with an incentive to untie their aid programme. This offer initially attracted the interest of Australia, Canada, and Switzerland (DAC 2007), but eventually only one agreement was signed, with Australia in March 2009 for access to aid contracts in Asia, except for Indonesia (European Commission 2009). In the words of a European Commission official, 'the reciprocity card, clearly, has not worked' (Interview, July 2013).

At the same time, the issue of aid untying was being discussed in the context of the second high-level forum on aid effectiveness held in Paris in May 2005. Celebrated as one of the most important achievements in the area of development, the *Paris Declaration on Aid Effectiveness* acknowledged that aid untying would enhance aid effectiveness by reducing transaction costs, strengthening recipient ownership, and improving donor alignment. Thus, it urged DAC members to make more progress along the lines indicated in the DAC Recommendation. While there was no disagreement on the principles underpinning the 'new' aid relationship between donors and recipients, the EU's insistence on the inclusion of indicators of progress was resisted by the USA (Interviews, September 2013). Eventually, the EU succeeded, and managed to include one specific indicator on aid untying (Indicator 8). The follow-up decisions that were made within the DAC, however, were of marginal significance. In March 2006, it was decided to remove the coverage thresholds, with the aim of rebalancing the share of the burden between donors (some donors had remained largely unaffected by the Recommendation) and making it easier for firms in developing countries to access smaller aid-financed procurements. In May 2008, it was decided to extend the geographical coverage to all HIPCs – that is, only eight additional countries – for an initial period of five years (DAC 2011). The more ambitious proposal to include all low-income countries, supported by the European Commission and various European donors, met with significant resistance from non-EU donors, most notably Japan (Interviews, September 2013).

The third high-level forum on aid effectiveness, held in Accra in August 2008, further refined the aid effectiveness agenda. The EU was perceived as a 'progressive voice in the negotiations', by developing countries as well as by traditionally sceptical NGOs (*European Voice*, 5 September 2008), yet its efforts to achieve results on a more comprehensive approach to aid untying were in vain. The EU attempted to introduce 'more binding language' on the untying of food aid, but 'the USA did not want the words "food aid" even to be mentioned in the final consensus' (Interviews, August 2013). Conversely, untying technical assistance was resisted by Japan, although several EU Member States (e.g. Germany and Portugal) also had a lukewarm attitude towards this. Another important aspect concerned the use of the recipient country (and public procurement) systems. The European Commission argued that local enterprises and services should be given (some forms of) preference, but was blocked by the DAC Secretariat: the DAC has always promoted international competitive bidding, which however, tends to increase the chances of large firms from donor countries winning contracts (Interviews, September 2013;

The Guardian, 7 September 2011). In the words of a DAC official, 'the main priority for the DAC is effective competition and getting the best price for aid tenders: contracts must be awarded to the cheapest bidder, regardless of its long-term development impact' (Interview, September 2013). Eventually, the *Accra Agenda for Action* stipulated that donors would 'elaborate individual plans to untie their aid to the maximum extent', although neither a specific timeline nor targets were set, and that they would use recipient country systems as the 'default option' (Keijzer 2013).

The same issues reappeared in the context of the fourth high-level forum on aid effectiveness held in Busan in November 2011. In that context, much of the attention was concentrated on ensuring that emerging powers endorsed the final document, and yet tied aid was among the most controversial issues (*The Guardian*, 1 November 2011). The submission of the aid untying plans, as established in Accra, and the official survey on the implementation of the Paris Declaration showed that little progress had been made since 2005 (DAC 2011, OECD 2011). Thus, the proposal to eradicate the use of tied aid by 2015 met with open and silent resistance. Open resistance came from the USA – the then Secretary of State Hilary Clinton stated that 'one of the reasons tied aid has persisted is in order to get political support for the budgets that we turn into official development assistance' (*Financial Times*, 30 November 2011) – as well as from various EU Member States, notably Germany and Italy, which maintained that it was not the most propitious time to untie aid owing to the financial and economic crisis. Silent resistance came from the *untying champions*, who concentrated on other issues, such as aid transparency and private sector development. Moreover, the emerging powers did not show any interest in this issue – although their tying practices were expected to become more prominent in the coming years (Knack and Smets 2013). In the midst of these dynamics, the voice of aid recipients – this time stronger than ever in invoking the end of aid tying practices – was barely heard. Thus, the ensuing *Busan Declaration on Development Effectiveness* did not contain any new commitment for donors but a rather vague exhortation to 'accelerate efforts to untie aid'. That 'in the post-Busan development framework, the issue of aid untying has disappeared from the radar of donors' (Interview, September 2013) cannot come as a surprise.

A tale of two failures

At the risk of slight exaggeration, this historical account, albeit brief, points to a dual failure on aid untying: first, a failure of the European Commission to achieve an EU-wide approach, and second, a failure of the EU to make a difference in global negotiations. An official of the European Commission admitted that in the early 2000s there were high expectations, but 'the persistence of tied aid, formal and informal, represents one of the least visible failures of the European Union, as well as the European Commission, to have a significant impact in the field of international development' (Interview, August 2013). Interestingly, while in 2007 the DAC peer review praised the European Commission for playing 'a proactive and positive role in the debate on aid untying and encourag[ing] Member States to follow its lead' (DAC 2007, p. 58), the 2012 edition criticised it for its limited progress in even implementing the DAC Recommendation, thus dismissing its attempt to federate the development policies of the Member States (DAC 2012). The remainder of this section deals with these two failures.

The European Commission and EU development policy

Since the early 2000s, the European Commission has expressed the overt ambition to 'federate' the development policies of the Member States (Orbie 2012). The proliferation of initiatives – most notably the adoption of the European Consensus on Development, the commitments on policy coherence for development, and the initiatives on aid coordination – was not necessarily meant to result in a full transfer of policy authority to the supranational level but, more simply, represented an attempt to promote a common approach to international development issues (Orbie and Lightfoot forthcoming). Reactions by EU Member States to these initiatives have been largely shaped by two factors: first, their general commitment to European integration, particularly in the area of external relations; and second, their overall performance in foreign aid (including issues of quantity and quality). Thus, on one side, we can find a group of countries in northern Europe which are good performers in terms of foreign aid – high volumes, to poor and relatively democratic governments, mainly in the form of programme aid and/or sector-wide approaches – but lukewarm towards (further) European integration, or even coordination. On the opposite side, we can find a group of countries in southern Europe (as well as in Central and Eastern Europe), which lag behind in terms of aid performance – low volumes, largely to less poor and relatively undemocratic governments, mostly in the form of project aid – but are generally more supportive of EU-driven coordination efforts, and even further European integration. Other countries, most notably France and Germany, do not fall into either category, but their policy position depends on the issue under discussion (Carbone 2007, Carbone 2013a).

The case of tied aid represents another, yet little known, attempt to federate the development policies of EU Member States. The adoption of the 2001 DAC Recommendation, with all its limitations, was perceived by the European Commission not only as the first step towards further aid untying at the global level, but also as a way to promote an EU-wide approach to the issue (Interviews, January–February 2004). Thus, the merit of the proposal launched in November 2002 by the European Commission, which drew on its success in the context of the FfD conference, was not only that of proposing a full untying of the EU's supranational aid programme, but also that of challenging EU Member States to follow suit. Opposed to the use of political and ideational arguments made by the European Commission, the *untying laggards* resisted by hiding behind the competence issue: 'deliberating on the bilateral policies of the Member States is against treaty provisions was the refrain heard many times in the Council', to quote a policy-maker from an untying champion (Interview, February 2004). For an official of the European Commission, 'this was a loud defeat not only for the European Commission, but also for the cause of international development: the EU could have set an important example for other donors to follow' (Interview, January 2004).

This debacle did not mark the end of the efforts of the European Commission. First, it used the annual reports monitoring the FfD commitments to 'legally' challenge the Member States, including the newcomers in Central and Eastern Europe (which actually could be included among the *untying laggards*). More specifically, it threatened them with initiating infringement procedures if they did not untie their aid in relation to all other EU Member States (European Commission 2004, 2007). Second, it sought to 'frame' the issue of aid untying differently, subsuming it within the EU's contribution to the global agenda on aid effectiveness. In particular, it supported the publication of two studies which, albeit crudely (and thus controversially), showed that by promoting EU-wide aid coordination, the EU could save between €3 and 7 billion per year and, in the case of the untying of aid, between €400 and 900 million (HTPS 2009, Soges 2011). Neither attempt, however, was successful. By the end of the 2010s, the entire agenda of aid effectiveness – and with that, the ambition of the European Commission to play a federating role – entered a period of fatigue. Moreover, the European Commission, with the 2011 *Agenda for Change*, indicated that the promotion of inclusive and sustainable growth, including strengthened support to the private sector and emphasis on new forms of development financing beyond foreign aid, would become more central to the EU's relations with the developing world (Carbone 2013b).

Apparently, the main obstacle to the EU-wide approach on aid untying was the group of countries in southern Europe. Examining the formation of preferences in individual donors is beyond the scope of this article (cf. Pincin 2013), yet it is clear that the negotiation positions of the *untying laggards* seem to reflect the prevalence of commercial over ideational pressures on foreign aid. An official of the European Commission has admitted that 'business groups have not targeted the European Commission, but from conversations with my counterparts in the Member States I have learnt that they are very active at the national level' (Interview, August 2013). Conversely, the *untying champions*, contrary to what generally happens with other aspects of EU development policy (Carbone 2007), seemed more receptive to a common European vision on aid untying, with the aim however, of making further progress globally. It should nonetheless be noted that this scenario changed when the European Commission attempted to promote a more pro-poor agenda of aid untying. In fact, the *untying champions* took more than a lukewarm attitude towards the use of recipient country systems and any initiatives that allowed developing countries to enjoy greater benefits from aid untying. According to a DAC Secretariat official, 'the UK is certainly a leader in formal aid untying, but it is also a master of informal aid tying practises' (Interview, September 2013). Data from the DAC (2013) support this view: the allocation of aid contracts denote that the UK and other *untying champions* may informally tie a much larger share than is generally acknowledged (Table 2). In particular, it was found that in the UK, aid went to a small number of British firms and consultancies and that this share had risen in recent years (*The Guardian*, 21 September 2012; see also Clay *et al.* 2009). For an official of the European Commission, 'it is clear to us that tied aid benefits a small number of well-connected firms at the national level. And the UK and the Nordic countries are not exempted from this practise' (Interview, August 2013).

While resistance from national firms may not be unexpected (cf. Petermann 2013), the lukewarm attitude of NGOs, at least from the late 2000s onwards, is surprising. For an official of the European Commission, 'some NGOs were very vocal in the late 1990s and early 2000s, but they have gradually lost interest in this issue' (Interview, August 2013). Indeed, in 1999 ActionAid International and other European NGOs launched a formal complaint against the European Commission, arguing that tying aid breached both the EU competition policy and Single Market rules: this complaint was very influential in the building of the European Commission's discourse on aid untying (Interview, February 2004). For an official of the European Commission, 'before the UK announced that it would have untied its aid by April 2001, there is no doubt that NGOs were the most vocal actors in the EU' (Interview, February 2004). NGOs are generally perceived as strong supporters of the principle of aid untying, and yet this battle has been fought only by a selected group of international NGOs operating at the EU level. For a representative of an European NGO, 'a large majority of NGOs within the EU Member States benefit significantly from tied aid, so I am not surprised that, albeit not openly, they are sceptical about using recipient country systems and supporting organisations in developing countries' (Interview, July 2013). For a representative of a non-European NGO, 'the issue of untying aid has been of interest only to NGOs in Europe, while NGOs in the developing world have been more preoccupied with other issues, for instance, gender equality, human rights, and economic growth' (Interview, September 2013).

The EU and international development

The role of the EU in international development is contested. Some scholars argue that the EU follows trends set by various international organisations. Even the attempt to produce, with the European Consensus on Development, an alternative to dominant international practices by including progressive concepts such as ownership, participation, and capacity building, in reality it resonates with the language used by the World Bank (Arts and Dickson 2004, Farrell 2008). Conversely, other scholars argue that the EU throughout the 2000s has managed to shape outcomes in a number of crucial international development issues and negotiations (Carbone 2007, Gänzle *et al.* 2012, Holland and Doidge 2012). More generally, a number of recent studies on EU external affairs have examined the impact of the EU in international contexts. Many observers have noted that the EU's external stature has been boosted by the EU's involvement in the full spectrum of international issues and by several institutional reforms. However, a number of factors, such as the slow implementation of these reforms, a less favourable external environment, and the prolonged economic crisis, have cast doubts upon the EU's effectiveness in the international arena (Carbone 2013b, Niemann and Bretherton 2013, Smith 2013). Thus, whether the EU makes a difference in international development depends not only on its (in)ability to speak with one voice but also on the negotiating context.

The EU's effectiveness – that is, whether the EU achieves the goals it sets for itself – in the case of aid untying has met with different types and levels of resistance of three groups of actors: traditional donors, emerging powers, and developing countries. Most of the credit for the adoption of the 2001 DAC Recommendation is given to the DAC Secretariat, yet an official from the DAC Secretariat conceded that 'the instrumental role played by the European Commission in the final stages of the negotiations' (Interview, September 2013) cannot be disregarded. In fact, it is in this context that the European Commission started to play a sort of federating role: 'this does not mean that the EU acted as a monolith, but it was still possible to identify the Europeans at the one end of the table, and the USA and Japan at the other end of the table' (Interview, September 2013). Moreover, to use the words of another official from the DAC Secretariat, 'the issue of aid untying has often been a European show and the European Commission has been one of the protagonists' (Interview, September 2013). Japan sought to curb the EU's activism in the early 2000s by publicly blaming its reluctance to fully untie its supranational aid programme: thus, for a senior policy-maker from the Japanese Ministry of Foreign Affairs, while Japan had mostly untied its aid to LDCs, 'in order to make efforts for untying aid sustainable, donor countries [that is, the EU] should promote similar efforts' (*Financial Times*, 26 June 2000). The EU–USA dualism became manifest on two occasions. First, in the negotiations of the 2005 Paris Declaration, the USA resisted the EU's attempt to include aid untying among the indicators of progress on aid effectiveness. Second, in the negotiations of the Accra Agenda for Action, the USA resisted the EU's attempt to extend the coverage of the 2001 DAC Recommendation to food aid. Interestingly, the USA has gradually adopted a more progressive stance on aid untying. In 2012, despite mounting pressure from firms uneasy about losing business, it announced that it would open its aid contracts to all developing countries, rather than countries in specific regions as the EU does – and it should be noted that purchase of goods and services for the Millennium Challenge Account is open to aid recipients and all DAC members (*The Guardian*, 21 September 2012; La Chimia 2013).

The EU has also faced the sceptical attitude of the DAC Secretariat, which has not only viewed with scepticism any attempt made by the European Commission to coordinate EU Member States, but has also projected a very formalistic approach on aid untying (Interview, September 2013). Officially, the view of the DAC is that initiatives that offer some advantage to suppliers in developing countries are not fully compatible with the agreed definition of untied aid (DAC 2006, p. 8). More radically, for a representative of a European NGO, 'the DAC is not a development forum, but another instrument of the prevailing neo-liberal paradigm' (Interview, September 2013). Indirectly, the EU's effectiveness has been compromised by the rise of new powerful actors on the international development scene. In fact, the rise of China and India has called into question the (emerging) consensus on aid effectiveness and aid untying, and has also threatened the commercial interests of traditional donors. Most EU

Member States, particularly those facing economic problems, have expressly stated that any further untying of aid would end up favouring China (Interviews, July–August 2013; *The Guardian*, 1 November 2011). These problems, together with the global financial crisis of the late 2000s, have put foreign aid under pressure in a number of European countries, which have either reduced their aid budgets or have become more eager to attribute direct results to them – regardless of any potential negative consequences for aid effectiveness (Carbone 2013b).

The EU has also found it more difficult than usual to count on the support of developing countries. Some aid recipients are concerned about a reduction of aid flows, while others fear the imposition of new conditionalities, and still others feel that they would not be able to benefit substantially from untied aid because they do not produce the required goods (Interviews, May–June 2009; May–June 2010). More generally, there is a divergence of views on the meaning and implications of aid untying, as cogently stated by an official of an African country: 'For donors, it is a matter of complying with legal and administrative requirements. For recipients, it is a matter of promoting ownership and offering business opportunities to local firms' (Interview, May 2009). Most European donors are inclined to increase the use of recipient country systems, but in return demand that developing countries reform their procurement policies and practices: they claim that they cannot 'buy locally' because of inefficiency, corruption, and the high fiduciary risks posed by doing business in developing countries (Chinnock and Collinson 1999, Ellmers 2011). This conflict has resulted in tense negotiations on public procurements (particularly within the World Trade Organisation): the call for equal treatment for domestic and foreign companies made by developed countries (the ultimate aim of which appears to be the acquisition of new commercial opportunities for their firms) meets with the opposition of developing countries for which public procurements play a very important role, as they can be used to promote specific industries or sectors (Chinnock and Collinson 1999, Ellmers 2011). Incidentally, a similar conflict also exists within the European Commission. The view of development circles is that of moving away 'from a trade approach limited to the issue of reciprocal access between donors to a more pro-poor approach centred on developing countries' (European Commission 2007, p. 164), whereas the line taken by trade circles is that 'public procurement is an area of significant untapped potential for EU exporters' (European Commission 2006, p. 17).

Conclusion

The fact that the trade policies of developed countries, including those in the EU, have detrimental effects on countries in the developing world has been widely studied. Some attention has been drawn by the fact that donor trade interests, through aid tying, directly impinge on foreign aid. Thus, most donors have fulfilled pledges to 'formally' untie aid. Less acknowledged is the phenomenon of informal untying: a number of donors still allocate a large portion of aid contracts to their firms, with the result that the developmental potential of foreign aid remains untapped. This article has discussed both forms of aid tying, and has investigated the global politics of aid untying, from the adoption of the DAC Recommendation in May 2001 to the fourth high-level forum on aid effectiveness in Busan in November 2011 (through other key aid summits held in Monterrey in 2002, Paris in 2005, and Accra in 2008). More specifically, it has argued that the EU's leadership aspirations exemplified in the 'radical approach' to aid untying proposed by the European Commission in the early 2000s and reiterated by the EU in all the international contexts mentioned above, have remained largely unfulfilled: in other words, much ado about nothing. Thus, the EU has failed to adopt a EU-wide vision on aid untying; persuade non-EU donors to untie their aid, even when it has played the reciprocity card; and promote a pro-poor use of foreign aid, by supporting local ownership and facilitating greater access of developing country firms to aid contracts.

There are also a number of other interesting findings that, indirectly, have emerged from this study and that undoubtedly deserve further attention. First, the formal untying of aid is a first necessary step, but to truly increase the development impact of foreign aid, greater consideration – including by the academic literature – should be given to informal aid tying. Second, those countries that have been praised for their achievements in formal untying – the so-called *untying champions* – in reality seem to privilege their own firms, which suggests that their aid is less untied than they claim. Third, the EU has been one of the strongest promoters of the 'aid for trade' agenda and more recently has pledged to support private sector development in developing countries. Yet, with the partial exception of the EDF, it has failed to use aid as a catalyst for business development, and see the enormous benefits of 'trade for aid' (La Chimia 2013): a tendering process that encourages bids from firms in developing countries has the potential to significantly boost the emerging private sector in developing countries and generate new employment opportunities. Finally, support from both NGOs and developing countries to aid untying, albeit for different reasons, has been less wholehearted than could have been expected.

Acknowledgements

This study was completed during a period of research spent at the German Development Institute, for which I want to thank Mark Furness, Christine Hackenesch, Stefan Klingebiel, and Svea Koch. I am also grateful to Chris Stevens, Niels Keijzer, Annamaria La Chimia, and Jan Orbie for helpful comments on earlier drafts of this paper.

Notes

1. These interviews were conducted in several rounds: a first round in January–February 2004 in Brussels, a second round in May–June 2009 (in Senegal and Gambia) and May–June 2010 (in Ethiopia and Djibouti), and a third round in July–September 2013. They include policy-makers directly involved with the issue of the untying of aid within the DAC Secretariat, the European Commission (including its delegation at the DAC), some EU Member States (specifically those officials representing their countries at the EU and the DAC), the four countries in sub-Saharan Africa mentioned above, and some NGO representatives.
2. Most donors do not disclose in advance offers for untied aid for specific projects, nor do they report systematically or comprehensively on contract awards, claiming that they do not maintain central records of the value or the origin of contracts awarded, or that information lies with aid recipients (DAC 2013).
3. For a review of the Helsinki Arrangement, see Moravcsik (1989), Owen and Lammersen (2001), and Hall (2011).
4. The European Commission – except for a brief period of uncertainty in 1999–2001 caused by bureaucratic clashes – has consistently attempted to promote an EU-wide approach on aid untying since the early 1970s. In line with the positions of their native countries, Chris Patten, the British Commissioner for External Relations, supported full aid untying, whereas Poul Nielson, the Danish Commissioner for Development, was against it (*European Voice*, 11 January 2001; 25 January 2001).
5. For a thorough analysis of these regulations, see La Chimia (2013).
6. This was partially modified in 2010, when it was decided to align the EDF to EU-budget aid rules.

References

Arts, K. and Dickson, A.K., 2004. *EU development cooperation: from model to symbol*. Manchester: Manchester University Press.

Bhagwati, J.N., 1967. *The tying of aid*. UNCTAD Secretariat, TD/7/supp. 4, United Nations, 1–57.

Carbone, M., 2007. *The European Union and international development: the politics of foreign aid*. London: Routledge.

Carbone, M., 2013a. Between EU actorness and aid effectiveness: the logics of EU aid to sub-Saharan Africa. *International Relations*, 27 (3), 341–355.

Carbone, M., 2013b. International development and the EU's external policies: changing contexts, problematic nexuses, contested partnerships. *Cambridge Review of International Affairs*, 26 (3), 483–96.
Chinnock, J., 1998. In whose benefit? The case for untying aid. London: ActionAid.
Chinnock, J. and Collinson, S., 1999. *Purchasing power: aid untying, targeted procurement and poverty reduction*. London: ActionAid.
Clay, E.J., Geddes, M. and Natali, L., 2009. *Aid untying: is it working? An evaluation of the implementation of the Paris Declaration and of the 2001 DAC recommendation of untying ODA to the LDCs*. Copenhagen: Danish Institute for International Studies.
Development Assistance Committee (DAC), 2001. *DAC recommendation on untying official development assistance to the least developed countries*. Paris: OECD.
Development Assistance Committee (DAC), 2006. *Implementing the 2001 DAC recommendation on untying official development assistance to the least developed countries: 2006 progress report to the high level meeting*. DCD/DAC(2006)/26/REV1, 22 March.
Development Assistance Committee (DAC), 2007. *Peer review of the European Community, 2007*. Paris: OECD.
Development Assistance Committee (DAC), 2011. *Implementing the 2001 DAC recommendation on untying aid: 2010–2011 review*. DCD/DAC(2011)4/FINAL, 18 April.
Development Assistance Committee (DAC), 2012. *European Union: peer review 2012*. Paris: OECD.
Development Assistance Committee (DAC), 2013. *Aid untying: 2012 report*. DCD/DAC(2012)39/FINAL, 7 January.
Easterly, W. and Williamson, C.R., 2011. Rhetoric *versus* reality: the best and worst of aid agency practises. *World Development*, 39 (11), 1930–1949.
Ellmers, B., 2011. *How to spend it: smart procurement for more effective aid*. Brussels: Eurodad.
European Commission, 2002. *Untying: enhancing the effectiveness of aid*. COM (2002) 639, 18 November.
European Commission, 2004. *Translating the Monterrey consensus into practice: the contribution by the European Union*. COM (2004) 150, 5 March.
European Commission, 2006. *Global Europe: competing in the world*. COM (2006) 567, 4 October.
European Commission, 2007. *Keeping Europe's promises on financing for development*. COM (2007) 164, 4 April.
European Commission, 2009. *Aid effectiveness after Accra. Where does the EU stand and what more do we need to do?* SEC (2009) 443, 8 April.
Farrell, M., 2008. Internationalising EU development policy. *Perspectives on European Politics and Society*, 9 (2), 225–240.
Gänzle, S., Grimm, S. and Makhan, D., eds., 2012. *The European Union and global development: an 'Enlightened Superpower' in the making*. Basingstoke: Palgrave Macmillan.
Hall, S., 2011. Managing tied aid competition: domestic politics, credible threats, and the Helsinki disciplines. *Review of International Political Economy*, 18 (5), 646–672.
Hendra, J., 1987. Only 'Fit to be Tied': a comparison of the Canadian tied aid policy with the tied aid policies of Sweden, Norway and Denmark. *Canadian Journal of Development Studies/Revue canadienne d'études du développement*, 8 (2), 261–281.
Holland, M. and Doidge, M., 2012. *Development policy of the European Union*. Houndmills: Palgrave Macmillan.
HTSPE, 2009. *The aid effectiveness agenda: benefits of a European approach*. Brussels: European Commission.
Jepma, C.J., 1991. *The tying of aid*. Paris: OECD.
Jepma, C.J., 1994. *Inter-nation policy co-ordination and untying of aid*. Aldershot: Avebury.
Keijzer, N., 2013. *Unfinished agenda or overtaken by events? Applying aid- and development-effectiveness principles to capacity development support*. Discussion Paper, Bonn: Deutsches Institut für Entwicklungspolitik.
Knack, S., Rogers, H. and Eubank, N., 2011. Aid quality and donor rankings. *World Development*, 39 (11), 1907–1917.
Knack, S. and Smets, L., 2013. Aid tying and donor fragmentation. *World Development*, 44 (1), 63–76.
La Chimia, A., 2013. *Tied aid and development aid procurement in the framework of EU and WTO law: the imperative for change*. Oxford: Hurt.
Lammersen, F., 2001. The untied aid debate. Development choices: opening up markets. *International Trade Forum*, 4, 23–24.

Lloyd, T., McGillivray, M., Morrissey, O. and Osei, R., 2000. Does aid create trade? An investigation for European donors and African recipients. *European Journal of Development Research*, 12 (1), 107–123.

Moravcsik, A., 1989. Disciplining trade finances: the OECD Export Credit Arrangement. *International Organization*, 43 (1), 173–205.

Morrissey, O., 1993. The mixing of aid and trade policies. *The World Economy*, 16 (1), 69–84.

Niemann, A. and Bretherton, C., 2013. EU external policy at the crossroads: the challenge of actorness and effectiveness. *International Relations*, 27 (3), 261–275.

Nilsson, L., 1997. *Essays on North-South Trade*. Lund Economic Studies 70. Lund: University of Lund.

OECD, 2011. *Aid effectiveness 2005–10: progress in implementing the Paris Declaration*. Paris: OECD.

Orbie, J., 2012. The EU's role in development: a full-fledged development actor or eclipsed by superpower temptations? *In*: S. Gänzle, S. Grimm and D. Makhan, eds. *The European Union and global development: – An Enlightened Superpower in the making?* London: Palgrave, 17–36.

Orbie, J. and Lightfoot, S., forthcoming. The Europeanization of development policy. *In*: A. Hadfield, I. Manners, and R.W. Whitman, eds. *The foreign policies of the EU member states*. Abingdon: Routledge.

Owen, A.D. and Lammersen, F., 2001. The Helsinki arrangement: its impact on the provision of tied aid. *International Journal of Finance and Economics*, 6 (1), 886–894.

Petermann, J-H., 2013. *Between export promotion and poverty reduction: the foreign economic policy of untying official development assistance*. Wiesbaden: Springer.

Pettersson, J. and Johansson, L., 2013. Aid, aid for trade, and bilateral trade: an empirical study. *The Journal of International Trade & Economic Development*, 22 (6), 866–894.

Pincin, J.A., 2013. Political power and aid-tying practises in the development assistance committee countries. *Oxford Development Studies*, 41 (3), 372–390.

Smith, M., 2013. Foreign policy and development in the post-Lisbon European Union. *Cambridge Review of International Affairs*, 26 (3), 519–535.

Soges, 2011. *The aid effectiveness agenda: the benefits of going ahead*. Brussels: European Commission.

Tajoli, L., 1999. The impact of tied aid on trade flows between donor and recipient countries. *Journal of International Trade & Economic Development*, 8 (4), 373–388.

White, H. and Woestman, L., 1994. The quality of aid: measuring trends in donor performance. *Development and Change*, 25 (3), 527–554.

Young, A.R. and Peterson, J., 2013. 'We care about you, but ... ': the politics of EU trade policy and development. *Cambridge Review of International Affairs*, 26 (3), 497–518.

The value of *pointillism*? Integrating trade and development and the European Union as a global actor

Alasdair R. Young

The Sam Nunn School of International Affairs, Georgia Institute of Technology, Atlanta, GA, USA

As the contributions to this volume make clear, the intersection between the European Union's (EU) trade and development policies is populated by a diverse array of policies. The EU's selection of policies reflects, in part, the level of development of the developing country and competing understandings of how to best foster development. The contributions also hint at significant contributions to wider debates about the EU as a global actor, particularly the extent to which it is motivated by normative considerations and how affective it is in achieving its objectives. This article reviews the main findings of the contributions to this volume and advances some suggestions so as to enable a clearer picture to emerge that could more readily inform wider debates.

The European Union (EU) is undoubtedly both a trade power and a leading development actor. The articles in this volume focus on the nexus between those two critical and particularly well-developed aspects of the EU's external relations. In doing so, they give a vivid impression of the breadth and complexity of the EU's efforts to promote development through trade. Stepping back from the individual chapters to make sense of the whole, as with a *pointillist* painting, suggests a number of conclusions of relevance to wider debates about the EU as a global actor. I will begin by drawing out what I can discern about the overall picture of the EU's engagement at the intersection of trade and development policies. I will then highlight how these glimpses suggest valuable contributions to our understanding of the EU as a global actor. I conclude by suggesting some ways in which the painting might be fleshed out so as to render the picture clearer and thus enhance how it relates to the wider debates.

Making sense of the picture

Reading across the contributions yields three strong impressions, each of which shares the common feature of diversity. First, even within the confines of the trade-development nexus, the EU pursues multiple, dramatically different policies. Second, this diversity of approaches is in part a product of the EU treating countries at different levels of development differently. Third, to a lesser extent, the diversity of approaches reflects different, sometimes competing, understandings of how best to foster development.

A diversity of instruments

The most striking image from this volume is the diversity of ways in which the EU's efforts to promote development intersect with trade. Some are purely unilateral. The EU's Everything but

Arms (EBA) initiative under which it offered duty-free, quota-free access to all exports save arms from the world's poorest countries, which appears in passing in a number of contributions, is the archetypical example. The EU's initiative to untie aid – allow aid recipients to purchase goods and services from any country not just the donor – is another, much less commonly acknowledged example (see Carbone this volume). The EU's implementation of the Aid for Trade initiative is another (see Holden this volume). Other EU policies are unilateral, but require developing countries to undertake obligations in order to qualify. Portela and Orbie (this volume) focus on the EU's withdrawal of preferential market access under its General System of Preferences (GSP) and GSP + schemes in response to violations of human rights. With regard to these policy initiatives, developing countries are effectively recipients.

As a number of the contributors note, however, the EU is increasingly engaging in bilateral, reciprocal trade negotiations with developing countries (see the contributions in this volume by Heron, Langan, Siles-Brügge and Woolcock). In these instances, the developing countries are more explicitly partners and are obliged to make commitments to liberalize imports. The EU's switch to such reciprocal agreements with the former European colonies after the 2000 Cotonou Agreement – the so-called Economic Partnership Agreements (EPAs) – have received the bulk of the attention to date. Even though the explicit aim of this volume is to look at the EU's trade and development nexus beyond the EPAs, there is no getting away from them, as several contributions to this volume (Heron, Holden, Langan and Woolcock) focus extensively on them, although each situates them in a broader trade and development context. In particular, Woolcock treats the EPAs as a specific case of the EU's push to pursue reciprocal trade agreements, which intensified after 2006.

The EU's trade and development nexus is also evident at the multilateral level. What commitments developing countries should undertake within the multilateral trading system have been a central bone of contention within the on-going Doha Development Round of World Trade Organization (WTO) talks (see Ahnlid and Elgström this volume). The EU has also sought to get agreement among the main aid donors, within the Development Assistance Committee of the Organisation for Economic Co-operation and Development, to untie their aid donations (Carbone this volume). Thus the EU's trade-development nexus involves a wide variety of policies that it pursues through multiple channels.

Differentiating among developing countries

Several contributions to this volume explain the diversity of the EU's policies, at least in part, by treating developing countries of different level of development differently. The prominence of such 'differentiation' is a particularly clear conclusion from this volume. That the EU treats countries differently depending on their level of development may not seem surprising, but until the mid-1990s the EU's development policy differentiated between the former European colonies (known as the African, Caribbean and Pacific (ACP) countries) and other developing countries irrespective of their level of development (Young and Peterson 2013, p. 501).

The EU's new basis for differentiation is manifest across the spectrum of policies at the trade-development nexus. Within the Doha Round negotiations, for example, the EU is willing for the least developed countries (LDCs) to make no concessions, but wants the emerging economies – notably Brazil, India and China – to make substantial concessions, particularly with respect to market access for non-agricultural goods (Ahnlid and Elgström this volume). Woolcock (this volume) draws attention to how the EU is willing to accept less generous concessions in its reciprocal trade agreements with poorer developing countries than it is with those that are more developed. In addition, a central feature of the 2012 reform of the EU's GSP was 'graduating' more developed countries out of the preferential system (see Siles-Brügge this volume). Even in the debate over untying aid, a distinction was drawn between the least developed and heavily indebted poor countries and the rest (see Carbone this volume). Consequently, the differential treatment of developing countries is evident across the unilateral, bilateral and multilateral dimensions of the EU's trade-development nexus.

The contributions in this volume also suggest two challenges associated with differentiating among countries on the basis of their level of development. One concerns how to classify countries. While it is relatively clear which countries are the poorest (the UN's list of LDCs is used) and therefore warrant particularly good treatment, it is much less clear, and thus much more controversial, which states no longer qualify as developing countries and thus warrant no special treatment (see the contributions by Ahnlid and Elgström and Siles-Brügge). The second challenge is that treating some developing countries better than others has implications for the EU's ability to pursue some of its policies and has adverse side-effects for less privileged developing countries (see below). The EU's new basis for differentiation, therefore, is not unproblematic.

Different understanding of how to foster development

The contributions in this volume, at least implicitly, suggest another reason for the variety of policies at the nexus of the EU's trade and development policies: different understandings of how best to foster development. There is general agreement that export-led growth is beneficial for development and thus that preferential market access for developing countries is appropriate. As Woolcock (this volume) points out, however, despite preferential access, the share of GSP imports in EU imports has fallen. The same pattern can be observed in ACP imports (Young and Peterson 2013, p. 502). A central aim of the Aid for Trade agenda (Holden this volume) is to try to enhance the capacity of developing countries to exploit the preferential market access that is available to them. In addition, while more exports might be better than fewer, increased export opportunities do not necessarily translate into better living conditions (see Langan this volume).

In part in response to the assessment that unilateral market access has not boosted exports, in part reflecting neoliberal economic ideas about the benefits of competition for increased efficiency and in part in response to WTO rulings against EU policies that discriminate among developing countries on historical grounds, the EU has begun to emphasize reciprocal trade liberalization with developing countries, albeit it with asymmetrical coverage and pacing (see Heron and Woolcock this volume; also Young and Peterson 2013, pp. 501–504). Holden (this volume) argues that Aid for Trade, with its emphasis on export-led growth and recognition that capacity needs to be developed as a precondition for liberalization, is a somewhat interventionist policy, and thus qualifies the shift towards a more neoliberal approach to development. Nonetheless, there has thus been a shift in the EU's trade policy, although an incomplete one, from non-reciprocal to reciprocal trade liberalization.

Another recent, related shift in how the EU uses trade policy to promote development is its increased emphasis on fostering regional integration among developing countries. This is most commonly observed with reference to the EPAs, which the EU has sought to conclude with groups of developing countries, only some of which had cooperated previously (see Woolcock this volume). Promoting regional integration, however, is also a distinctive characteristic of the EU's use of Aid for Trade (see Holden this volume). What is less clear is whether the EU merely simply seeks to replicate itself or whether it considers, in the light of its own experience, that fostering south–south trade is beneficial for development (see Ahnlid and Elgström this volume, Woolcock this volume).

Beyond whether the granting of trade preferences or the negotiation of reciprocal agreements is the appropriate way to use trade policy to foster development, there is a third consideration. That is the imposition of political conditions – respect of human rights, promotion of good governance and protection of the environment. In this volume, only Portela and Orbie address such political conditionality at length and their focus is on whether these conditions are enforced in line with wider foreign policy objectives, not whether or how such conditionality fosters development. Thus the EU's trade-development nexus contains at least three different understandings about how to promote development.

It is worth noting that the different understandings of how to foster development through trade policy are applied differentially to developing countries. In particular, the EU, not entirely by design, promotes only export-led growth strategies with respect to the LDCs and it pursues reciprocal trade liberalization with other developing countries. The EBA is a unilateral, export-led growth opportunity open to only the LDCs. In the Doha Round, the EU was willing to accept that the poorest countries make no concessions of their own, but benefit from concessions offered by others (see Ahnlid and Elgström this volume). While the EU has sought to include those LDCs that are also members of the ACP in reciprocal EPAs, this has not occurred as the LDCs have chosen not to make concessions in exchange for no improvement on the market access they already have under the EBA (see Heron this volume, Woolcock this volume). By contrast, countries at the other end of the developing-country spectrum are losing their unilaterally granted preferential access and have to negotiate reciprocal agreements if they want to keep it (see Siles-Brügge this volume) and/or have been expected to make significant concessions in the context of the Doha Round (see Ahnlid and Elgström this volume). Thus the two clearest conclusions from the volume – that the EU treats developing countries differently on the basis of their level of development and that different understandings of how to prompt development through trade coexist within the EU – interact.

Relevance to the main collection

While these are non-trivial contributions they are very firmly contributions to the literature on the EU as a development actor. Only three contributions – Ahnlid and Elgström, Portela and Orbie, and Siles-Bügge – engage actively with wider debates about the understanding the EU as a global actor, the consistency of the EU's development and foreign policies and whether EU policy is informed by norms, respectively. Other contributions – Carbone, Heron, Holden – do so indirectly. Nevertheless, trade and development policies are two areas where the EU is widely regarded to have the greatest capacity to act and most substantial power resources. Moreover, the contributions hint at the potential to contribute to central debates about the EU as a global actor, notably what motivates its policy (what kind of actor is it?) and whether it achieves its objectives (how effective an actor is it?).

The EU as a flawed normative actor

Most of the contributors assert that the EU's policies at the trade and development nexus are motivated primarily by normative considerations, although this is done largely in passing. The contributions by both Ahnlid and Elgström and Carbone point to the EU wanting to be a development 'leader', while Langan contends that the EU aspires to be a 'benevolent' development actor. Heron notes that the EU's shift towards ambitious, reciprocal negotiations with the ACP countries might be motivated by pursuing market access, but concludes that the EU's policy is meant to foster development and the form of the policy reflects the impact of neoliberal ideas on how best to foster development. Ahnlid and Elgström contend that the EU has adopted a more developing-country friendly stance than the USA in the context of the Doha Round, being willing to accept less from developing countries in exchange for its concessions. Woolcock also notes that the EU tends to be more 'progressive' than its peers in its bilateral relations with developing countries. Portela and Orbie focus on the EU's use of trade policy to promote human rights. Thus these would seem to support the depiction of the EU as 'normative power Europe' (Manners 2002), the dominant perspective on the EU as a global actor (Peterson 2012).

There are qualifiers, however. Heron notes that how the EU has pursued concluding EPAs has not been as 'non-coercive' and 'development friendly' as the EU likes to portray its behaviour. Carbone and Woolcock both note that the EU's aims are motivated by the desire to foster development, but that economic interests can deflect the substance of the policy (see also Young and Peterson 2013, 2014). Siles-Brügge, who explicitly considers whether the EU's policy is more consistent with normative or interest-based explanations, argues that the EU's decision to 'graduate' richer countries from its preferential GSP scheme is not motivated primarily by the articulated desire to benefit the poorest countries, but more by the aim of enhancing the EU's leverage in bilateral trade negotiations with emerging economies by cancelling their preferential access. Accepting Siles-Brügge's argument does not necessarily challenge that the EU is a normative actor motivated by the desire to aid developing countries. Arguably the EU has concluded that the norm no longer applies to these countries because of their level of development and (less plausibly) that other, less developed countries are sufficiently competitive in some sectors that they no longer need a leg up for those exports. Siles-Brügge's argument does, however, point to a gap between the EU's stated – normative – aim and the effect of its policy. The gap between the EU's words – stated aims – and the impact of its policies is also highlighted by Holden and Langan. Such gaps may reflect the use of normative arguments to justify policies pursued for other reasons or they may reflect problems of effectiveness in realizing desired objectives.

How effective an actor is the EU?

The literature on the EU as a global actor has tended to focus on the EU's ability to agree common positions to the exclusion of consideration of whether it has been able to convert those positions into outcomes (Jørgensen *et al.* 2011, Niemann and Bretherton 2013, Young and Peterson 2014, Conceição-Heldt and Meunier forthcoming). Addressing this shortcoming is the focus of several recent special issues (Jørgensen *et al.* 2011, Niemann and Bretherton 2013, Conceição-Heldt and Meunier forthcoming). The effectiveness of EU policies is central to some of the contributions to this volume.

Much of the existing literature on the EU's external effectiveness has focused on the coherence of its policies: between levels of policy-making (vertical coherence); between policy sectors (horizontal coherence); as well as within and between the EU institutions (institutional coherence) (Bretherton and Vogler 2013). Contributions in this volume address the first two types of coherence in particular. Carbone, for instance, contends that the EU's progress in formally untying aid has been undermined by member state practices that mean that much aid remains tied informally. Portela and Orbie find that the coherence between the EU's withdrawal of trade preferences with foreign policy sanctions is greater than would be expected, given that they pursue different aims under different decision rules and involve different institutions.

The contributions in this volume also point to problems of coherence among more closely related policies (see also Young and Peterson 2013, 2014). The logic of Siles-Brügge's argument is that granting GSP preferences made it harder for the EU to conclude bilateral trade agreements with some emerging economies. In addition, by liberalizing trade within the Doha round (Ahnlid and Elgström) or through bilateral agreements (Langan), the EU reduces the value of the preferences that it has granted to developing countries. More distinctively, a number of contributions in this volume point to problems of coherence among policies located within the trade-development nexus. Holden, for instance, highlights the tensions among the EU's pro-poor, regional integration and human development discourses in the context of aid for trade. More significantly, several other contributors note that some of the EU's trade and development policies undermine others. Heron notes how granting the LDCs tariff-free, quota-free access to the EU's market under the EBA undermined their incentive to participate in EPAs, complicating the EU's efforts to conclude such agreements. In these cases, one EU trade and development policy makes it harder for the EU to realize another.

Other contributions highlight other challenges to the EU's effectiveness. Ahnlid and Elgström, for instance, note that the EU's efforts to establish itself as a leader on development within the Doha Round has not been recognized by other participants in the negotiations. Woolcock notes that the EU's granting of unilateral trade preferences has not prevented a decrease in the share of EU imports from developing countries. Langan contends that reciprocal trade liberalization has not translated into better working conditions in the beneficiary countries. These observations are significant because they shift the focus from what the EU aspires to do to what it achieves.

A particular contribution of this volume is to draw attention to the limits of the EU's market as a source of influence. Ahnlid and Elgström note that the EU's concessions on agriculture were not sufficient to induce China and India in particular to offer concessions in the Doha Round. Heron, Siles-Brügge and Woolcock all note, albeit in different ways, the problems that the EU has had in getting supposedly weaker countries to conclude reciprocal agreements with it. Implicit in Portela and Orbie's account of the EU's withdrawal of trade preferences for violations of human rights is how little impact the EU's action had on the behaviour of the targeted states (see also Young and Peterson 2014). That the EU has had trouble using its market power to influence the policies of others is particularly significant as the literature on the EU as a global actor overwhelmingly cites the size of its market as a crucial power resource (Peterson 2012, Bretherton and Vogler 2013, p. 386). The contributions in this volume suggest that, while the EU's market is undoubtedly a critical power resource, there are limits to its fungibility. This suggests the need to shift away from the prevailing emphasis on the EU's power capabilities to a more relational understanding of power.

Sharpening the image

As the preceding discussion underlines, the contributions in this volume advance a number of interesting observations about the trade-development nexus and suggest a number of valuable contributions to the broader analysis of the EU as a global actor. These observations, however, could be sharpened to make the image of the EU's trade-development nexus clearer. Doing so would also make their contribution to the wider debate on the EU as a global actor more evident.

Norms versus ideas

While all of the contributions in this volume discuss the extent to which the EU's policies at the intersection of trade and development are normatively informed, they differ significantly in terms of what they understand those norms to be. More importantly, they differ in terms of what they understand a norm to be. Some contributors (Ahnlid and Elgström and Holden) do not spell out what the relevant norms are. Other contributors (Langan, Siles-Brügge, Portela and Orbie) explicitly refer to 'progressive ideas', such as decent work, international labour standards and, presumably, helping the poor (international social solidarity), although this is taken as understood. A first step, therefore, is to be specific about what norms are thought to be (or might be) informing the EU's policy.

A more significant issue is a lack of common understanding of what a norm is. Heron sometimes uses the term 'norm' interchangeably with rules or law, as in 'WTO trade norms'. This is certainly a common use of the term, but in the context of whether the EU is a normative power it muddies the water. In other contributions (Carbone, Heron and Woolcock), the term 'norm' seems to be equated with common understandings, but it is unclear whether these are understandings about ends or means. For instance, both Heron and Woolcock refer to the EU's promotion of a neoliberal approach to development, including through fostering regional integration, as normatively informed, but describe it in terms that suggest the real norm is helping the poor and that neoliberal policies are understood to be the best way to achieve that end. Although Manners (2002, p. 239) equates normative power with 'ideological power', it is quite clear that the ideology in question is constituted of norms in the sense of values: liberty, democracy, rule of law, respect for human rights, and, to a lesser extent, social solidarity, anti-discrimination, sustainable development, good governance. The use of the term 'norm' in this volume seems broader than Manners's original formulation and is more akin to 'beliefs' or 'ideas'.

If the discussion of the trade-development nexus is to get to grips with what motivates the EU policy, let alone for it to engage with what kind of actor the EU is, greater precision about what the relevant norms are is required. Goldstein and Keohane's (1993, pp. 8–9) distinction among three types of belief might provide a way forward. First, and most fundamental are 'world views', which are ideas that define the universe of possibilities and which are 'entwined with identities'. Second are 'principled beliefs', which consist of normative ideas that 'specify criteria for distinguishing right from wrong and just from unjust' and 'mediate between world view and particular policy conclusions' by 'translat[ing] fundamental doctrines into guidance for human action'. These are norms as understood by Manners and most of the contributors. Goldstein and Keohane's third category is 'causal beliefs', which reflect understandings about cause–effect relationships. As such they suggest how to go about securing objectives. Some of the contributions in this volume are thus concerned about the impact of principled beliefs on what objectives the EU pursues, while others consider how prevailing ideas inform choices about how to pursue those objectives. Strictly speaking, only the former understanding speaks to what kind of international actor the EU is.

Does the EU achieve what it wants?

The preceding discussion has highlighted the importance of drawing a clear distinction between the EU's desired ends and the means it chooses to get there. As goal attainment is a crucial indicator of the EU's effectiveness (Jørgensen *et al.* 2011, Dee 2013), in order to assess the EU's effectiveness, it is necessary to be precise about what the EU's goal is. One thing that complicates drawing conclusions about the EU's overall effectiveness from the contributions in this volume is that the authors assess very different types of objectives.

In some cases, the focus is whether the EU got other countries to change their *policies*. This includes enforcing international labour standards (Portela and Orbie), concluding preferential trade agreements (Heron, Siles-Brügge, Woolcok), securing concessions in multilateral trade negotiations (Ahnlid and Elgström), and untying aid (Carbone). In others, the issue is whether a policy change had the intended effect. For instance, making Aid for Trade 'pro-poor' is difficult because larger firms are the ones more likely to be able to take advantage of any opportunities created (Holden). Informal practices have undermined the formal untying of aid where it has occurred (Carbone). In some cases, the question is whether the EU's policies affect private actors' *behaviour* the way they are intended to. For instance, whether granting preferential market access has led to an increase in developing-country exports to the EU (Heron and

Woolcock). Ultimately the question is what is the *outcome* of the policy? Do the EU's policies actually foster development and improve the lives of poor people (Langan)? While all of the policies, at least arguably, strive for the same, ultimate end, the assessments in this volume consider very different types of objectives.

The difference in these objectives matters because some are prior to others. The EU's efforts to promote decent work (Langan) illustrate this point. Even assuming that the EPAs are the appropriate policy to pursue to achieve this objective, which Langan disputes, for the EU's policy to have any impact requires first that a developing country conclude an EPA (a change in policy). What impact the EPA has on working conditions hinges on whether, which and how many firms in the developing country are able to weather the increased competition and increase exports and whether and when they begin to increase wages (a change in behaviour). While focusing on different types of objectives is understandable, even desirable, awareness of the length of the causal chain between the EU's action and the observed objective is important both in terms of setting expectations and in terms of comparison across cases.

Takeaways

The contributions in this volume are valuable, particularly collectively, in several ways. They illustrate the diversity of the ways in which the EU's trade and development policies intersect, including several that have not received much attention to date. The contributions also provide clear evidence of the EU's shift away from engaging with developing countries based on historical colonial relationships to differentiating among them based on their level of development. Although the focus of this volume is on understanding the interaction between the EU's trade and development policies, the articles, when viewed together, suggest contributions to the burgeoning literature on the EU as a global actor. They provide qualified support for the normative power Europe view that the EU is motivated by norms. Strikingly the contributions also universally illustrate the limits of the EU's effectiveness even in a policy domain where its power resources are considerable. There are thus real limits to the fungibility of the EU's market power. There is also real value to be added by stepping back from detailed cases so as to appreciate their collective impression.

References

Ahnlid, A. and Elgström, O., 2014. Challenging the European Union: the rising powers and the United States in the Doha Round. *Contemporary Politics*, 20 (1), 77–89.

Bretherton, C. and Vogler, J., 2013. A global actor past its peak? *International Relations*, 27 (3), 375–390.

Carbone, M., 2014. Much ado about nothing? The European Union and the global politics of untying aid. *Contemporary Politics*, 20 (1), 103–117.

Carbone, M. and Orbie, J., 2014. Beyond Economic Partnership Agreements: the European Union and the trade–development nexus. *Contemporary Politics*, 20 (1), 1–9.

Conceição-Heldt, E. and Meunier, S., forthcoming. Speaking with a single voice: internal cohesiveness and external effectiveness of the EU in world politics. *Journal of European Public Policy*.

Dee, M., 2013. Challenging expectations: a study of European Union performance in multilateral negotiations. Thesis (PhD). University of Glasgow.

Goldstein, J. and Keohane, R.O., 1993. Ideas and foreign policy: an analytical framework. *In*: J. Goldstein and R.O. Keohane, eds. *Ideas and foreign policy*. Ithaca: Cornell University Press, 3–24.

Heron, T., 2014. Trading in development: norms and institutions in the making/unmaking of EU-ACP trade and development cooperation. *Contemporary Politics*, 20 (1), 10–22.

Holden, P., 2014. Tensions in the discourse and practice of the European Union's Aid for Trade. *Contemporary Politics*, 20 (1), 90–102.

Jørgensen, K.E., Oberthür, S. and Shahin, J., 2011. Introduction: assessing the EU's performance in international institutions – conceptual framework and core findings. *Journal of European Integration*, 33 (6), 599–620.

Langan, M., 2014. Decent work and indecent trade agendas: the European Union and ACP countries. *Contemporary Politics*, 20 (1), 23–35.

Manners, I., 2002. Normative power Europe: a contradiction in terms? *Journal of Common Market Studies*, 40 (2), 235–258.

Niemann, A. and Bretherton, C., 2013. EU external policy at the crossroads: the challenge of actorness and effectiveness. *International Relations*, 27 (3), 261–275.

Peterson, J., 2012. The EU as a global actor. *In*: E. Bomberg, J. Peterson, and R. Corbett, eds. *The European Union: how does it work?* 3rd ed. Oxford: Oxford University Press, 203–223

Portela, C. and Orbie, J., 2014. Sanctions under the EU Generalised System of Preferences and foreign policy: coherence by accident? *Contemporary Politics*, 20 (1), 63–76.

Siles-Brügge, G., 2014. EU trade and development policy beyond the ACP: subordinating developmental to commercial imperatives in the reform of GSP. *Contemporary Politics*, 20 (1), 49–62.

Woolcock, S., 2014. Differentiation within reciprocity: the EU approach to preferential trade agreements. *Contemporary Politics*, 20 (1), 36–48.

Young, A.R. and Peterson, J., 2013. 'We care about you, but . . . ' the politics of EU trade policy and development. *Cambridge Review of International Affairs*, 26 (3), 497–518.

Young, A.R. and Peterson, J., 2014. *Parochial global Europe: 21st century trade politics*. Oxford: Oxford University Press.

Index